Perspective.

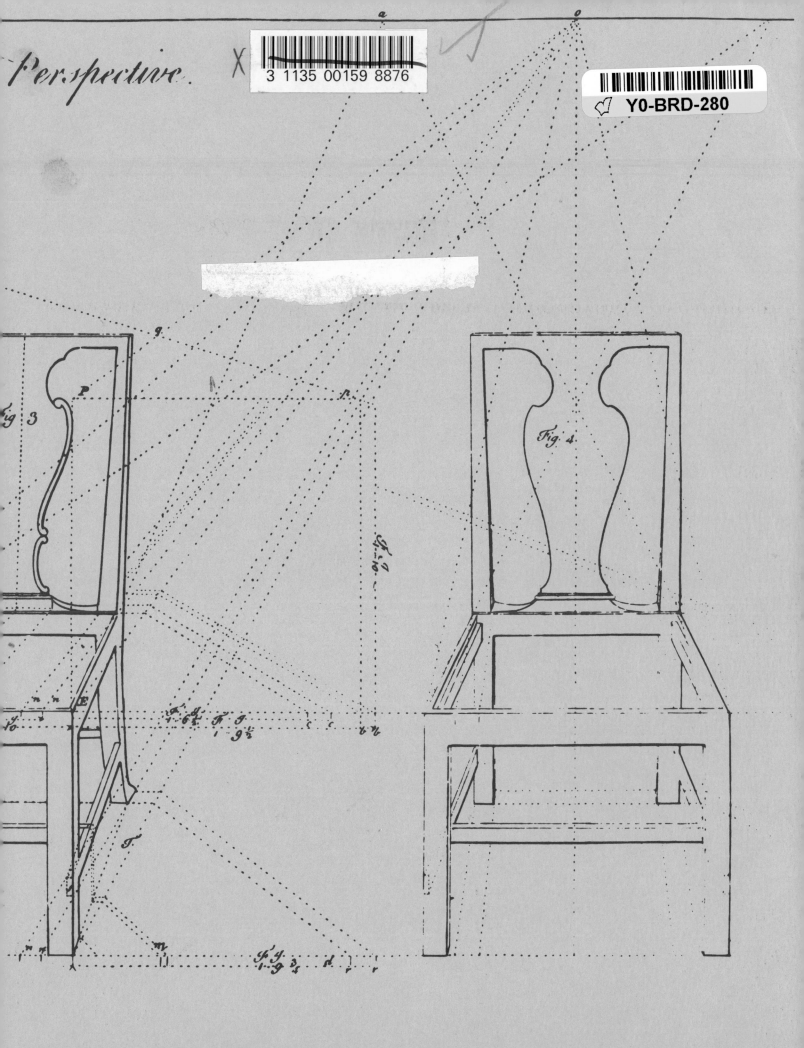

Fig 3

Fig 4

FURNITURE OF WILLIAMSBURG
AND EASTERN VIRGINIA

1710-1790

Figure 59

Furniture of Williamsburg and Eastern Virginia

1710-1790

by Wallace B. Gusler

VIRGINIA MUSEUM
Richmond

The publication of this book was made possible, in part, by a grant from the National Endowment for the Arts
in Washington, D.C., a federal agency.

LIBRARY OF CONGRESS CATALOGING IN PUBLICATION DATA

Gusler, Wallace B.
  Furniture of Williamsburg and eastern Virginia, 1710-1790.

  Bibliography: p. 184
  Includes index.
  1. Furniture—Virginia—Williamsburg—History—
18th century. 2. Furniture—Virginia—History—18th
century
I. Title.
NK2438.W54G87   749.2′155′4252   78-27282
ISBN 0-917046-05-6

Dedicated to the late William A. R. Goodwin, whose understanding and knowledge of early Williamsburg and its furniture was far ahead of his time:

"Some houses should be deliberately furnished with the style of furniture which was made in Williamsburg by Anthony Hay and other cabinet makers whose craftsmanship doubtless supplied in large measure the native local demand, or otherwise they could not have conducted their business."

William A. R. Goodwin to *Colonel Arthur Woods*
October 11, 1930

(Colonial Williamsburg Foundation Archives and Records)

NOTE

This book is the culmination of a two-part project undertaken jointly by the Virginia Museum and the Colonial Williamsburg Foundation. Beginning with the seminal concept—the need to underscore the importance of the decorative arts in American culture—and proceeding with the idea that an exhibition and catalog of the fine products of Virginia's colonial cabinetmakers would best express that concept, Wallace B. Gusler, Curator of Furniture at Colonial Williamsburg, was invited to organize the exhibition and to prepare the catalog that would document the display.

With the expert guidance of the Museum's development director, Paul B. Hood, and associate curator Frederick R. Brandt, financial implementation for the project was secured. Appropriately, funding was received from both public and private sectors: the bequest of Christopher T. Chenery, and the National Endowment for the Arts and the National Endowment for the Humanities, both federal agencies in Washington, D.C.

Furniture of Eastern Virginia: The Product of Mind and Hand was proudly unveiled at the Virginia Museum on March 13, 1978, and remained on view through April 30. Carolyn J. Weekley, curator of decorative arts at the Virginia Museum, coordinated the efforts of the staff members at both institutions, and was responsible for the laudable suggestion that the scope of the project should include design sources, models of furniture construction, and archaeological evidence, as well as the furniture itself. Mr. Gusler, assisted by Sumpter Priddy III, studied and selected appropriate examples of the finest works available from generous public and private lenders throughout the region.

Mr. Gusler was further aided in his organization of the exhibition by the Museum's registrar, Lisa Hummel, and by Programs Division staff members William Gaines and William Rasmussen. Guest installation designer Vincent Ciulla transformed the assembled furniture into a stunning and cohesive display, while Barbara Carson of Colonial Williamsburg translated the exhibition into a fascinating and informative film.

The second half of the project—this book and the exhibition checklist—became a reality through the combined efforts of the Museum's chief editor, George Cruger, publications coordinator Monica Hamm, graphic designer Raymond Geary, and design assistant Gene Rudy. Photographic documentation for both the exhibition and its related publications was ably provided by photographers Delmore A. Wenzel and Hans E. Lorenz of Colonial Williamsburg, and by Ronald Jennings, Katherine Wetzel, and Dennis McWaters of the Virginia Museum staff.

Contents

Foreword

American furniture studies date to the nineteenth-century fascination with "relics." The turn of the century saw little change in this antiquarian attitude, although a few key exhibitions, such as the 1909 Hudson-Fulton show at the Metropolitan Museum brought new, almost sudden, popular awareness of America's early arts. The progress of research from then until now has seen continual expansion, redefinition, and scientific examination. Ultimately, we have come to identify regional traditions and technological idiosyncrasies. More importantly, we now recognize that these objects can be studied by the art historical methods of style analysis and iconographical interpretation, and American furniture now has a rightful place in our fine-arts institutions.

The sophisticated furniture analyzed here by Wallace Gusler underscores this new awareness. As a milestone in southern furniture research, this book comes more than twenty years after the only other in-depth study of the same subject, the late Milby Burton's *Charleston Furniture: 1700-1825*. Continuing research by Henry D. Green, and Frank L. Horton's work at the Museum of Early Southern Decorative Arts and its *Journal* have revealed additional information on southeastern furniture.

But this book is not just a regional study; it also synthesizes both new and traditional methods of furniture analysis, thereby offering new insights into furniture's aesthetic and historic values. Its roots are in early regional publications, such as William Horner's *Blue Book, Philadelphia Furniture*, that first revealed evidence of art in American furniture and signaled the need to investigate stylistic patterns and to document provenance. Later, catalogs by Joseph Downs and Richard H. Randall, Jr. outlined styles by emphasizing iconography, and determined provenances according to wood usage. Then, Charles F. Montgomery's book on federal furniture at Winterthur awakened scholars to the crucial questions that still needed to be answered—to establish where, when, by whom, how, and why American furniture was made. Mr. Montgomery's work touched everyone connected with *Furniture of Williamsburg and Eastern Virginia*. His untimely death occurred last spring, on the eve of the exhibition that preceded this publication. Yet in so many ways, both that exhibition and this book are tributes to his inspired scholarship and teaching.

It is particularly fitting that the premiere museum institutions in Virginia pooled their talents and resources to produce the exhibition and this document. The Virginia Museum recognizes the support of Colonial Williamsburg's Chairman of the Board, Carlisle H. Humelsine, its President, Charles Longsworth, and Graham Hood, Director of Collections, whose early encouragement of Mr. Gusler's work resulted in this research.

Finally, undertakings of this magnitude are made possible by responsive Board members. I wish to acknowledge the fine support of the Virginia Museum's Board of Trustees, particularly that of William H. Higgins, Jr., and Eugene B. Sydnor. It was their initial idea to organize a major show proclaiming that the decorative arts deserve equal recognition in the museum field, alongside the traditional fine arts.

R. PETER MOOZ
Director
Virginia Museum of Fine Arts

Eighteenth-century Williamsburg and its environs have been the subject for more than fifty years of one of the most intensive investigations ever conducted into a relatively small place over a comparatively short period of time. Researchers—architects, archaeologists, craftsmen, curators, to name but a few —have approached it from innumerable vantage points. Thus one might be excused for thinking, a few years ago, that little of major importance remained to be discovered about the colonial capital, and that attempts to improve our understanding of it would be rewarded more by lateral movements than by forward ones. Yet to assume that would have been to discount the sharpness of the human eye and the inextinguishable curiosity of the human mind— two qualities with which Wallace Gusler is endowed, in abundant measure.

Approaching the subject of furniture made in this area in the eighteenth century with the insights of a craftsman and the instincts of an historian (in both capacities self-trained), Mr. Gusler has undertaken a major revision of accepted theories. By sifting old evidence with a newly-fine mesh and relating it both to previously-known and to hitherto-unknown objects; by making extremely precise visual analogies between various objects; and by incorporating evidence not normally taken into account by furniture historians, such as the finding of the archaeologist, Mr. Gusler has pieced together a remarkable picture of cabinet-makers in Williamsburg and the products of their craft. As a result of his discoveries, the idea of the abundance of English imports overwhelming the native product is no longer tenable, while the local production of elaborate ceremonial objects should cause us to look at Virginia society in the eighteenth century anew.

Not only do we watch here the emergence of the Peter Scott shop, for example, active over a longer period than any similar colonial establishment yet known, but we also see the appearance of probably the most sophisticated ceremonial chair in the colonies, a virtuoso piece fully marked by a Williamsburg cabinetmaker. At this late date in studies of American regional furniture—the categorization of which is probably the greatest accomplishment of furniture historians in this country—it is extraordinary to witness the delineation of a new and major regional school, the Williamsburg group. No longer need the South be regarded as the repository of mainly rural, regional styles. Indeed, the discoveries embodied in this book should force us to look again for the products of the South's major and remarkable urban centre, Charleston, South Carolina. If little Williamsburg can compare so favorably in quality to Philadelphia or Boston, what might Charleston not have done?

Colonial Williamsburg is very grateful to William Gaines of the Virginia Museum for his initial suggestion of an exhibition of eastern Virginia furniture, which thus precipitated the idea of this book, and to R. Peter Mooz and Carolyn J. Weekley of the same museum for then making the exhibition and the book realities; to Frank Horton for generously providing information from the research files of the Museum of Early Southern Decorative Arts, Winston-Salem, N.C.; to Harold B. Gill, Jr. for his professional historian's advice, to Sumpter Priddy III for assistance and contributions far beyond the call or expectation of duty; but above all, and in a permanent way, to Wallace B. Gusler for the originality, energy, tenacity, and brilliance with which he has expanded our knowledge and appreciation.

GRAHAM HOOD
Vice-President and Director of Collections,
The Colonial Williamsburg Foundation

Figure 49

Preface

The furniture covered by this work is divided into a number of related groups, with major emphasis on production in Williamsburg. The reasons for this latter concentration are threefold. Primarily, the research and study of furniture made there is many years ahead of efforts in any other area of eastern Virginia. Secondly, the documentation, together with the surviving furniture, indicates that Williamsburg was the leading furniture-producing center of colonial Virginia. Finally, the time has long passed for general surveys. Notwithstanding the importance of Williamsburg, the subject of colonial furniture from eastern Virginia could, from present knowledge, comprise a number of books equal in scope and volume to this work.

The extensively detailed approach taken in this book utilizes evidence provided by both the furniture and its related documents. It has resulted in a technical work that examines and interprets a number of complex relationships. Some of the conclusions reached through this process may seem overly specific, some perhaps startling. However, the evidence for these conclusions is illustrated and discussed, and its interpretation is explained in detail.

If the study of furniture is to progress beyond a pseudo-science, an intense analysis of both artistic and constructional features must be painstakingly pursued. Only when the results of such studies are correlated with documentation, however, does an accurate picture begin to emerge. In the past, furniture scholarship has centered on documentary research, in many cases skillfully handled and interpreted. But there are few furniture studies that attempt to analyze the evidence offered by the objects themselves—either artistically or technologically—although several books and some excellent articles have appeared in the last few decades. These mark a valuable beginning, but the essential questions regarding English and American furniture of the eighteenth century go unanswered and, in many instances, have yet to be asked. Earlier studies, many of which create an air of legitimacy by mentioning individual characteristics, may make fine coffee-table books, but they do not make a lasting contribution to a further knowledge of the subject.

Here, a number of related pieces have been brought together in groups that share constructional and artistic characteristics. Each is designated according to a shop group, although it must be admitted that little is known regarding the movement of journeymen or apprentices. As research and study progress, the intricate relationships used to define each group here will undoubtedly prove to be more complex and result in additional sub-groups. The captions accompanying each illustration carry the shop attribution and an approximate date that suggests the most probable time of production. Therefore, if a piece is dated "circa 1770," the time bracket is 1765 to 1775, with the midpoint favored. In pieces where historical circumstances suggest a more exact time, these will be indicated by a date range. Within each shop group, the pieces are arranged in chronological order.

In the second half of the book, pieces from areas other than Williamsburg are shown. These are not covered with the intense approach that was possible with the Williamsburg examples. The impracticality of thoroughly dissecting all of the furniture groups from eastern Virginia is evident, for the time spent in researching the documents and seeking out the pieces from any one of these areas is astounding. These pieces are included to give an overview of cabinet-making in eastern Virginia and to put Williamsburg production in perspective. More than anything else, this section points out not only the production of other localities, but also the need for intense studies to clarify their valuable contribution to cabinetmaking in the colonial South.

ACKNOWLEDGMENTS

During the past two decades several people have influenced and contributed greatly to the development of the analytical and typological approach I have taken in this book. Although I never met the late Dr. Torsten Lenk, his work *The Flintlock: its origin and development* has served as a monument of inspiration. Likewise, *Thoughts on the Kentucky Rifle in its Golden Age* by Joe Kinding, Jr. revealed the tremendous understanding that is possible when a detailed and intensive study is carried out on objects that were created under the dictates of function and style. John Bivins Jr. and William F. Muller have, by their incisive and discerning observations, also contributed to this methodology. Harold B. Gill Jr. has been an equivalent source of values and principles in historical research, and his substantial material contribution is evident throughout this book.

This work would not have been possible without the financial support of a grant from the National Endowment for the Arts in Washington, D.C., and the personal efforts of the staffs of both the Colonial Williamsburg Foundation and the Virginia Museum. In particular, Graham Hood and Carolyn Weekley provided essential help, as did editors George Cruger and Monica Hamm; designers Raymond Geary and Gene Rudy; and the photographers Delmore A. Wenzel, Hans Lorenz, Ronald Jennings, Katherine Wetzel, and Dennis McWaters.

The Museum of Early Southern Decorative Arts in Winston-Salem, North Carolina, was a major resource. Its research files furnished much information and brought to my attention many objects without which this study would have been severely fragmented. In addition to the files, Frank Horton and Bradford Rauschenberg, research fellows, were extremely helpful.

Many others, both museum colleagues and private individuals, have made substantial contributions, and a special thanks is due the owners of pieces illustrated and studied in this work. While it is not practical to recognize everyone, there are others who have made exceptional contributions as well: Mr. and Mrs. William Adams, Bernard Caperton, John D. Davis, Christopher Gilbert, Margaret Gill, Marshall Goodwin,

Charles Granquist, Leroy Graves, Lindsey Grigsby, Mack Headley, Brock Jobe, Joe Kindig III, Rebecca Lehman, Mr. and Mrs. James Melchor, J. Roderick Moore, Albert Skutans, Earl Soles, Jr., Mary Ellen Stumpf, Peter Thornton, Thomas W. Wood. The typists were Deborah Laubach, Gwen Schwartz, Emeline Wood, Joette Headley, Deborah Wallace, and Sandra Green.

The largest contribution to this work was made by Sumpter Priddy III, who served as my assistant throughout the preparation of this book, put in countless hours of research and editing, and did the principal research and writing of the general introduction.

And, a final acknowledgement to my wife, Georgia Allen, for her encouragement and constant support in this endeavor.

—WALLACE B. GUSLER
Curator of Furniture
The Colonial Williamsburg Foundation
June 30, 1978

Figure 46

Introduction

Twenty-six years have passed since *Furniture of the Old South 1640-1820* opened in Richmond during January of 1952. That landmark exhibition, sponsored jointly by the Virginia Museum, *The Magazine Antiques*, and the Colonial Williamsburg Foundation, was the first large-scale presentation of southern furniture to the American public, and it spurred an increased awareness of the subject that has been followed by extensive and revealing research. This has resulted in a steady stream of furniture discoveries showing that cabinetmaking in the early South reached an exceedingly high level of sophistication from both stylistic and technical standpoints.[1]

Yet, despite the advances of recent decades, the South's appreciation of its decorative arts matured noticeably more slowly than in other regions of the nation. Collections of antique furniture were begun as early as 1793 in New England, when an American chair in the "antique fashion" was bequeathed to the Massachusetts Historical Society. By 1842, when antique collecting was still virtually unheard of in the South, the movement was gaining considerable momentum in the Northeast, prompting the librarian of the American Antiquarian Society in Worchester, Massachusetts to proclaim that old furnishings were eagerly sought as "the most cherished ornaments of the drawing room. . . ."[2]

There is currently little indication that nineteenth-century Virginians expressed any great curiosity about the lifestyles and furnishing of their early forebears. With the exception of individuals who preserved objects that had descended in their own families, or the unusual collector who purchased a furnishing that had belonged to a revolutionary hero,[3] little value was attached to such pursuits. The founding of the Mount Vernon Ladies' Association of the Union in 1853 and the campaign to return Washington's possessions to his home are among the earliest attempts at historic preservation in the country.[4] But alas, the inspiration for doing so did not come from within, and Virginia must be seen not as the leader in the movement, but as a follower.

Popular interest in antique collecting in the Northeast was further reflected during 1876, when two exhibits at the Centennial Exposition in Philadelphia emphasized the growing curiosity of nineteenth-century Americans toward the homes and lifestyles of their ancestors. The Connecticut Cottage, which portrayed "the character of American houses of a century ago," was filled with early furniture on loan from Connecticut residents. A more rustic approach was found in the "Old Log Cabin," where a series of rooms, including a New England kitchen, were filled with furniture and cooking utensils "whose very simplicity made them incomprehensible to the victim of modern improvements."[5]

There was little southern participation in the Centennial Exposition, and despite an invitation to do so, the government of Virginia "declined to make any contribution."[6] No documents are currently available to verify the reactions of southern visitors to the Connecticut Cottage or the Old Log Cabin, but it is doubtful that New England interiors held much meaning to the South, which was still deeply embittered by the Civil War and by the economic depression that followed. The post-war period was, of necessity, a time for redefining southern society, and the recreation of a colonial Virginia home would have undoubtedly brought to mind the loss of a way of life, and not the nostalgic remembrances that these images inspired in the North.

As an indication of public awareness during this period, it is important to note that the Virginia Historical Society, which led the movement to preserve the state's historical documentary materials, received its first gift of furniture in 1882.[7] The Society did not have a permanent home during its early years, which may well have discouraged potential donors. But the gift—a table on which George Mason had written the Bill of Rights—came nearly fifty years after the founding of the Society, and almost a century behind the first recorded donation in Massachusetts. Like many furnishings associated with historic figures during the nineteenth century, George Mason's table stood among a class of objects often referred to as "relics," a word often used to mean a remembrance or a souvenir. Its religious definition, however, as "a memorial to a departed saint, martyr, or holy person,"[8] may actually better explain the sentimentality that spurred nineteenth-century collectors to gather these historic possessions. Beyond the realm of such objects, however, there was little interest in collecting antique furnishings in the South. Other "old" furniture was often given away, discarded, or relegated to outbuildings and back porches. There were few museums, and fewer historical societies, and the shortage severely hampered the preservation of valuable historical materials. At the critical time when historians from Pennsylvania to Maine were salvaging important artifacts for public or private collections, there were no decorative arts scholars and few collections emerging in the South.

One of the earliest exhibitions in Virginia to include furniture was the *Art Loan Exhibition* held in Norfolk during May of 1879. Over 300 objects were displayed there, the vast majority of them paintings. A small representation of the decorative arts was also shown, including a "looking glass brought over in the Mayflower," two tables owned in Williamsburg, and a chair "formerly the property of Lord Dunmore"— the latter piece is included in this study (fig. 58).[9] The last three examples were owned by Miss Sallie Galt of Williamsburg and came from a house that virtually burst at the seams with ancestral furniture. Miss Galt was an outstanding woman in many respects, certainly one to be lauded for her farsightedness, but she is also important because she represents a generation of Virginians who cautiously preserved the memory of their forebears by preserving the material possessions they had owned.[10] It was this reverence for family heritage that was to play an important role in preserving the furniture that makes this study possible. And yet, the impetus for knowing something about it—how, when, and by whom it was made—was not to come from within.

By the 1920s the steady interest in antiques among collectors and dealers in the Northeast had resulted in dozens of books that explored the decorative arts of that region and attempted to define its regional schools. Yet, there was not the first volume to examine the South's contribution to colonial cabinetmaking. Many northern scholars took note of the South's lack of interest in their arts, but neither private collectors nor dealers hesitated to take advantage of the availability of antiques found there at reasonable prices. One publication from 1928 told of an imaginary excursion by three collectors who ventured to "Richwood" and "Petersville" in Virginia, where ". . .two thirds of the poultry in the suburban districts have reared their broods for more than half a century in rare old Hepplewhite sideboards, magnificent old cabriole-legged scrutoires, or exquisite old block-front chests-on-chests that the old families of old Virginia long ago relegated to the old barn."[11] Dealers from Maryland northward ventured into the South to help stock their shops, and by 1931 one author was prompted to comment, somewhat shortsightedly, that the South had been practically "cleaned of its finer pieces."[12]

Not all who were interested in southern furniture carried it north for collections or for sale. By the early 1920s a New England printer, Paul H. Burroughs, settled in Clinton, South Carolina and found to his dismay an abundance of southern furniture either neglected or discarded. In 1931 he published *Southern Antiques*, the first text on the subject and one that is still considered a classic despite the findings of more recent research.[13] Unfortunately, Burroughs' book spurred no major contributions to southern decorative arts scholarship, and it was nearly two decades before southerners were again poignantly aware of the dearth of information available on their arts. In 1949, Joseph Downs, curator of the American Wing at the Metropolitan Museum, stood before a crowd at the first Williamsburg Antiques Forum and boldly declared that little of artistic merit was made in the region south of Baltimore.[14] By the time the Forum had ended, strong sentiments expressed the need for a response. At the insistence of Helen Comstock, then an editorial consultant for *The Magazine Antiques*, it was decided that an exhibition should be organized to show the scope of southern furniture production. Leslie Cheek, Jr., director of the Virginia Museum of Fine Arts, volunteered his museum's facilities, and with the aid of the Colonial Williamsburg Foundation, *Furniture of the old South 1640-1820* opened to an enthusiastic crowd in Richmond in January of 1952. That exhibition, accompanied by the February issue of *The Magazine Antiques*, reintroduced the subject to the American public.[15]

Since 1952 there has been a slow but steady increase in scholarship regarding the decorative arts of the American South. E. Milby Burton's pioneering work on *Charleston Furniture* was the first major regional study, and it has been followed, largely in articles, by work by a number of scholars.[16] The 1960 founding of the Museum of Early Southern Decorative Arts in Winston-Salem by Frank Horton was a major step in establishing a focal point for regional studies, and the first printing of MESDA's biannual *Journal* in 1975 provided an important forum for introducing new discoveries and for consolidating past research.[17]

Work by the Colonial Williamsburg Foundation has also contributed to furthering the knowledge of southern furniture, and from the outset, at the insistence of Dr. W. A. R. Goodwin, a concerted effort was made to fill the newly restored buildings with Virginia-made materials. After his death in 1939, however, the Foundation slackened its pursuit of his sound philosophy, and despite an occasional purchase of southern-made furniture, there was little attempt to isolate regional schools. As late as 1971, there was still not a single indisputably identifiable piece of Williamsburg furniture.[18] Thanks to the research of the last half decade, there are now literally hundreds.

A number of factors have contributed to a misidentification of the sophisticated furniture that was produced in colonial Virginia. Not the least of these factors is its striking similarity to English design—a point that has met with some degree of misunderstanding by traditional historians, who prefer to think of the "divergence" of American furniture styles. This was further complicated by a traditional southern bias that goods produced in England were better than those made here, a viewpoint that probably developed as much from nineteenth-century experience—when regional tensions were increasing and the South turned to England as a source of manufactured goods—as it did from colonial ties with England in the eighteenth century. Added to this is a prejudice often encountered in the twentieth-century—that "English" means "inferior"—and a clearer image begins to emerge. Since southern furniture was often considered "English" by its owners, it never received the close scrutiny of scholars because the label was taken at face value. However erroneous the viewpoint, the piece was automatically deemed unworthy of further examination. Some furniture historians, at a loss to identify stylish furniture of southern origin, concluded that little or none was produced there. Others, lacking published sources for the subject, sometimes interpreted this to mean that no primary materials existed at all.

Once the art historians had "established" the fact that little of artistic merit was produced in the South, social historians, lacking an ability to interpret the physical evidence themselves, often drew upon documents for evidence that would "reinforce" these findings. They usually came to the conclusion that Virginia's taste for "things English" condemned its native craftsmen largely to repair work; that artisans were forced to "confine their activities principally to the retailing of imported goods and the making of repairs."[19] An incomplete understanding of the cabinetmaker's trade also contributed greatly to this misrepresentation. The true scope of talent of capable artisans was never discussed because, in addition to making furniture, they did repair gunstocks, set up bedsteads, and put up fencing—jobs that "might well have been done by ordinary carpenters or a handyman."[20] There was also little understanding of the hierarchy established in larger cabinet shops, where a range of workmen, from the servant, to the journeyman, and finally to the master, bespeaks a clearly delineated division of labor.

It cannot be denied that Southerners sometimes imported furniture from England, but the assumption that Virginia's wealthier families filled their homes with imported furnishings in the highest fashion, leaving their native artisans "to cater to those who could not afford the best"[21] is untenable. Two factors support this denial; first, one must consider the surviving furniture and the documents, and then, one must carefully scrutinize the very products that were imported. Take, for example, the work of Philip Bell, a London cabinetmaker who exported furniture to Virginia.[22] Much of Bell's cabinet work is known for its stark simplicity, and some of it undoubtedly fulfilled the many requests made by wealthy planters through their London agents for furniture that was "plain but neat." Perhaps the phrase "perfectly plain," used by Robert Beverley of Blandfield, sums it up best.[23] The very criticism often leveled against standard Virginia furniture, that of its sheer austerity, was also a hallmark of imported English examples. It will probably prove to be typical as well of venture cargo that was shipped south from New England once more research is completed. It becomes increasingly apparent, then, that the character of much southern colonial furniture reflects not so much the ability of the local cabinetmakers, but the tastes of their patrons instead.

Much of the time and material expended in the production of representative "plain but neat" Virginia furniture is invisible when contrasted with more elaborate examples found in the Northeast. Despite the fact that early furniture is admired because it is so well constructed, the final analysis of a piece has traditionally lain solely in the artistic merit, or flamboyance, of its exterior. Unfortunately, there have been few comparative studies of regional constructional traits, and none have been carried out whatsoever for case pieces. In this area, *Furniture of Williamsburg and Eastern Virginia* makes a particularly valuable contribution, for its in-depth structural analysis is essential not only for a technical understanding of this furniture, but also for a full appreciation of its aesthetic worth. For example, full dustboards between drawers, paneled backs, and "composite" feet are rare features in more elaborate pieces from other areas, but they are standard on quality furniture from eastern Virginia. Although these features do little to enhance the outward appearance or to affect the artistic merit of a piece, they were time-consuming refinements that assured permanence, and they reflect an aesthetic that differed significantly from the one usually expressed in the North.

Among historians who have viewed the topic of Southern furniture, a common fallacy occurs when they cite seventeenth- and eighteenth-century sources lamenting the shortage of craftsmen as proof of little or no production throughout the colonial period. Robert Beverley's observation, taken from the introduction to his *History of Virginia* published in 1705, is perhaps the most frequently cited of all:

> ". . .tho their country be overrun with Wood, yet they have all their Wooden-Ware from England; their cabinets, chairs, tables, stools, chests, boxes, cartwheels, and all other things, even so much as their bowls, and Birchen Brooms, to the eternal reproach of their laziness."[24]

Another observation from the early eighteenth century attempted to explain the reason: "For want of towns, markets, and money, there is but little encouragement for Tradesmen and artificers, and therefore little choice of them, and their labour very dear in the Country." By the mid eighteenth century, however, marked changes were visible along Virginia's coast and fall line. A series of towns, previously little more than communities of a few houses, had emerged, creating an atmosphere conducive to business in a colony that might otherwise be considered dependent upon agriculture. Historians, nonetheless, have traditionally emphasized the rural character of the South to explain that "beyond basic needs, almost no crafts developed" there in the eighteenth century.[25] They have been so thoroughly schooled in the relationship between concentrated urban population and well developed crafts that high-quality products have never been considered remotely possible in Virginia, where no major city, outside of Norfolk, existed. Compensation was offered in the admission that "architecture became the most successful art form in the region,"[26] and compared to the dearth of research available for its furniture, this was not a totally unwarranted view. Architecture has been studied with enthusiasm in the South for over half a century, while the analysis that comprises the majority of this study has been assembled in the last five years. Oddly enough, at least in the case of Williamsburg, it has become apparent that the artistic quality of its cabinet production actually surpasses that of its buildings, which are usually restrained in character.

But even after the old prejudices and misconceptions have been dispelled, someone will invariably ask; "How can Virginia-made objects that display so close an affinity to English precedent, or are attributed to English-trained artisans, be honestly considered American?" The answer might be found in a comparison of southern furniture with the products of seventeenth-century New England—where furniture was also inspired by English designs or made by transplanted cabinetmakers. Admittedly the products of New England and the Middle Colonies expressed an ever-increasing freedom from English archetypes, and by the middle of the eighteenth century northern artisans were building on decades of independence that made their styles distinctly different. But the very concept of measuring an object's "American-ness" is in many respects a self-defeating exercise unless one places the furniture in a larger social context. Southern furniture of the eighteenth century has sometimes been denigrated because it does not show the same strong independence from English design exemplified by pieces from the middle colonies and New England. Yet the products of eighteenth-century Williamsburg, Baltimore, Annapolis, Norfolk, or Charleston should not under any circumstance be viewed merely as English styles transplanted into colonial America while other colonies were producing sophisticated furniture of "native design." Nor should they be regarded as less creative or less "indigenous." Instead, they should be valued as a reflection of another segment of the multi-faceted character of American society—the segment that maintained the closest ties with England, that turned to England as the source for her law and custom, her architecture, literature, and taste. Southern furniture of the eighteenth century is closely allied to the styles used in England because that was the direction in which southern society focused itself.

By the end of the American Revolution, the towns that flourished along the coast and the fall line were considerably larger than they had been in mid-century. Documentary evidence indicates that they attracted an increasingly diverse community of craftsmen and, as one would expect, a large number of furnishings survive from the post-Revolutionary period. Initial observation seems to indicate that they represent sophisticated production not only from the larger towns of eastern Virginia, but from those west of the Blue Ridge as well. Only in-depth study, however, will further clarify the scope of their contributions to cabinetmaking in early America, and it will be years before a picture is complete that will fully portray the products of this region. If the examples discovered to date give any indication of the total, it promises to be an impressive and exciting panorama.

—SUMPTER PRIDDY III
Colonial Williamsburg

FOOTNOTES

1. "Furniture of the Old South, 1640-1820," Alice Winchester, ed., *The Magazine Antiques* 61 (February 1952):38-100.

2. Richard H. Saunders, "Collecting American Decorative Arts in New England," *The Magazine Antiques* 109 (May 1976):996-1003. See also Rodris Roth, "Relic Furniture of the Nineteenth Century," *The Magazine Antiques* 101 (May 1972):874-878.

3. One of the earliest purchases of antique furniture in Virginia was made at an undetermined date in the middle of the nineteenth century when Mann Valentine, later founder of the Valentine Museum in Richmond, acquired a federal shield-back side chair that had originally belonged to George Washington. Information courtesy of Elizabeth Childs, curator, the Valentine Museum.

4. Mount Vernon Ladies' Association of the Union, *Mount Vernon in Virginia* (Mount Vernon: Mount Vernon Ladies' Association of the Union, 1960).

5. Saunders, "Collecting."

6. *International Exhibition 1876 Official Catalogue: Complete in One Volume* (Philadelphia: John Nagle and Company, 1876).

7. Letter from George Mason, Alexandria, Virginia, July 26, 1880, to Col. John Ott of the Virginia Historical Society. The George Mason Papers. (Virginia Historical Society, Richmond, Virginia. Information courtesy of Mrs. Kenneth Southall, curator of special collections, Virginia Historical Society, April 1978.)

8. *The Oxford English Dictionary* 8 (Oxford: Clarendon Press, 1961): 405.

9. "Art Loan Exhibition for the Benefit of the Ladies Parish Aid Society of St. Paul's Church, Norfolk, Va. at Mechanics Hall, May 27, 1879" (Norfolk: no publisher), p. 8, entry 302. Research Library, Colonial Williamsburg Foundation, Williamsburg, Virginia.

10. A collection of Galt family papers in the Earl Gregg Swem Library of the College of William and Mary has correspondence and notes referring to furniture and household inventories written by Miss Sallie Galt during the late nineteenth century. Her interest in colonial Virginia furniture is a subject worthy of further pursuit.

11. Kenneth L. Roberts, *Antiquemania* (New York: Doubleday, Doran and Company, Inc., 1928), p. 17. This source is quoted in the introduction to Barry Greenlaw's *New England Furniture at Williamsburg* (Williamsburg: Colonial Williamsburg Foundation, 1974).

12. Mary Ralls Dockstader, "Simple Furniture of the Old South," *The Magazine Antiques* 20 (August 1931):84.

13. Paul H. Burroughs, *Southern Antiques* (Richmond: Garret and Massie, 1931).

14. Susan Stitt, *Museum of Early Southern Decorative Arts* (Winston-Salem, North Carolina: Old Salem, Inc., 1970).

15. "Furniture of the Old South."

16. E. Milby Burton, *Charleston Furniture 1700-1825* (Charleston, South Carolina: Charleston Museum, 1955).

17. *Journal of Early Southern Decorative Arts* 1 (May 1975).

18. This fact hampered the interpretation of objects excavated from both the Anthony Hay and Peter Scott shops. For further information on these excavations, see Ivor Noël Hume, *Williamsburg Cabinetmakers: The Archaeological Evidence*, Colonial Williamsburg Archaeological Series No. 6 (Williamsburg: Colonial Williamsburg Foundation, 1971).

19. Carl Bridenbaugh, *Seat of Empire: The Political Role of Eighteenth-Century Williamsburg*, Williamsburg in America Series No. 1 (Williamsburg: Colonial Williamsburg Foundation, 1950), p. 30.

20. Mills Brown, "Cabinetmaking in the Eighteenth Century" (unpublished research report, Colonial Williamsburg Foundation, Williamsburg, Virginia, 1959), p. 141.

21. Ibid., p. 105.

22. George Washington was among those who ordered furniture from Bell. See Mt. Vernon Ladies' Association of the Union, *Washington Furniture at Mount Vernon* (Mt. Vernon, Virginia: Mount Vernon Ladies' Association of the Union, 1966).

23. Thomas T. Waterman, *The Mansions of Virginia* (Chapel Hill: University of North Carolina Press, 1945), p. 143

24. Robert Beverley, *History and Present State of Virginia*, ed. Louis B. Wright (Chapel Hill: University of North Carolina Press, 1946), p. 295.

25. Carl Bridenbaugh, *The Colonial Craftsman* (New York: New York University Press, 1950), p. 9.

26. Carl Bridenbaugh, *Myths and Realities of the American South* (New York: Atheneum, 1963), p. 47.

PART I

The
Furniture
of
Williamsburg

Figure 47

An Introduction to Williamsburg

When Williamsburg became the capital of Virginia in 1699, it quickly assumed an important role in many phases of life there. As the capital of the wealthiest and most populated of the thirteen colonies, it served not only as a political focal point, but as the dominant cultural center as well. From the very beginning it was inevitable that Williamsburg would influence taste throughout the Colony. The Capitol and the College were among the most remarkable examples of architecture of their time; British Royal Governors, who furnished the "Palace" in the most fashionable manner, set standards in style and taste that were emulated among leading Virginians. It was logical that cabinetmaking, dependent upon a style-conscious and wealthy patronage, would flourish in such a center.

Although Williamsburg contained a static population of approximately 3,000 on the eve of the Revolution, its ranks were often swelled by temporary influxes of citizens. The reasons were varied, although legislative activities predominated. Two Burgesses came from each of the fifty-nine counties in the Colony, and one each from the cities of Norfolk, James City, and Williamsburg, to attend the meeting of the House of Burgesses. In April and October the General Court met, and others came to be heard before the Colony's judicial body, known as the Court of Oyer and Terminer, in June and December. The Hustings Court convened the first Monday of each month, and local citizens came into town the second Monday when the Court of James City County was held. It was inevitable that business would accompany legal work, and in the fall, usually at the time of the General Court, merchants from all over the Colony met in Williamsburg to set the annual rate of exchange.[1]

Williamsburg tradesmen profited from the continual influx of wealthy planters and merchants, and cabinetmakers were no exception. Accounts reveal that they had wide patronage, including a large representation rather distant from the city—a fact that differs with beliefs that were previously held about the craft in colonial Virginia. A compilation of these accounts and their illustration on a map demonstrate the documented usage of Williamsburg products in other areas during the eighteenth century, and reinforce Williamsburg's status as the major cabinetmaking center of the colonial Tidewater (fig. 1).

Most of the documents related to the purchase of furniture from Williamsburg list but a single object or, in many cases, only the cash amount of the transaction. Two series of accounts are more extensive, and give far greater detail. The most important pertain to Robert Carter of Nomini Hall, one of the wealthiest planters in colonial Virginia. Carter's surviving accounts contain only a single order for English furniture—that of a bed—and otherwise emphasize his reliance on Williamsburg artisans. While living adjacent to the Governor's Palace in Williamsburg for approximately eleven years (1761-72), he purchased a number of items from Benjamin Bucktrout, a Williamsburg cabinetmaker; among them was an expensive desk-and-bookcase costing £16.[2]

By 1772 Carter had grown weary of the rapidly changing political situation in the colonial capital, and in May he moved his family back to Nomini Hall, his Westmoreland County plantation. This involved much preparation, including a major remodeling of the country house, purchase of furniture for their new living quarters, and the delivery of his Williamsburg belongings to Nomini. Some of these were transported by wagon; others were sent by ship.

Bucktrout assisted in the move by making a packing case for a harpsicord, and in October of 1772 he billed Carter for "4 Elbow Chares" and 8 "Mohogany Chares Stuffed over the Rails with Brass nails." Costing over £2 each, these latter chairs are described in identical fashion by Thomas Chippendale in his *Director* and are deemed by him appropriate for a gentleman. About the same time, Carter also bought tables from Peter Scott, another Williamsburg cabinetmaker, although the exact date is not recorded.[3]

It is worthy of note that Robert Carter did not limit his purchase of furnishings for Nomini to tradesmen in Williamsburg, for he patronized craftsmen in Westmoreland County for less expensive items as well:

"The Honourable Robert Carter Esqr Dr
1770
To making two bedsteads @ 22/6   2 . . 5 . .0
To making three Tables @ 10/   1 . .10 . .0
To making 1 doz. Windsor Chairs
    @ 11/   6 . .12 . .0
                                         £10 . . 7 . .0
Dec. 5th Received the Contents of the Above
    Acct. & all
        Demands p.
                            John Attwell[4]
Test: Henry Francks"

The identity of John Attwell is not clear, but he was probably the "Mr. Atwell ship carpenter" to whom Carter referred in a 1789 letter.[5] The important point, however, is verification that one of Virginia's wealthiest and most influential citizens was patronizing Williamsburg cabinetmakers for elaborate furnishings, while turning to local artisans

for less expensive objects used in secondary areas of his large country house.

Extensive patronage of Williamsburg cabinetmakers can also be found among the accounts of Thomas Jefferson, although many of the entries in his papers are not itemized. His accounts with Anthony Hay and Benjamin Bucktrout must be cautiously considered, however, since Hay served as proprietor of the Raleigh Tavern, an establishment often frequented by Jefferson, and Bucktrout operated a retail store in addition to his cabinet shop. Nonetheless, Jefferson's papers contain indisputable specifications for furniture he ordered from Peter Scott; and his patronage of Edmund Dickinson, who operated no other business, is probably for cabinet-work.

Jefferson depended almost entirely on Williamsburg cabinetmakers before the Revolution, and though he bought a few furnishings in his native Piedmont, these are generally thought to have been used or second-hand items. Furthermore, evidence of Jefferson's orders for English or French furniture is unknown until his European sojourns in the period after the Revolution.[6]

Additional insight into the importance of Williamsburg as a cabinetmaking center and the extent to which its products were employed can be gained through furniture that is attributed to Williamsburg on the basis of style and construction but has a reliable tradition of ownership in other areas. These examples include a pair of armchairs at Shirley plantation and several pieces at Mount Vernon. The evidence such objects present, assembled on a second map, is quite revealing and indicates an extensive and sometimes distant market for Williamsburg-made furniture (fig. 2).

Further evidence of Williamsburg's dominance in the cabinetmaking trade of colonial Virginia can be found in a study of advertisements from the *Virginia Gazette*.[7] There one can find fifty-seven advertisements by cabinetmakers, including appeals for journeymen and apprentices, notices of runaways, and occasional pleas for commissions. There are also several announcements of new, or terminated partnerships. Other vaguely related advertisements are not considered here, largely because they include casual references to individuals not involved in the trade, or are notices by cabinetmakers who are concerned with other subjects.

As Williamsburg was the political center for colonial Virginia and the common meeting place of the wealthy and influential, it is not surprising to find that its cabinetmakers advertised more than any other group in the Colony. Major customers lived and spent most of their time some distance from the

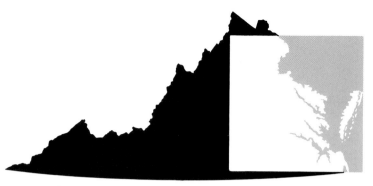

1. *Each symbol on the map represents documented patronage of the four major Williamsburg cabinetmakers discussed in this book.*

Outline map of Virginia. Detail maps drawn from the Fry-Jefferson map of 1751.

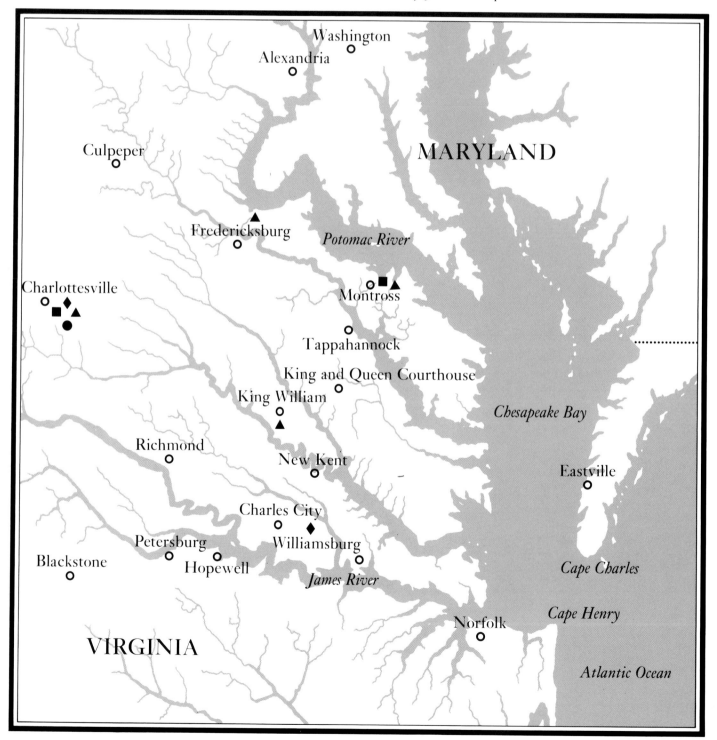

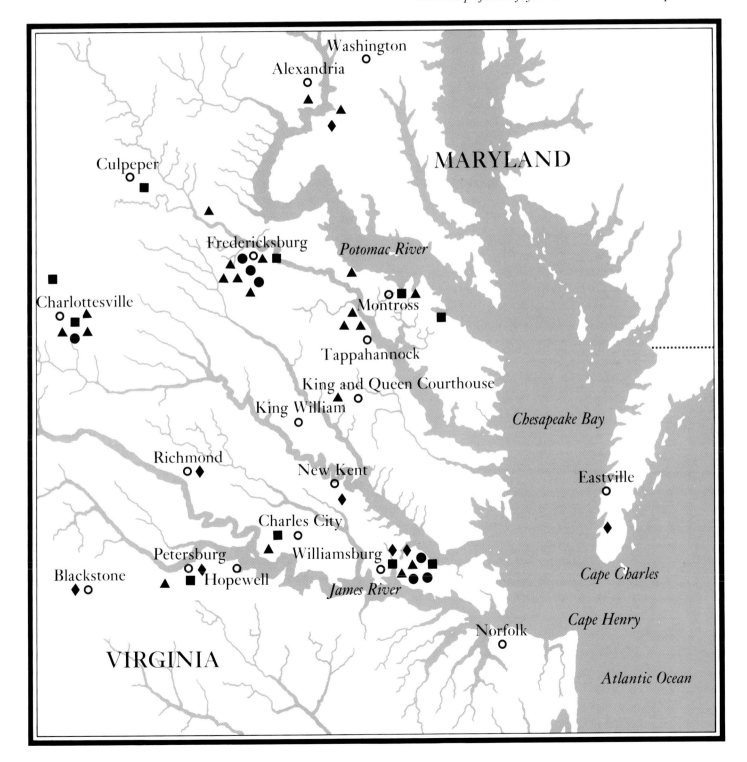

▲   Peter Scott

◆   Anthony Hay

■   Benjamin Bucktrout

●   Edmund Dickinson

2. In this map, the symbols show where pieces attributed to Williamsburg cabinetmakers were owned, according to their histories. It should be noted that not all Williamsburg groups are represented, and of those shown, many examples are omitted. This is especially true of Williamsburg and Fredericksburg, where the profusion of symbols would clutter the map.

Washington

Alexandria

MARYLAND

Culpeper

Potomac River

Fredericksburg

Charlottesville

Montross

Tappahannock

King and Queen Courthouse

King William

Chesapeake Bay

Richmond

New Kent

Eastville

Charles City

Petersburg   Williamsburg

Blackstone   Hopewell

Cape Charles

James River

Cape Henry

Norfolk

VIRGINIA

Atlantic Ocean

5

town. The competitive factor consequently appears to have been greater than in other areas of the Colony, but it is surprising, nonetheless, to find such an overwhelming one-sided dominance. Contrary to popular belief, cabinetmakers were fairly numerous during the colonial period. At least one is documented in every Virginia county for which records survive, and most counties supported a great many more. As a rule these craftsmen did not advertise, though when they did on rare occasions it was usually to request apprentices and journeymen and not to appeal for business. Many maintained lucrative trade for decades without the aid of newspaper notices, indicating that the demand for their products far exceeded available supply. This is not difficult to understand when one considers the phenomenal growth that took place in colonial Virginia during the third quarter of the eighteenth century.

Of the fifty-seven *Virginia Gazette* advertisements, thirty-three—over one-half of the total—were placed by Williamsburg tradesmen. This statistic alone is impressive, but when compared to the runner-up, Fredericksburg, with only four, it becomes very important. Richmond, Blandford, Yorktown, Charles City County, and Mecklenburg County are represented by two each, while the remaining eleven are single advertisements from various areas of Virginia. There is also one from North Carolina. Although only Williamsburg had a significant number of these, it appears that cabinetmakers in other Virginia towns had sufficient local business, which eliminated the need to advertise. The average level of production in smaller towns could be handled by apprentices, servants, and slaves who were readily available, but in Williamsburg, where wealthy patrons of the colony congregated, the use of advertising for trained professionals indicates that the quality of their trade attained a higher caliber. Over fifty percent of the Williamsburg advertisements are appeals for journeymen, and two professional carvers advertised their services from the Anthony Hay shop there.

This effort of Williamsburg cabinetmakers to attract journeymen is impressive when compared to practices seen in other areas of the Colony, where such notices are rare. Conversely, of the four Fredericksburg advertisements, only one sought the services of journeymen, while others were for runaway servants, two of them convict cabinetmakers. In fact, the single Fredericksburg advertisement for journeymen was placed by Thomas Miller on August 31, 1768, just three days after his convict servant had run away.[8]

The hiring of journeymen in Williamsburg and the use of convict servants in Fredericksburg make an important commentary on the state of the trade in these two centers. At the present time no documents are available to indicate that convicts were employed in Williamsburg cabinet shops. Anthony Hay's lone appeal in 1751 is the only contemporary reference to a servant of any kind having been associated with the city's cabinetmakers, and it is not known if he actually ever employed a servant in his own shop.[9] In contrast, servants were often offered for sale in the Rappahannock River basin, and their employment by Fredericksburg cabinetmakers seems to correspond with the general practice of that area. This suggests a poorer level of craftsmanship than that of Williamsburg where journeymen, who were salaried or worked "by-the-piece," played a major role.

The argument might be presented that Williamsburg cabinetmakers had a considerable advantage by residing in the city where the *Gazette* was published. This may have been an important factor, but it cannot be considered the major one. The postal system negated much of the geographic disadvantage, a fact that is reinforced by the sheer profusion of advertisements from other locales. The *Gazette* was the sole outlet for advertising within the colony, and access to the paper had little influence on Williamsburg merchants and artisans, who simply did not feel the need to advertise their businesses. Among them was Peter Scott, cabinetmaker, who carried on a flourishing business for fifty years without the benefit of *Gazette* notices.

The evidence thus assembled points to Williamsburg as the primary cabinetmaking center in colonial Virginia, possibly second only to Charleston, South Carolina in the colonial South. Unfortunately, the colonial production of Annapolis, Baltimore, and Norfolk has not yet been sufficiently isolated to make an accurate comparison.

The Williamsburg furniture assembled to date provides ample opportunity to determine general stylistic trends in the city's production and the adaptation of English stylistic development. The first phase of this development appears to date from the 1720s and 1730s and is consistent with English furniture in the George I and early George II styles representative of these two decades. Erroneously labeled Queen Anne (see fig. 8 and note), these pieces are characterized by an emphasis on overall form, a very conservative use of carving, and cabriole legs that end in pad feet. In English examples veneer and banded inlay were important refinements, although Williamsburg pieces rely on the use of solid woods.

This austere style gave way to a later phase of the George II style in the 1730s and 1740s. With increased elaboration and the use of carving, it was a prelude to more elaborate rococo taste. This style had a major impact on Williamsburg furniture and, by extension, on eastern Virginia. Details such as paw feet, animal-head terminals on chair arms, and splats with geometric designs and foliate carving are characteristic. Straight bracket feet and desk interiors with flush straight drawers are typical of case furniture. All of these features, representative of furniture in the George II style, can be seen in the Williamsburg groups shown here.

The Capitol chair (fig. 46) gives the earliest evidence of the rococo style in Williamsburg. Dating from the mid 1750s (see discussion of dating with figs. 46, 47, 48), the chair's basic design is the George II style, although its knee carving is an asymmetrical design incorporating tattered shells and C-scrolls, and is clearly rococo. This latter style was often applied to earlier forms in Williamsburg and, in fact, candlestands and fret-work china tables are the only pure rococo pieces from Williamsburg. During the decade from 1765 to 1775 an abstract form of rococo design developed. Its approach, although sometimes elaborate, was not well coordinated and is characterized by a lack of unity. Examples of this abstract style can be seen in chairs (figs. 30, 58) and a table (fig. 93). This style was not uniform and appears to have co-existed with more refined rococo approaches (figs. 51, 52, 98).

Neo-classic taste appears to have been introduced in Williamsburg with Lord Botetourt, Royal governor and successor to Francis Fauquier in 1768. The earliest references to this style are associated with him. In the fall of 1770, just about the time of Botetourt's death, a monumental cast iron stove (fig.3) arrived in Williamsburg. This elegant "warming machine," ordered by Lord Botetourt for the House of Burgesses, bears the name of its designer, "Buzaglo," the date 1770, and the Virginia coat of arms.[10] It is virtually covered with relief ornament in the style of Robert Adam, although a few rococo details linger, and it is the earliest documented example of the neo-classic style in Virginia. The impact of this monumental object from London, bearing an abundance of ornament in the new and fashionable "Antick manner," must have been tremendous.

3. *Warming Machine, designed by Abraham Buzaglo, London, 1770.*
Cast iron.
The Commonwealth of Virginia, on loan to the Colonial Williamsburg Foundation.

4. *The Botetourt Statue, Richard Haywood, London, 1772-1773. Marble.*
The College of William and Mary in Virginia.

At the same time that Buzaglo's warming machine arrived in town, Williamsburg silversmith William Waddill was fashioning silver furniture for Lord Botetourt's coffin. The handles, unfortunately now lost, were a naive attempt at neo-classic design, even though their companion escutcheons had profiles cut in the form of rococo scrolls.[11] Of great historical importance, they were certainly the earliest documented examples of this style actually produced in Williamsburg.

A further awareness of the neo-classic style is evident in a series of documents related to the commission of a statute of Lord Botetourt (fig. 4), whose death in 1770 was sorely grieved by the citizens of Virginia. On July 11, 1771 the Burgesses resolved:

> That an elegant Statue of his late excellency the Right Honourable Norborne, Baron de Botetourt be erected in Marble at the Public Expence, with proper Inscriptions, expressing the grateful Sense this House entertains of his Lordship's prudent and Wise Administration, and their great Solicitude to perpetuate, as far as they are able, the Remembrance of these many public and social Virtues which adorn his illustrious Character. . . .[12]

William Nelson, President of the Council, headed a committee of six appointed to obtain the statue. John Norton, a London merchant who represented many Virginia planters in England, was employed to commission the work, and he did so with Richard Hayward, a well-known London sculptor. Proposed designs for the statue were sent to Williamsburg for approval and Robert Carter Nicholas, a correspondent for the group, wrote to Norton regarding the committee's reaction to suggestions for the pedestal: "We highly approve eather of the Designs for the back-Front [but] of the two, should prefer that which has the Vine or Branch running up the inner Edge as we think it fills up better & makes the figure more compleat."[13] Unfortunately the designs have not survived, but the finished product has graceful neo-classic details, suggesting that Nicholas and his committee were clearly interested in how these contributed to an overall effect. In August of 1772, Norton informed his son in Yorktown, Virginia that "The Statue of Lord Bottentourt [sic] is in forwardness. . ." and in March that ". . .Ld. Botetourts Statue is on board the Virginia 'tis much admir'd here by all the Curious and Artists. . ." By June the statue had arrived in Williamsburg, where it was placed on the open piazza of the Capitol in full public view. Robert Carter Nicholas again wrote Norton, "It is a Masterly piece of Work" and later, "The Statue is universally admired."[14]

The Botetourt statue was the only tribute in America to a Royal Governor and was one of four public statues erected in the colonial period. Two of the others, both of William Pitt, expressed gratitude for his part in repealing the Stamp Act. They were carved by Joseph Wilton of London and were brought here in 1770, one to New York and the other to Charleston, South Carolina. Wilton also carved a statue of George III for New York.[15]

Although Hayward's statue of Botetourt and Buzaglo's iron stove represent imposing public monuments that firmly established neo-classicism in Williamsburg before the Revolution, more personal items also found their way to the city. These smaller items, including wallpaper, a variety of metalwork, prints, and ceramics, were imported in large volume, and were carried by numerous merchants. Furniture with neo-classic detail was apparently produced in Williamsburg as well. George Hamilton, a carver and gilder from Britain who worked in the Anthony Hay shop, advertised work in the "New Palmyrian Taste" upon his arrival in 1774 and thus documented the first indisputable record of the new style in Virginia.[16]

Lord Botetourt was succeeded as Royal Governor by John Murray, Earl of Dunmore, who left Williamsburg in 1775 as a result of growing political unrest. The following summer his personal property was sold by the state at public auction. As the text of this book will show, a surprising number of items survive with traditions dating to this sale, but a single chair is of utmost importance to this discussion of the early neo-classic style in Virginia (fig. 5). According to tradition, this piece was purchased by James Ambler of Jamestown, a tradition that is supported by another chair from the same set that descended through a different branch of the Ambler family. The exact time the pair was separated is unknown, but it was well before 1900 when the other example was illustrated in *Furniture of Our Forefathers*.[17]

The form of these chairs would be considered by most standards to date later than the Dunmore sale of 1776. In fact, their first impression is one of purely neo-classical style. Closer inspection, however, reveals that they are transitional in nature. While they have the familiar undulating crests of later shield-back chairs, it should be noted that the bottom of the splat is mortised into the rear seat rail, a characteristic typical of rococo chairs that preceded the full development of the shield. Most of the carving is also neo-classical, but there are vestigial remnants of rococo "tattered shells" in the ears of the crest, and its legs are reinforced by earlier H-stretchers. This combination of stylistic and constructional evidence indicates that the chairs

5. *Side Chair, probably English, 1771-1775.*
Mahogany primary; beech secondary.
Height 36¼", width 21½", depth 20¾".
Private collection.

were made in the transition from the late rococo to the neo-classic style. This evolutionary design, in conjunction with strong evidence supplied by the separate but identical traditions, strongly suggests their use in the Palace during the early 1770s.

It is doubtful that these chairs are so early in date that they could have been part of the shipment brought by Lord Dunmore when he arrived in 1771, and they appear to date closer to the 1776 sale.[18] This hypothesis is supported by the earlier style of a Scottish chair (fig. 6) that descended in the same family and also has a Dunmore tradition. The origin of the neo-classic examples is obscure and at present is difficult to determine. The rails are beech, and though this would normally be accepted as good

6. *Side Chair, probably Scottish, circa 1765.*
Mahogany primary; beech secondary.
Height 37⅝", width 22¼", depth 22½".
Private collection.

evidence of English construction, it is not safe to assume so in the study of Williamsburg furniture. Beech was used by at least two shops there for upholstered pieces. It is possible that George Hamilton, working in conjunction with Edmund Dickinson, produced such a chair. Hamilton's advertisement is clear regarding the neo-classic style in which he worked, and it is documented that Dunmore patronized Dickinson's shop.[19] Another confusing circumstance regarding this chair's origin is the fact that Dunmore had a cabinet shop, including three workbenches and their accompanying tools, on the Palace grounds.[20] Apparently he manned the shop with indentured servants, some of whom may have come directly from England, thus possessing a familiarity with this style. New evidence will have to surface before final conclusions can be drawn, but regardless of their origin, these are highly important examples and appear to be the earliest neo-classic chairs used in America.

Pre-revolutionary Williamsburg pieces with neo-classic influence are understandably scarce. The style was not introduced until after 1770, and the direct flow of British neo-classic development terminated with the outbreak of the Revolution. The war also seems to have significantly disrupted the cabinetmaking trade in Virginia, although the extent to which this is true is difficult to ascertain. Only scattered accounts exist for cabinet work executed during that period, and many *Gazette* ads referring to the trade suggest a serious economic situation. The seven years covered by the conflict were extremely important ones in England for the development of the new style, and during that period the evolution from the rococo to the neo-classic was completed. It is doubtful that newer tastes were arriving in America during the war, and styles were apparently "fixed" here from its outbreak. A new development had to await an end to hostilities, and by that time the mature neo-classic had developed.

A chronological summary of the styles that dominated cabinetmaking in Williamsburg include George I and George II, 1725-50; rococo or Chippendale, 1750-80; and the neo-classic, 1770-1810. These bracket dates represent the major period each style was in use, although each phase has some features that carry into the following style.

The cabinetmakers of Williamsburg were able to dominate their trade in colonial Virginia. By utilizing the political and economic advantages of the city, and combining them with an astute sensitivity to the perpetual flow of English furniture development, they produced a unique school that often incorporated academic features unknown even in the production of larger American centers.

FOOTNOTES

1. Rutherford Goodwin, *A Brief and True Report Concerning Williamsburg in Virginia* (Richmond: A. Dietz and Son, 1941), pp. 35-38. Information courtesy of Harold B. Gill, Jr., historian, Colonial Williamsburg Foundation.

2. Robert Carter Papers, Virginia Historical Society, Richmond, Virginia. Courtesy of Harold B. Gill, Jr., from his forthcoming book *Arts and Crafts in Virginia*.

3. Ibid.; Robert Carter Day Book, Vol. 14 (1776-1778), p. 146, and Robert Carter Letter Book, Vol. 6 (1784-1785), pp. 134-135, Manuscripts Division, Duke University Library, Durham, North Carolina.

4. Carter Papers, M-82-8.

5. Carter Letter Book, Vol. 8 (1787-1789), p. 261.

6. All Jefferson accounts are courtesy of Charles Granquist, assistant director, Thomas Jefferson Memorial Foundation, Monticello, Virginia.

7. Information from a statistical study made in 1978 by Sumpter T. Priddy III, curatorial intern, Department of Collections, Colonial Williamsburg Foundation, Williamsburg, Virginia.

8. *The Virginia Gazette*, ed. William Rind, September 22, 1768, p. 3.

9. *The Virginia Gazette*, ed. John Dixon, November 28, 1751, p. 4.

10. Accession File No. L1933-503, Department of Collections, Colonial Williamsburg Foundation, Williamsburg, Virginia.

11. Accession File No. L1956-535, Department of Collections, Colonial Williamsburg Foundation, Williamsburg, Virginia.

12. Marcus Whiffen, *The Public Buildings of Williamsburg* (Williamsburg, Virginia: Colonial Williamsburg Foundation, 1958), p. 167.

13. Ibid., p. 168.

14. Ibid.

15. Wayne Craven, *Sculpture in America* (New York; Thomas Y. Crowell Company, 1968), pp. 47-49.

16. *The Virginia Gazette*, ed. Alexander Purdie and John Dixon, July 28, 1774, p. 3.

17. Esther Singleton, *The Furniture of Our Forefathers* (New York: Doubleday, Page and Company, 1900), pp. 112, 113.

18. Papers of John Murray, Earl of Dunmore, Manuscript T1-488-folio 101, British Public Records Office, London. Information courtesy of Harold B. Gill, Jr.

19. Mills Brown, "Cabinetmaking in the Eighteenth Century" (unpublished research report, Colonial Williamsburg Foundation, Williamsburg, Virginia, 1959), p. 133.

20. List of cabinetmaking tools is in Lord Dunmore's Loyalist Claim, File A. O. 13-18, British Public Records Office, London. Reference courtesy of Harold B. Gill, Jr.

Figure 8

An Early Williamsburg Furniture Group

The earliest furniture that can be attributed with any assurance to Williamsburg is a group related to the Speaker's chair made for the Capitol and used there until the legislature moved to Richmond in 1780 (fig. 7). This group of furniture appears to belong principally to the decade of the 1730s.

The date of the Speaker's chair has been the subject of considerable discussion. An early attribution of circa 1710 has been suggested, due largely to the survival of the 1703 note ordering that the hall of the House of Burgesses "be furnished with a large Armed Chair for the Speaker to sit in . . ."[1] In recent years this was revised and the chair was re-dated to another extreme, circa 1753, owing largely to the rebuilding of the Capitol in that year after the disastrous fire of 1747.[2] Both of these attributions, however, seem unlikely: 1710 is by far too early for the form of the cabriole legs, and 1753 far too late for the style of the arms.

Some have assumed that the disaster that befell the Capitol in 1747 destroyed all the building's furnishings, including the Speaker's chair. A surviving account of the tragedy, however, tells of a slow but steady fire that began in the attic and then moved downward, thus providing adequate time to rescue the more important objects on the lower floors.

> Last Friday, (Jan. 30) the fatal and ever memorable Day of the Martyrdom of King Charles the First, a most extraordinary Misfortune befel this Place, by the Destruction of our fine Capitol. Between 7 and 8 o'clock in the Morning the Inhabitants of the City were surprised with the Sight of a Cloud of Smoke, issuing from the upper Part after some of the Shingles began to kindle on Fire from within, and immediately a Blaze burst out, which presently reached the Cupola, and thence communicated the Fire to the Covering of the whole Fabrick. The Cupola was soon burnt, the two Bells that were in it were melted, and, together with the Clock, fell down, and were destroyed; and the whole Floor of the several Rooms took Fire, soon burnt thro', and decended to the second Floor, and so to (the) Bottom, till the whole Timber and Wood-work was destroyed, and the naked Brick Walls only left standing, which, however, seem good, except one or two small Cracks in the Semicircles. During this Consternation and Hurry, all the Records deposited in the Capitol, except a few loose, useless papers, were, by great Care and Diligency, and in the Midst of Danger, happily preserved; as were also the Pictures of the Royal Family, and several other things.[3]

The Speaker's chair was probably one of "several other things" saved from the fire and, as will be discussed later, strong evidence indicates that it was saved. The question also arises whether it is the first such chair made for the Capitol. While the only surviving order is dated 1703, there is good reason to believe that considerable time passed before it was

14

7a.

7. *Speaker's Chair, the Virginia House of Burgesses, Williamsburg, circa 1730.*
Walnut primary; poplar, yellow pine, and oak secondary.
Height 97½″, width 39⁵/₁₆″, depth 26⅜″.
The Commonwealth of Virginia, on loan to the Colonial Williamsburg Foundation (acc. no. L1933-504).

actually carried out. In the early years of the century the Capitol was perpetually in a state of construction. Lieutenant Governor Spotswood made tremendous progress on the building after his inauguration in 1710, but by 1720 he had become so frustrated with the council's lack of action and their charges against him for the misuse of funds, that he declined "all future Concerns in thease works." Answering their accusations, he made it clear that he had advanced his own money "by reason of the deficiency of Revenue at that time."[4] Testimony given on November 15, 1718 seems to indicate, as well, that there were security problems, for on that date "John Broadnax was called in again and demanded by order of the House to give an account of the furniture belonging to the Capitol, Whereupon he answered that the Doors were broke open and the chairs removed without his knowledge."[5]

From a stylistic standpoint it appears that the Speaker's chair post-dated this period. The late 1720s or early 1730s seem most probable, and this conclusion is confirmed by other pieces of Williamsburg furniture that are related to it. Further, a series of pieces showing continuity from this early group can be traced through four decades to the 1770s. Lastly, and perhaps most importantly, is the survival of another chair made for the Capitol that dates to the 1750s (fig. 46). This chair, too, is a Williamsburg product, and it proves without doubt that in Williamsburg the style of the Speaker's chair had long since passed by that time.

The Speaker's chair is made of American black walnut and has oak and poplar as the secondary woods. The cornice and pediment are finished on the back and the sides have a deep rabbet that originally received a paneled back. Since the chair was finished on all sides, it appears that it was originally intended to be used as a free-standing form. This is confirmed by the virtually indentical form of Speaker's chair that was used in the British House of Commons, a chair that stood in the central area of the room.[6] By 1777, when Ebenezer Hazzard visited the House of Burgesses and made a sketch of the Speaker's chair, its location may have changed. He noted that it stood with a large iron stove "at the upper end" of the room and that there were ". . .on Each Side the Seats for the Members & at the lower End a Gallery for the use of Spectators. . . ."[7] While the description does not note the chair's placement, it might be construed to imply that it stood against the wall, and it may already have lost its paneled back. Some support of this is seen in the Chowan County Courthouse in Edenton, North Carolina—a building that was strongly influenced by the design of the Virginia

Capitol. The Judge's tall, pedimented chair seen there is copied from the Speaker's chair and is built in, or attached to, the wall.[8] Since the Edenton Courthouse was built in 1766, nearly three decades after the burning of the first Capitol, it undoubtedly represents the influence of the second building and may reflect the usage of the Speaker's chair in Williamsburg at the time.

Of great symbolic and historical importance, the Speaker's chair is a cornerstone in the study of Williamsburg furniture. It served the House of Burgesses, the lower elected body, and thus forms a close parallel to one used by the British House of Commons. Its arms are lone survivals in an academic William and Mary style in Virginia or, for that matter, the South. But its cabriole legs, with their distinctive pad feet, and its knee brackets, which are applied to the face of the seat rails, provide important ties with other local productions.

These cabriole legs, with their bulbous pad feet, are of the same form seen on a mahogany tea table descended in the Galt family of Williamsburg (fig. 8). Displaying the elegance and proportion for which the Queen Anne style is renowned, it was inspired by oriental designs that came to America via England and Holland.[9] It would be difficult to find a better representative of the Chinese quality in American-made furniture of the eighteenth century.

Several features found on this table are very important to the study of later groups of Williamsburg furniture. The raised molding of the top is glued and nailed into a shallow rabbet that is cut on the upper edge of the table. It is interesting to note as well, that the pieces forming the skirt pass across the top edge of the cabriole legs and are mitered at the corners. A third feature found here is the removal of a small central section from the lower edge of the front skirt, cut away at a 45-degree angle. All of these characteristics appear again in later Williamsburg groups and will be discussed on pieces attributed to the Anthony Hay shop.

The main frame of this table is unusually constructed (see cross-section detail, fig. 8a). The top half of the rail is mahogany, the lower half is oak along the sides and walnut on the ends. A contoured skirt made in two pieces is applied over the lower portion. The visible outer portion of this skirt, like the upper part of the rail, is mahogany. Sandwiched between it and the lower rail is a long thin wedge of pine.

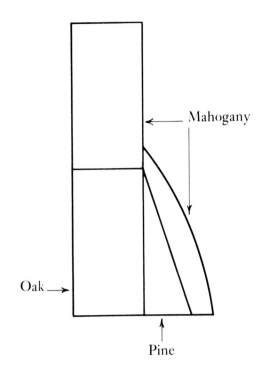

Mahogany

Oak

Pine

8. *Tea Table, Williamsburg, circa 1735.*
Mahogany primary; yellow pine, oak secondary.
Height 26¾", width 29½", depth 17⅜".
The Colonial Williamsburg Foundation (acc. no. 1978-11).

8a. *Tea Table, cross-section of skirt construction.*

A massive and impressive dining table (fig. 9) that traditionally belonged to Robert "King" Carter (died 1732) gives some support to the early date assigned to the Speaker's chair. Both have identical pad feet. There are secondary woods of oak and yellow pine, and its primary wood is a high quality mahogany. The three boards of the top are matched cuts from the same tree, with an extraordinarily bold curly grain, and the outer edges of the leaves have a narrow strip glued on to complete the top. These are not repairs but were done by the maker, and show the same curly grain as the larger boards.

This piece appears to be the earliest of a large group of tables made in Williamsburg, and is characteristic of that city's products in having a frame with cut-out bracket returns on the ends and applied brackets on the sides. Furniture in this group has legs that are square at the top, with slightly rounded corners that gradually taper into round legs and pad feet below. The offset in the gate-leg, which accomodates the side rail when the gate is closed, is finished with a graceful lamb's tongue that appears from the side as a cyma curve (figs. 10, 11a).

9. Dining Table, Williamsburg, circa 1730.
Mahogany primary; yellow pine, oak secondary.
Height 38¾", width 66¼", depth 21¼" closed, 71¼" open.
Private collection.

18

10. *Table Legs, Williamsburg, circa 1735.*
Walnut primary; yellow pine secondary.
Height (without caster), 27⅜″, width 2⁵/₁₆″, depth 2⅜″.
The Colonial Williamsburg Foundation (acc. no. 1977-266, 8 and 9).

11a.

Another table of this early period survives only in part, although enough remains to identify it as clearly belonging to this group (fig. 10). Its feet are the same as those on the Carter table, with the addition of casters—the one original that survives being severely worn down. Both the lamb's-tongue transition for the side rail and the marks where the brackets were attached to the legs are clearly visible. The wood is walnut with a small portion of the original yellow pine side rail remaining in a mortise. These legs were in the refuse of an early twentieth-century cabinet shop in Richmond and had apparently been discarded from a repair.

An important difference, both stylistically and technologically, separates early Williamsburg furniture into two phases of development. The earliest of these is represented by the preceding pieces, which have bulbous pad feet that were produced by carving. The second phase is characterized by flattened pads that were lathe-turned. The continuity between these groups is established by dining tables that are identical in style and construction, which were produced with both phases of pad feet development.

11. *Dining Table, Williamsburg, circa 1745.*
Mahogany primary; oak, yellow pine secondary.
Height 28"; width 59½"; depth 19" closed, 64" open.
Courtesy William M. Dickson.

12. *Dining Table, Williamsburg, circa 1745.*
Walnut primary; walnut and pine secondary.
Height 28¾", width 60¾", depth 55¼".
The Colonial Williamsburg Foundation (acc. no. 1930-169).

The next two tables (figs. 11, 12) are closely related to the preceding and show the later lathe-turned pad foot. The first is made of mahogany (fig. 11) and has yellow pine and oak secondary woods. Its top is held to the frame by small glue blocks and large wood screws with "dome" heads. These dome-top screws are typical of those used for this purpose in the first half of the eighteenth century, until counter-sunk examples with flat tops replaced them. This table and the walnut example (fig. 12) probably date from the decade 1735-45. The first has a history of ownership in Greenbrier County, West Virginia, and the second was found in the Petersburg, Virginia area. Many tables of this type, with the later pad feet, survive.

A walnut dressing table (fig. 13) has feet relating to the two tables just discussed and probably dates to the late 1730s. Its finely developed skirt has a small central pendant reminiscent of the larger pendant on the Speaker's chair (fig. 7). The cabriole legs of this dressing table appear slightly earlier in form than those of the Speaker's chair, and they have heavily hollowed areas on each side of the knee, forming wide flanges. This creates a pronounced "shin bone" effect just below the knee, continuing down to a point where the flanges taper into a round ankle. In profile this leg has a distinct "haunch," or offset, on the inside curve. While the design of the "shin bone" leg is archaic when compared to those of the Speaker's chair, this example is actually later in date and therefore the leg design must be considered a feature that was retained from an earlier style. The utilization of turned pad feet clearly establishes its later period of production. The brass pulls and their plates are original to this piece, and their pattern with the geometric design is consistent with the decade of the 1730s. Even though the backboard is yellow pine, the brackets of the rear knees are completely finished and the top is molded across the back. This finished approach for tops and backs of tables is encountered in much furniture of the Williamsburg area. This dressing table descended in a family of York County, Virginia.

The lower section of a high chest of drawers (fig. 14) is dramatically bolder than the preceding dressing table but is closely related to it. It descended in the Finch family of King George County and is the only example of this form, often called a highboy today, known to have been made in eastern Virginia. Considering the strong ties of Virginia furniture to English cabinetwork, the early date of this piece is somewhat explainable. The form was very popular in England through the end of the first quarter of the eighteenth century, and thereafter it quickly passed

13. Dressing Table, Williamsburg, circa 1740.
Black walnut primary; yellow pine secondary.
Height 28½", width 29⅞", depth 20⅞".
The Museum of Early Southern Decorative Arts.

14. *High Chest Base, Williamsburg, circa 1740.*
Walnut primary; yellow pine secondary.
Height 32", width 41½", depth 23".
The Colonial Williamsburg Foundation (acc. no. 1978-13).

14a.

14b.

15. *Tea Table, attributed to Williamsburg, circa 1710.*
Walnut primary.
Height 27½", width 26½", depth 21½".
The Colonial Williamsburg Foundation (acc. no. G1976-429),
    gift of Mr. & Mrs. Miodrag Blagojevich.

from use. On this piece not only has the top been lost, but all drawers have been replaced, as well.

The legs of this piece are highly developed. The shin-bone effect is much bolder than the preceding example, and the addition of the large trifid foot and small scallop shell, are further refinements. The distinctive gouge cuts on the backs of the feet, which undoubtedly relate to carved "hoof" feet, may help to identify other examples from the group. Three tables recorded in the research files of the Museum of Early Southern Decorative Arts show some relationship to these pieces. The C-scrolls flanking their knees appear to have developed from those in the preceding example. Further study is needed to determine whether they were made in Williamsburg, or whether they represent a style transplanted from that city. Their diverse provenances and relationship to two groups of Williamsburg furniture strongly suggest they were produced there.[10]

Another table that may be cautiously considered here has an unspecified Virginia provenance (fig. 15). The molding of the top on this table may be compared to that of the preceding tea table (fig. 8) and several later examples that follow. Here the molding is not set into a rabbet but is glued and nailed directly to the top. The columnar turnings of this table, together with the columnar arm supports of the Speaker's chair, are among the most academic of this form to come from colonial Virginia. The combination of these two features forms the basis of an extremely tentative attribution of this table to Williamsburg.

Early Williamsburg pieces are very rare, although the group here assembled exhibits a homogeneity of design and construction, with the possible exception of the latter tea table. They show a high quality, self-assured level of workmanship, and an amazing awareness of style. It has been possible to establish a chronology based on specific details and evolutionary trends, some of which are continued in later Williamsburg shops—particularly that of Anthony Hay. Before this continuity can be discussed, however, other early developments in Williamsburg should be analyzed, and attention is thus turned to Peter Scott, dean of cabinetmakers in Virginia's colonial capital.

FOOTNOTES

1. H. R. McIlwaine and J. P. Kennedy, eds., *Journals of the House of Burgesses of Virginia, 1619-1776* (Richmond: Virginia State Library, 1905-1915), Vol. 4 (1702-12), April 9, 1703, p. 30.
2. Accession File No. L 1933-504, Department of Collections, Colonial Williamsburg Foundation, Williamsburg, Virginia; John T. Kirk, *American Chairs: Queen Anne and Chippendale* (New York: Alfred A. Knopf, 1972), p. 151, fig. 202.
3. Marcus Whiffen, *The Public Buildings of Williamsburg* (Williamsburg, Virginia: Colonial Williamsburg Foundation, 1958), pp. 127-128.
4. *Journals of the House of Burgesses of Virginia*, Vol. 5 (1712-26), pp. 283, 284.
5. Ibid., p. 225.
6. H. M. Colvin, ed., *The History of the Kings Works* (London: Her Majesty's Stationery Office, 1976) Vol. 5 (1660-1782), plate 53.
7. Jane Carson, *We Were There: Descriptions of Williamsburg, 1699-1859* (Williamsburg: Colonial Williamsburg Foundation, 1956), pp. 37-38.
8. Frances Benjamin Johnston and Thomas Tileston Waterman, *The Early Architecture of North Carolina* (Chapel Hill: University of North Carolina Press, 1947), p. 249, plates p. 268.
9. The term "Queen Anne" is a misnomer when applied to this style. It is generally recognized that the style developed from Indian and Chinese prototypes during the reigns of George I and George II.
10. The provenances of these tables are recorded in: Photographic File Numbers 5300, southeast Virginia; S-3923, Isle of Wight County; and S-5979, Fredericksburg area, at the Museum of Early Southern Decorative Arts in Winston-Salem, North Carolina. This latter example descended in the same family as two Scott chairs (figs. 25, 28) and has a high trumpet-shaped pad foot that is associated with Anthony Hay's shop. The extruded scroll on the knee brackets are closely associated (in profile) with those on the Hay Shop card table (fig. 48).

Figure 18

The Peter Scott Shop

The career of Peter Scott (1694-1775) spanned five decades and is distinguished as the longest of any Williamsburg cabinetmaker. He is first documented in the town during 1722 and had established his shop on the south side of Duke of Gloucester Street, opposite Bruton Parish Church, by 1733.[1] Little is known of his early years, and most of the important details regarding his life and business are gathered from six *Virginia Gazette* notices. It is significant that the earliest of these, the only one placed by Scott, was printed more than three decades after his first known appearance in Williamsburg. It was not intended to promote his business but instead to settle his affairs and announce his intended departure for England:

> To Be S O L D
>
> BEFORE Mr. Finnie's Door, on the 23rd Day of October next, Two Lots of Ground, situate on the Back Street, near Col. Custis's in Williamsburg; on which there is a good Dwelling House, containing Six Rooms and Closets, a good dry Cellar, with all convenient Out-Houses, and a good Well: Twelve Months Credit will be allowed the Purchases giving Bond and Security. At the same Time and Place will be sold, for Bills of Exchange or ready Money, Two Negroes, bred to the Business of a Cabinetmaker; likewise will be sold, at the Subscriber's Shop near the Church, sundry Pieces of Cabinet Work, of Mahogony and Walnut, consisting of Desks, Book-Cases, Tables of various Sorts, Tools, and some Materials. Six Months Credit will be given to those that purchase above the Value of Fifty Shillings, on their giving Bond and Security; and Five per Cent, will be allowed for ready Money.
>
> And as I intend to go for Great-Britain the latter End of next Month, therefore, I desire all Persons indebted to me, to make speedy Payment, otherwise they may expect Trouble without further Notice.
>
> Peter Scott[2]

Although this advertisement notes that Peter Scott owned two lots on "Back" (Francis) Street with a house and outbuilding, it does not tell us that he rented a dwelling and/or shop on Duke of Gloucester Street (colonial lot 354). This was granted in 1717 to John Custis, Martha Washington's first father-in-law, who will re-enter the story at a later date. It was a convenient business location, and Scott inhabited the house from 1733, until his death on the eve of the Revolution:[3]

> December 2, 1775
>
> Deaths . . . .
>
> Mr. Peter Scott, in the 81st year of his age, he was upwards of forty years a Common Councilman of this corporation.[4]

It is unfortunate that the early court records for James City County were destroyed and that no documentation of Scott's council activities or his estate survives. The only known reference to the settlement of his personal property is found in a notice shortly after his death:

January 13, 1776
To be SOLD before Robert Nicolson's Store,
    on Tuesday the 16th instant,
A GREAT variety of cabinet-makers tools, mohogany, walnut, and pine plank, likewise new walnut book cases, desks, tables, &c. belonging to the estate of mr. Peter Scott, deceased. Six months credit will be allowed for all sums above 51. the purchasers giving bond with good security.
    All persons indebted to the said estate, by bond or open account, are requested to pay off as soon as possible; and those to whom the estate are indebted are desired to call and receive payment, from
    ALEXANDER CRAIG,   EXECUTORS[5]
    ROBERT NICOLSON,

Less than two months after Scott's death, and shortly following the sale of his estate, the old house in which he had lived was a casualty of the American Revolution:

January 26, 1776
    Mr. Peter Scott's old house in this city, which he had rented and lived in for fourty-three years, was burnt down last Sunday night by accident.[6]

Further details concerning the cause of the blaze are found in a letter written by Edmond Randolph to George Washington on January 26, 1776: "About 5 Days since, Mr. Custis's Tenement, where Scott lived, Opposite the Church, was burnt to the Ground, by the Negligence of some of the Soldiers, who had been quartered there. The Wind, being due South, the out-House escaped the Flames; the Difficulty of saving the Church became thereby very great. . ."[7]

Although little information is available on Peter Scott's personal life, the *Virginia Gazette* advertisements that refer to him offer valuable insight into his business activity. The 1755 notice, in which he offered his property for sale and announced his intention to leave for Great Britain, indicates the success of his trade. Scott owned two lots on Francis Street at that time, but he continued to rent his dwelling and shop from Custis at Williamsburg's average rate of £10-£12 yearly.[8] The advantages of a business location on Duke of Gloucester Street must have been great, for one would otherwise expect his shop to have been on one of the Francis Street properties he owned. This same advertisement also discloses that Scott owned "two Negroes, bred to the business of a Cabinetmaker," a parcel of mahogany and walnut, and a stock of finished cabinet work.

Noticeably absent from the records concerning Scott's shop are advertisements of completed work

for sale. While he does not advertise custom cabinetwork for sale, the incidental ads in 1755 and 1776 list various items that must have been on hand for direct sale from his shop. Despite the time span between these notices, there is a striking similarity between the items listed, and a consistent pattern seems to emerge. The evidence strongly suggests that in addition to custom order, it was normal practice to keep a large stock on hand, that sales were regular, and that demand was so great as to eliminate the need for advertisement. This also held true in 1766 when Williamsburg cabinetmaker John Ormeston announced his intention to move to Wilmington, North Carolina. He, too, had completed furniture on hand to sell.[9]

Although there is no appeal for journeymen or apprentices in Scott's lone *Virginia Gazette* notice, it is highly likely that they were employed in his shop. The surviving records indicate that he had a fairly large operation, and over a period of five decades he undoubtedly trained apprentices and employed some journeymen. A large distribution of simple chairs, all having Scott construction, corroborates this assumption. Perhaps the answer to this lack of advertisements is his extreme popularity, for he was established in Williamsburg at an early date and was patronized by many wealthy Virginians by mid-century. He was so well-known, in fact, that in *Gazette* notices about the burning of the house, which actually belonged to the Custis family, it was referred to as "Mr. Peter Scott's old house in this city." Scott's residence is mentioned, matter of factly, as a familiar landmark. Presumably his prominent location and his popularity attracted prospective apprentices and journeymen thereby eliminating any need to advertise. This appears to have been the case regarding custom orders and direct sales of his shop's products, since no advertisements for these goods are known to have ever existed.

Scott's 1755 *Gazette* notice of his plan to go to Great Britain mentions his ownership of two black cabinetmakers. If indeed Scott ever left, and if he sold them prior to his departure, then he had purchased or hired another by November 2, 1772, when Thomas Jefferson noted in his account book "pd. Peter Scott in Full £16 gave negro man at Peter Scotts 5s."[10] By the time of Scott's estate sale in 1776, there were no black cabinetmakers listed, indicating that the one mentioned in 1772 had been hired from another owner or was sold in the meantime, or perhaps his fate was decided by Scott's will, which no longer exists. These incidental references seem to indicate that black cabinetmakers were an integral part of his shop operation, and that they played an important role in cabinetmaking in early Williamsburg.

Occasional documentation for Scott's custom orders survives, and from them we learn something of his production and activity. One of the earliest is a 1748 entry regarding a desk in Colonel William Bassett's account book.[11] A desk that descended in the Bassett family of Hanover County may be the same one referred to in this account and will be discussed in depth later in this book (fig. 35). In 1748, 1749, and 1750, Scott received payments from John Mercer, a lawyer who lived near Fredericksburg, but the work was probably for Mercer's two children who studied at the College of William and Mary during those years. One of the more enlightening entries in Mercer's daybook is a debit to Scott for "mending of a table for my sons." This account is listed under the entry "Peter Scott joiner at Williamsburg."[12] In another receipt, unfortunately not dated, Scott charged Robert Carter of Nomini Hall for two card tables, a sideboard, and four picture frames.[13] It was not until April of 1785, almost 10 years after Scott's death, that Carter authorized payment of £21.9.3, plus interest, to Scott's estate for these items.[14]

Thomas Jefferson also had numerous accounts with Peter Scott. From 1771 until the cabinetmaker's death in 1775, Jefferson seems to have patronized him more than any other Williamsburg artisan. Several accounts are listed only as cash sums paid, but a few are more detailed, such as an order recorded in 1772: "wrote to Scott to make table 4f 1 I. sq and 2 f. 4 I. high. My tea tables were directed to be 3. f. by 2.f. & 2. f. 3.2 I. high."[15] A ball-and-claw-foot table at Monticello may relate to the first portion of this account (fig. 31). A memorandum, also dated 1772, gives measurements that may be preliminary plans for the tea tables in the second portion of the Jefferson account: "Tea table when leaves down 2f by 1f 7½ I, when leaves up 2 f by 2 f 9 I Height 2 f 3⅜ I."[16] Another order, dating 1773-74, specified "clothes presses to be made by Scott 4 f 6 I wide. High as a desk and bookcase."[17] It is fortunate that a clothespress matching this very unusual description (fig. 42) survives among the furnishings owned by Robert Beverley of Blandfield.

No signed or labeled piece of Scott furniture is known at this time, but strong circumstantial evidence argues for the attribution of a large group to the Williamsburg area, and more specifically to Peter Scott's shop. A summary of this evidence, divided into several groups, is necessary to make the basis for this attribution as clear as possible. The first provides strong reasons for assigning the group to the city of Williamsburg.

—A clothespress in this group descended in the Galt family of Williamsburg (fig. 36).
—Case pieces in this group share a relationship with other Williamsburg shops (figs. 50, 77, 85, 86).
—A set of Scott chairs, including a matching settee and corner chair, has a firm history from the Governor's Palace (figs. 32-34).
—The chairs in this group have strong constructional ties to other Williamsburg shops (figs. 49, 58-62, 64, 96).
—The application of their knee blocks over the seat rail is the same as that found on the Speaker's chair in the Capitol (fig. 7).
—Scott chairs are also related in construction to a set that descended in the Benjamin Waller family of Williamsburg (fig. 62) and to a lone example with a history in the Governor's Palace (fig. 58).

Two furniture fragments excavated at the Anthony Hay site also suggest a Williamsburg origin for this group. One of these, an easy-chair leg, is related to chair legs in the Scott group (see fig. 65). The second, a fragment of a slip seat, utilizes the same upholstery technique as the two Palace sets (figs. 58 and 67).

Since constructional features common to this group are also found in other documented Williamsburg shops, particularly those from the Hay site, it is necessary to consider the documentary evidence in order to specifically attribute these pieces to Peter Scott:

—The Jefferson ball-and-claw-foot table (fig. 31), possibly conforming to Jefferson's 1772 order to Scott.
—The Bassett family desk-and-bookcase (fig. 35), possibly the one recorded in Colonel Bassett's 1748 account due Scott.
—The Blandfield clothespress (fig. 42) matching the description of one ordered by Jefferson from Scott.

Finally, the long period of time spanned by the objects within this group corresponds to Scott's cabinetmaking career. While other cabinetmakers were working in Williamsburg, no other Williamsburg cabinetmaker is known to have been working throughout this period. The geographic distribution of this group, as well, corresponds closely to the documented patronage of Scott and other Williamsburg cabinetmakers.

Having discussed Scott's background and having set out the basic points that substantiate the attribution of this group to him, we can proceed to a stylistic and chronological study of the pieces. The George II style and the construction of earlier pieces within the group parallel English development in the

1730 period. From that point a chronology is indicated as the George II style gives way to the rococo. That change is paralleled by a gradual decline in the quality of carving, which is not surprising considering Scott's advancing age. Several of these pieces can be associated with documents or historical circumstances that help to establish an approximate date. A list of the details that characterize the chairs in this group helps clarify their relationship:

—Knee brackets. These are applied to the face of the seat rails that pass behind them (fig. 19a). The clear outline of the missing bracket remains on the face of the seat rail.

—Shoe. The shoe and the rear rail are a single piece, with the bottom profile of the rear rail cut out. Occasionally the outer portions of the shaped bottom edge are separate pieces that have been glued on (fig. 16b).

—Stiles. Invariably parallel, they flare outward just below the crest rail.

—Splats. The splats are heavily undercut on the back, with a pronounced bevel that is very well finished (fig. 16b).

—Arms. These are dovetailed into the stile and are reinforced with a screw. This dovetailing is visible from the rear of the stile (fig. 22a).

The first five chairs shown (figs. 16, 18-21) are of the highest quality and are stylistically termed George II, with controlled carving that accents large, plain spaces. The scale of the carving is well proportioned in relation to the chair elements, producing a clarity of overall design that is often not present in later, rococo examples. Here the design "reads" well and is not cluttered or confused.

The first chair (fig. 16) has several details that indicate it is closest to its London counterparts and, theoretically, the earliest of the group. Its cabriole legs have a more pronounced curve, which is most noticeable on the inside at the top behind the knee. More wood has been removed from this area than on later chairs, giving it a graceful, flowing character. Likewise, the finish work of the undercutting on the bottom profile of the seat rails is more refined than on later examples, and the carved shell with bellflower pendants and plain knee brackets are the earliest type. According to tradition this chair descended in the family of Alexander Spotswood (1676-1740), lieutenant governor of Virginia from 1710 to 1722.

16. Side Chair, attributed to the shop of Peter Scott, Williamsburg, circa 1740.
Mahogany primary; beech slip seat.
Height 38⅞", width 21⅜", depth 17¼".
The Colonial Williamsburg Foundation (acc. no. G1938-199).

16a.   16b.

17. *Side Chair, London, circa 1730.*
Walnut and walnut veneer primary.
Height 42¾", width 20¼", depth 20¼".
The Colonial Williamsburg Foundation (acc. no. 1936-219).

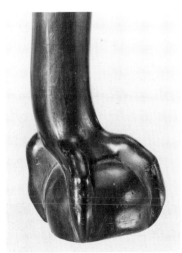

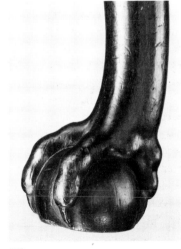

16c.   *17a.*   *16d.*   *17b.*

A pair of impressive armchairs (fig. 18) that are original furnishings of Shirley Plantation have design elements related to the Spotswood chair. Their arms are well formed, with serpentine supports that terminate in carved dog's heads. A pair of side chairs in the Virginia Historical Society (fig. 19) was probably a part of this set. These are also made of cherry and are identical in height and carved detail.

Less elaborate than the preceding example, and fashioned of black walnut, is a side chair recently found in Rhode Island that has an obscure Virginia background (fig. 20).[18] Its carving is very well executed and it retains several original voluted knee brackets. The splat is a less expensive variation of the earlier examples, as is the crest rail.

19. *Side Chair, attributed to the shop of Peter Scott,*
    Williamsburg, circa 1745.
Cherry primary; beech slip seat frame and cherry blocking.
Height 39⁵/₁₆″, width 21¾″, depth 17⅜″.
Virginia Historical Society.

18. *Armchair, attributed to the shop of Peter Scott,*
    Williamsburg, circa 1745.
Cherry primary.
Height 39⁵/₁₆″, width 24³/₅″, depth 18⅜″.
Shirley Plantation, Charles City County, Va.

18a.   *18b.*   *19a.*

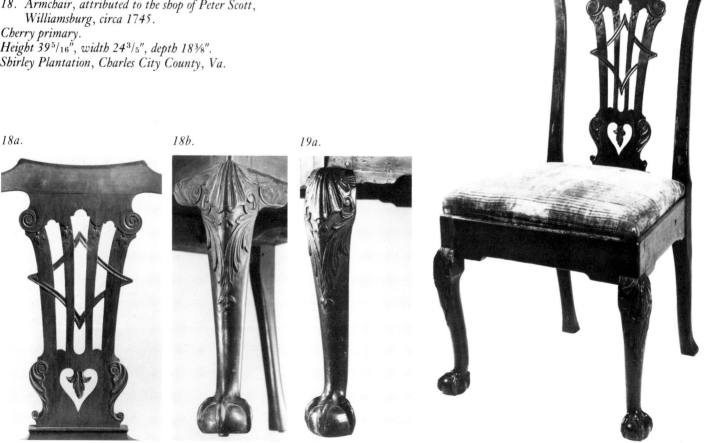

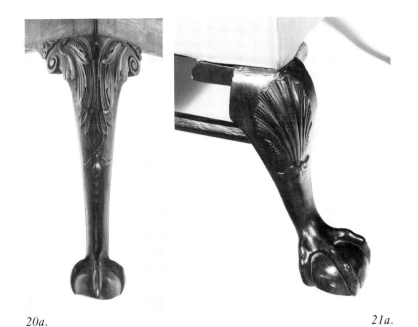

20a.   21a.

21. *Easy Chair, attributed to the shop of Peter Scott,*
    Williamsburg, circa 1750.
Mahogany primary; beech secondary.
Height 46", width 32", depth 30½".
Mount Vernon Ladies' Association.

20. *Side Chair, attributed to the shop of Peter Scott,*
    Williamsburg, circa 1750.
Walnut primary; oak slip seat and yellow pine blocking.
Height 37⅞", width 22¾", depth 20½".
The Colonial Williamsburg Foundation (acc. no. 1972-230).

One of the rarest American easy chairs (fig. 21) descended in the Washington family and is thought to have belonged to Mary Ball Washington. The bold legs and feet are typical of other examples in this group, but their visual impact would be much improved by the restoration of the knee brackets and the removal of the added stretchers. The support blocks of the brackets survive and suggest large volutes similar to the preceding chair and to several corner chairs as well (figs. 28, 29). The rear cabriole legs, with ball-and-claw feet, are the only known examples from colonial America, although several Philadelphia chairs of this form have pad or trifid feet on the rear.

Stylistically there are two additional features that tie these pieces to the second quarter of the eighteenth century. The dog's-head terminals found on several of the armchairs offer an interesting alternate to the more popular eagle's- and lion's-head terminals found in quality English work. Occasionally, New York chairs have eagle's-head terminals, but Williamsburg is the only other center in America that produced sculptural animal forms on the arms of chairs. A second feature, originally found on the

Washington easy chair (fig. 21), are large volutes flanking the knees. Their design is closely related to the feet and knee blocks on two desk-and-bookcases (figs. 37, 39).

The first definite indications of the rococo style evident in this group are found on the knee brackets of a side chair (fig. 20). Above the large volute on each bracket is carved a short C-scroll with a slight shell appendage on its top. A small segment of this same design can be seen on the ends of a gadroon molding on the front of an armchair (fig. 22b).

A mahogany armchair (fig. 22) also shows signs of the change to rococo style. The ears of the crest rail have lost their vigorous expanding volutes and are replaced by weak scrolls that are molded across their fronts. This molding originates beneath a small acanthus carved at the juncture of the crest and stiles and continues until it rolls over the ear and disappears around the curve. Unfortunately, the knee blocks are missing, but their carving was probably the same as those on the walnut side chair (fig. 20). The design of the knee carving is identical throughout, although the finish work of the armchair is slightly inferior. This workmanship is particularly noticeable in the background behind the relief carving, which shows many tool marks. This armchair has an oral history in the Ferneyhough family of Fredericksburg and is virtually identical to another armchair in a private Richmond collection, which has a long verbal tradition of ownership by Jefferson. This example came to the author's attention too late to be illustrated in this study, but it is extremely important in light of Jefferson's numerous accounts with Scott.

22c.

22a.

22. *Armchair, attributed to the shop of Peter Scott,*
    Williamsburg, circa 1755.
Mahogany primary.
Height 38½", width 28½", depth 18".
The Mary Washington House of the Association for the
    Preservation of Virginia Antiquities.

22b.

33

Another side chair with a Fredericksburg history has a simple design without carving and typifies the sober approach of the largest number of chairs surviving in the Scott group (fig. 23). This and a matching armchair from King and Queen County (fig. 24) show many concessions to the rococo style. A change in the handling of the voluted ears on the crest rail of the preceding mahogany armchair (fig. 22) has already been discussed. Here, however, the crest has evolved into a completely different form, and the voluted ears of earlier examples have become rounded into large, swelled lobes. The form is clearly rococo, although the saddle in the center of the crest, the parallel stiles, and the splat design remain from the earlier style. On the armchair the S-shaped arm support is retained, considerably weaker in form, and a dog's-head terminal has been dropped in favor of a small, down-curved volute. The construction is the same as carved armchairs in the group, where shoe and rear seat rail are an integral piece with horizontal shaping, and the arms are dovetailed into the stiles.

23. *Side Chair, attributed to the shop of Peter Scott,*
    Williamsburg, circa 1760.
Walnut primary; beech slip seat frame.
Height 37½", width 22⅝", depth 17".
The Kenmore Association, Inc.

24. *Armchair, attributed to the shop of Peter Scott,*
    Williamsburg, circa 1760.
Walnut primary; yellow pine blocking.
Height 37½", width 17", depth 22⅝".
Private collection.

25. *Child's Chair, attributed to the shop of Peter Scott, Williamsburg, circa 1760.*
Walnut primary.
Height 27", width 18", depth 13".
Ms. Turner Ashby.

26. *Child's Chair, attributed to the shop of Peter Scott, Williamsburg, circa 1760.*
Walnut primary; yellow pine secondary.
Height 18¾", width 14", depth 11".
The Colonial Williamsburg Foundation, gift of Mr. & Mrs. Ray Power.

Quite consistent with these examples in its construction is a child's armchair (fig. 25). Its serpentine arm support, with a dovetailed arm fitting, is closely related to the preceding chair (fig. 24). The arm terminal is a variation seen on several later chairs in the group. Unfortunately, the crest rail, splat, and front seat rail are replacements. The original crest was probably the squared form, as are the other known examples in this group. The knee brackets, too, are replaced, although the originals were types that overlapped the rail. According to tradition, this chair was an original furnishing of Belmont at Falmouth near Fredericksburg. Also worth noting here is a corner chair with the same history, which has similarly shaped arm terminals (fig. 28).

Another child's chair (fig. 26), found in Dinwiddie County near Petersburg, is closely related to the preceding. It, too, has lost its original splat, its crest rail, and the top one-third of its stiles, which appear to have been broken just below the arm joint. This chair has cabriole legs similar to the preceding example and retains its original knee brackets overlapping the rails. It differs in two respects, however. The arm supports, now cut off even with the rails, were originally an extension of the front legs; the shoe is a separate piece, although the rear rail has horizontal shaping conforming to the group. This separate shoe, however, could be an alteration that accompanied the loss of the original splat and crest rail.

Possessing elements of the previous simple and elaborate examples is a walnut side chair with a tradition of ownership by George Washington at Mount Vernon (fig. 27). Its splat, though not original, is a very old mahogany replacement, the design of which was probably taken from the original, since it is continuous with the design of the crest rail and is heavily undercut in imitation of the Scott group bevel. All other elements that survive

27. Side Chair, attributed to the shop of Peter Scott, Williamsburg, circa 1760.
Walnut primary; beech slip seat.
Height 39", width 22⅝", depth 20½".
Mount Vernon Ladies' Association.

27a.

27b.

are original. Here the rounded ear of the crest rail is completely rococo in design, with the top profile formed by three C-scrolls (fig. 27a). The quality of the carving has declined from that of the earliest chairs; this is most apparent on the acanthus leaves of the rounded ears, and on the central leaf element of the crest rail. The cabriole leg and foot also show a loss in quality: the leg is very straight and the foot is somewhat smaller than the earlier examples. There was also carving on the skirt, which originally had a gadroon molding glued along the lower front edge, identical to construction seen in the Ferneyhough chair (fig. 22). Although now lost, the glue mark and undercutting for it are quite obvious. In addition to the rococo back and crest, the symmetry of earlier knee carving has been broken by adding a curled ending to the acanthus leaf.

The following corner chairs (figs. 28, 29) are unusually constructed. Their crests have an arch on each side of the central column and the joining of the skirt to the cabriole leg is very uncommon. One other chair of this form is pictured in the MESDA files (#S-6591), although it is much plainer and has straight chamfered legs. These chairs, particularly the two illustrated here, fall solidly within the Scott group. Their carving and major design elements are identical to, or variations of, details seen on the earlier chairs, and they continue the decline in the quality of carving already noted in the preceding examples.

The first of these corner chairs (fig. 28) is conceptually related in design and execution to other chairs in the Scott group. The knee carving, while initially appearing somewhat different, reveals upon closer study that virtually all of the elements come from the preceding examples and are merely rearranged. The basic formula was used in designing the earlier chairs (figs. 18b, 19a). It was altered by reducing the shell and moving it upward, away from the knee (fig. 28a). The inward-facing volutes flanking the large shell have been moved up until they touch each other and surmount the small reduced shell. Oddly, the bellflower, which is in the center of the knee's maximum protrusion, has not been moved in the new design but sits awkwardly between the extended acanthus leaves. At the top, branches of the acanthus flare toward the knee blocks, on which they would have continued but now, unfortunately, the blocks are missing. This feature, too, is remarkably similar to the wing-like features that extend beneath the shell and toward the knee block (fig. 18b). The knee blocks on figure 18 are replaced, however, and the continuation of these wings cannot be trusted as correct. Below the central bellflower is a series of grains very similar to those that terminate the knee

28. *Corner Chair, attributed to the shop of Peter Scott, Williamsburg, circa 1765.*
Walnut primary; walnut secondary.
Height 34", width 23", depth 26".
Ms. Turner Ashby.

28a.

carving of figures 20a and 22b and are interspersed on figure 16c. These sit upon a large acanthus flanked by overlapping fronds, virtually identical to those on figures 20a and 22b. Finally, the major acanthus terminates in a folded-back overlap, which is a slight variation of the curved termination of figure 27.

This chair was produced by employing a combination of designs that were in use two decades earlier. While the foot carving approximates the earlier quality, the knee carving is more crudely executed and is not as successful. The recombination of these elements produces a slightly clumsy, cluttered design, and the sculptural quality is flatter and somewhat cruder. This example is important, however, as an indication of the extreme effects traditional training could instill in the eighteenth-century tradesman.

The left splat of this corner chair is an old replacement and is coarser in execution than the original on the right. Their design is reminiscent of the interlaced diamond pattern found on some of the earlier Scott side and arm chairs (figs. 16, 18, 22). This example represents a major departure from traditional corner chair construction by employing four pieces of wood in the crest and arms rather than three. The arms do not meet in the back and the extra piece, centrally glued to the bottom of the crest, is mortised to receive the rear column. An apparent offshoot of this construction exists on several chairs belonging to another Williamsburg group. Found in the MESDA research files, they too have arms that are not joined. These examples, however, lack the arches in the crest and are fashioned from a single piece of wood. This construction replaces the small glued-on block found on the chairs illustrated here. Another chair in this latter group (fig. 96) does not have this solid construction, although it has a splat nearly identical in outline to that seen on the first Scott corner chair illustrated (fig. 28).

29a.

29b.

29. *Corner Chair, attributed to the shop of Peter Scott,*
    Williamsburg, circa 1770.
Walnut primary; walnut slip seat and blocking.
Height 31¾", width 30", depth 26".
Museum of Early Southern Decorative Arts.

The second corner chair (fig. 29) is closely related to the preceding piece. This example, however, has a ball-and-claw foot with a noticeably different approach (figs. 29a, 29b). It is higher, and probably represents a conscious attempt to depart from the early flattened ball, thus producing a piece more in line with changing fashion. Despite this difference, its affinity with earlier examples is evident in its smooth, slightly knuckled "toes" and its lack of webbing. The claws are angular points with little definition to separate them from the toes—carving that is typical of the entire group although several examples have more detailed definition on the claws. The knee carving is a variation of double overlapping fronds seen on several other chairs, although greatly degenerated in quality (fig. 29a). The acanthus leaves are an elaboration of those on a side chair, an armchair, and a corner chair (figs. 20, 22, 28) but end in such extended points that they take on the appearance of hooks. The splat of this chair is

a simplification of that design most often used in the group. It has an inverted vase-shaped base with a central heart opening below a series of parallel vertical piercings. The carved volutes that terminate the arms are nearly identical to those on the crest rails of early chairs in the group.

Six side chairs owned by Thomas Jefferson are thought to be a part of a set acquired by him from George Wythe of Williamsburg (fig. 30).[19] These chairs, one of them numbered "XX," are the only examples with this splat design and crest rail known to the writer, although they have some similarity to the walnut side chair with a Palace history (fig. 58). Two piercings of the splat splay downward and out, and both have seat rails with well-developed moldings. However, it appears that the crest rail on the Jefferson examples was produced for carved decoration, considering the shell outline at the extremes. In fact, their crest rails were cut to allow an extra thickness for the carving of the shell, but as they were never executed they have a simple scallop cut just above the joint of the stile to disguise the offset (fig. 30a). The Washington chair (fig. 27) is an example in which this allowance was actually carved. There are other pieces with this unusual feature, including a settee and chairs (figs. 32, 34) from the Governor's Palace. These are interesting examples and relate not only to the Jefferson chairs in the unused allowance for carving but also to the Washington chair in the profile of their ears. In those from the Palace (fig. 32, 34) the offset is left straight at the joint and lacks the refinement of the slight scallop.

This allowance for carving, without the follow-through, seems to indicate a large shop production of chairs. Where many sets were being made from patterns designed to accommodate carving, an order for the plainer chairs could have been supplied from the uncarved inventory examples, thus producing the somewhat awkward result seen in these chairs.

In addition to these chairs and several case pieces yet to be analyzed, one other furniture form survives in this group—a ball-and-claw-foot table. Having a tradition of ownership by Jefferson, it is possibly the piece he ordered from Scott in 1772 (fig. 31; see footnote 15). Once a full-sized dining table, it was cut to its present "breakfast" size in an alteration that is thought to have been done at Monticello during Jefferson's lifetime. The heavy ankles and rounded knuckles are related to other feet in this group—particularly those on the side chair owned by Washington (fig. 27) and those on a corner chair (fig. 29). Its small claws, while differing from most in the group, are like the surviving claw on the Mary Ball Washington easy chair (fig. 21). The rear toe (fig. 31b) protrudes at the top and is concave just above the claw—as are many in this group. It is not carved as a separate element but flows down from the ankle in a smooth curve, and in this respect it is more like English examples (fig. 17b). The only comparable toe in this group is found on the rear feet of the easy chair (fig. 21), but since this is the only table in the group the difference may be a stylistic allowance for the taller leg. The front of all the toes have lost some definition through wear, but despite this allowance they are shallow and the overall result is a cruder foot than others in the group.

The stiff, rather straight cabriole legs of this table are similar to later chairs of the group. The pointed knees of these legs are consistent with those found on case pieces (figs. 37, 39) and suggest a continuation of the corner of the case. Unfortunately, the knee brackets are missing, but some evidence remains and it is clear they were not the type that overlaps the rails of chairs in this group.

30a.

31a.

30. Side Chair, attributed to the shop of
    Peter Scott; Williamsburg, circa 1770.
Cherry primary; oak slip seat.
Height 39", width 20", depth 17".
The Thomas Jefferson Memorial Foundation.

31b.

31. Dining Table, attributed to the shop of Peter Scott,
    Williamsburg, circa 1772.
Mahogany primary; yellow pine, oak secondary.
Height 28", width 33", depth 18" closed.
The Thomas Jefferson Memorial Foundation.

The knee bracket on the gate was not attached to the leg but was nailed and glued to the table skirt. When the leg swung out, it stayed on the skirt rather than moved in the typical manner. This feature, like the sharp knee, parallels case construction with cabriole legs in which knee brackets are glued beneath the case and not to its face. This unusual constructional feature may help in identifying other related tables, and it is reminiscent of the shaped brackets on the skirts of dining tables in the early Williamsburg group (figs. 9, 11a).

The latest examples in the Scott group comprise a very large set of seating furniture with a history in the Governor's Palace (fig. 32-34). According to tradition, they were sold in 1776 at the sale of Lord Dunmore's property, having been left at the Palace when he fled Williamsburg the preceding year. They are said to have been purchased by Thomas Lewis of Augusta County and to have been presented by him to John Stuart and Agatha Frogg Lewis of Greenbrier County, Virginia (now West Virginia) as a wedding gift. They remained in "Stuart Manor" near Lewisburg, West Virginia until 1975, when they were purchased by Colonial Williamsburg from Stuart

descendants. It is quite important that the tradition of ownership is supported by a book which descended in the same family. This has the engraved bookplate of John Murray, the Earl of Dunmore, surmounted by those of Thomas Lewis and John Stuart.

Evidence indicates the set was very large. One side chair seat is marked "XIII" and apparently there was another settee, since the surviving example has a middle stretcher that was removed from another in an early repair.

These pieces probably date between 1771, when Dunmore arrived, and 1775, when he fled the colony. They display the coarsest workmanship of the entire group. As already discussed, they possess offset crest rails with an unused allowance for carving. In addition to this, the lower portion of the splat has the same vase-shape seen on many of the earlier chairs. Near the top of the splats are volutes emphasized by relief carving. These terminate the continuous flowing line of the crest rails lower profile and are similar to their antecedents (figs. 16, 18, 19, 20, 22), although not fully carved. Similar carving of splats occurs again and again in this group and

32. *Side Chair, attributed to the shop of Peter Scott, Williamsburg, 1771-1776.*
Cherry primary; oak slip seat with original black leather upholstery.
Height 36½", width 20¼", depth 17⅜".
The Colonial Williamsburg Foundation (acc. no. 1975-23,8).

33. *Corner Chair, attributed to the shop of Peter Scott, Williamsburg, 1771-1776.*
Cherry primary; poplar blocking; white oak slip seat with original black leather upholstery.
Height 29", width (across arms) 34" (measurements are approximate).
Private collection.

34. Double Chairback Settee, attributed to the shop of Peter Scott, Williamsburg, 1771-1776.
Cherry primary; poplar blocking; white oak seat with original black leather upholstery.
Height 36½", width 73", depth 21½".
Colonial Williamsburg Foundation (acc. no. 1975-23,1).

appears as well on two chairs from the Hay shop (figs. 59, 60). The awkward terminals of the arms of the settee are closely related to those on one of the corner chairs (fig. 29). On the settee, however, they have been simplified by the omission of the side volutes. Constructionally, these have all the features of the group outlined at the beginning of this section, with the exception of the substitution of a notch for the dovetails on the arms of the settee and the omission of undercutting on the splat. The settee has a rear seat that is integral with both shoes but lacks the horizontal shaping. These, plus the obvious differences in the corner chair, are probably due to the decline in quality seen all along—and to the cheaper aspects of this set in general.

Having completed an examination of the forego-ing chairs and table, and having established a chronology for them, the case pieces of this group can now be studied. They relate to the chairs through their identical ball-and-claw feet, common use of beech, and employment of primary woods in secondary usage. Constructionally, these cases exhibit a remarkably consistent approach:

—Case construction. Tops and bottoms are dovetailed into sides with hidden dovetails. The drawer blades are one-half dovetailed into the sides and enter from the front. They are then covered along the vertical front edge by a glued-on strip. The back is set into a rabbet on the top and sides and is secured by nails.

—Dustboards. These are thinner than the drawer blades and are wedged into grooves in the sides of the case by pine strips that run beneath them from front to back (fig. 37d). The dustboards are half-lapped onto the drawer blades.

—Base molding. The base molding is not applied to the sides of the case but to a series of rectangular blocks glued to the case bottom. The top edge of the base molding overlaps the bottom edge of the case very slightly and sometimes has a very shallow rabbet (fig. 37e).

—Ogee foot construction. The ogee-bracket feet are made of two pieces of wood. The primary wood that forms the exterior is glued to a piece of yellow pine which makes up the inside thickness of the foot (fig. 40b).

—Composite foot. The blocking of the feet is composed of several horizontally grained pieces of pine, with the grain of every other piece perpendicular to the preceding. This stacked blocking is neatly finished on the front feet (fig. 86b) but is left at random on the back feet (figs. 40b; 86b and c). Although figure 86 is from another shop, it conforms to Scott's in this respect; it is shown because those of the Scott examples have not survived completely intact. Since no terminology has been applied to this construction, that adopted here—"composite"—will be used throughout this work.

—Crown molding. The crown molding is glued to a series of large rectangular blocks across the front. On the sides it is glued to a continuous block that runs the depth of the case and is mitered at the front corners (fig. 37f).

—Drawer construction. The large case drawers have bottoms which are set into a very deep rabbet on the front and two sides and are then nailed into place (fig. 37g). The nails on the sides are covered from front to back with a continuous strip that also forms the drawer runners. This continuous piece butts against the drawer front, and is cut off at a 45-degree angle on the back. Across the front edge is a series of small blocks with open gaps between them. The lowest dovetail on the sides of each drawer is straight along the bottom, conforming to the upper edge of the rabbet that receives the drawer bottom (fig. 37h).

—Desk drawers. The small drawers in writing interiors also have a straight edge on the bottom of the lowest dovetails. The bottoms of these smaller drawers are set into a shallow rabbet on all four sides and are flush with the lower edge of the sides. They therefore have no runners and each drawer rides on the entire surface of its base.

—Door construction. The stiles and rails of the paneled doors are very broad, particularly the lower horizontal elements. They have blind tenons and are not usually pegged. The pine desk (fig. 39) is an exception, if, indeed, the pegging is original. The raised panels of these doors are not set into grooved stiles but fit into a rabbet. They are held in place by a small molding, either quarter-round or flat-bead, nailed around all four sides (fig. 36a). The pine desk is an exception here also.

—Fallboard supports. The fallboard supports of desks have a vertically grained facing that is joined by a tongue-and-groove joint. This joint is visible on the top and bottom.

—Waist joint. In large pieces consisting of upper and lower cases, the upper section sits on a series of shallow blocks that are arranged in identical layout to those of the cornice support blocking. The backboard of the lower section projects equally in height to these applied blocks and forms a support for the upper section across the back.

The walnut desk-and-bookcase (fig. 35) is apparently the earliest of these case pieces. It descended in the Bassett family and was sold from "Cloverlea" near Hanover, Virginia to the Talley family approximately seventy-five years ago. The present owner acquired it from them. The account book of Colonel William Bassett (d.ca.1742) dated 1730-48 contains an intriguing entry that may refer to this piece:

"Cash pd Dec. 9, 1748
To Mr. Peter Scott for a desk £5.0.0"[20]

While it is virtually impossible to research this desk to firmly associate it with this account, there are several points in favor of relating the two. The desk descended in the same family and resided in the same house with the account book until the twentieth century. Case pieces in this group are extremely rare and few have survived compared to later work. Documentation on Scott's furniture is very difficult to find, and the chances of correlating a document and a piece bearing family tradition is very slim. It is important when studying this piece to remember that the Bassett account book records payment for a desk—not a desk-and-bookcase. While the bookcase section of this example came from the same shop as others in the group, it was made at a later date than

the slant-top desk. The desk is finished off on top with a primary wood and is joined by a concealed, or "secret," dovetail, indicating it was made without a bookcase. This is reinforced within this group since the other desk-and-bookcase (fig. 37) has a pine top under the bookcase section and proves a different approach to the two types by the same maker. This later bookcase has a wall of Troy molding related to the type on the Blandfield press also attributed to Scott (fig. 42). The bookcase section probably dates to the 1760-70 period and was made at that time for the earlier desk.

The writing interior of this desk has drawers arranged on a single plane without stepping or blocking, and there are gracefully cut pigeonhole brackets and a burl walnut prospect door (fig. 35a). Mitered battens are found on the top and bottom of this door and serve to stabilize it from warpage. The match of wood grains has been made so cleverly that the joints are scarcely noticeable. The bracket feet have been heavily damaged and are partly replaced. It is difficult to determine their original shape.

35. Desk-and-Bookcase, attributed to the shop of Peter Scott, Williamsburg; desk circa 1740 (?), bookcase circa 1760.
Walnut primary; yellow pine and oak secondary.
Height 82⁷/₁₆", width 41³/₁₆", depth 21¾".
Mr. and Mrs. William C. Adams, Jr.

35a.

35b.

A fine clothespress made of mahogany is the only example of this wood within the case pieces (fig. 36). It descended in the Galt family of Williamsburg and is of large size with four fixed shelves on the interior. These are made of yellow pine and are faced with a bold, mahogany astragal molding. Although they are now lost, some evidence of wear remains on the shelves from the original sliding clothes trays. The cornice is distinguished by a well-designed wall of Troy molding. Likewise, the doors are well constructed with indented corners on the upper raised panels. The conforming molding that surrounds the panel is cut on the stiles, with the exception of the indented corners, where it is cut on two separate pieces mitered together and glued in place (fig. 36b). This piece stands on large, well-proportioned ogee-bracket feet that are double-ply, like all the ogee brackets in this group. Their composite blocking has been replaced.

36a. This clothespress was originally fitted with sliding trays that are now missing.

36b.

36c.

36. Clothespress, attributed to the shop of Peter Scott, Williamsburg, circa 1755.
Mahogany primary; yellow pine and walnut secondary.
Height 78¾", width 48", depth 21³/₁₆".
The Colonial Williamsburg Foundation (acc. no. 1951-205).

46

37a.

A second desk-and-bookcase attributed to Peter Scott is equally well executed but has a more imposing stance (fig. 37). Its unusually short cabriole legs are mortised into large, square, inch-thick pieces of beech that are nailed and glued to the bottom of the case (fig. 37e). The ball-and-claw feet on this piece and on the desk that follows are identical to the best quality chairs in this group and leave no doubt that both chairs and case pieces come from one shop.

To balance the taller bookcase section and the outward reaching ball-and-claw feet, the cornice molding of this desk has been made larger and is cut with a greater projection than those of the preceding two examples. Likewise, the molding on top of the desk, which receives the bookcase section, is more vigorously shaped. The raised panels in the doors have indented corners like those seen on other case pieces in this group, and the dentil molding of the cornice (fig. 37c) has small loops between the teeth—a design found in Chippendale's *Director* and seen on many pieces of English and American furniture. Their addition to the wall of Troy molding, however, (also seen on figs. 35 and 42) appears to be an unusual feature seldom encountered in other American furniture. The interior writing cabinet is finished with inlayed document drawers flanking a carved prospect door. Made from crotch walnut, this door is carved in a smooth concave depression terminating in a gothic arch, which is flanked by carved inset spandrels with a punched matt background. Originally, two drawers were behind the door.

37b.

37. *Desk-and-Bookcase, attributed to the shop of Peter Scott, Williamsburg, circa 1760.*
Walnut primary; poplar, yellow pine, and beech secondary.
Height 90¾", width 44½", depth 23½".
The Colonial Williamsburg Foundation (acc. no. 1976-95).

37c.

37f.

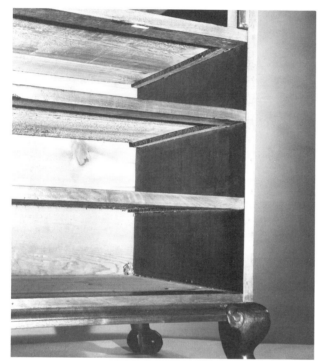

37d.

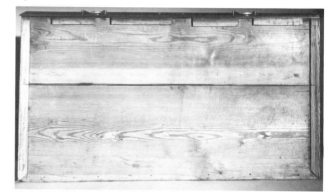

37g.

37e.

37h.

37i.

38a.

38. *Desk-and-Bookcase, London, circa 1735.*
Walnut and walnut veneer primary; spruce secondary.
Height 82½", width 29", depth 21".
The Metropolitan Museum of Art, Gift of Irwin Untermyer,
1964.

39. *Desk-and-Bookcase, attributed to the shop of Peter Scott,*
  Williamsburg, circa 1760.
Yellow pine primary; yellow pine and walnut secondary.
  Originally painted blue-green.
Height 91½", width 48⅝", depth 16¾".
Mount Vernon Ladies' Association.

The next piece has a history of ownership by the Jett family of Westmoreland and is one of the most unusual American desks (fig. 39). In its lower section are twelve vertical compartments suitable for storing ledgers, above which were two large drawers, now missing. The upper section has two narrow drawers below the fall board. Above the fall board is a bank of twenty-four drawers, and above these, two bookshelves with eight slots for height adjustment. These are flanked by a series of five pigeonholes.

39a.

The bookcase in figure 40 is one of a matched pair originally made for Blandfield, the home of Robert Beverley. It appears to derive from the same plan as the Galt family clothespress (fig. 36) and while it shares similar features, there are important differences. It is made of walnut and has the same type of dentil cornice, with a small loop between the teeth, that is found on the claw-foot desk-and-bookcase (fig. 37c). The most significant differences, however, are to be seen on the interior, where one finds, instead of a series of long shelves, a single vertical partition with shelves on either side. A large walnut foot approximately four inches square is double-mortised into a heavy walnut batten that is nailed and glued to the bottom of the case (fig. 40a). The presence of this extra foot, undoubtedly intended to bear the added weight of bound volumes, indicates that it served as a bookcase rather than a clothespress. The survival of this pair of handsome bookcases is remarkable testimony to the eighteenth-century practice of furnishing rooms en suite.

The primary wood of this desk, including the five ball-and-claw feet, is yellow pine. It was originally painted a blue-green color. Though now missing, there was once a block foot in the center of the back, opposite the central ball-and-claw. It was square in cross section and, like the five pine ball-and-claw feet, was mortised into a plinth of black walnut. Their addition to the desk was intended to support the weight of ledgers, books, and documents.

40. *Bookcase, attributed to the shop of Peter Scott, Williams-
     burg, circa 1765.*
Walnut primary; yellow pine secondary.
Height 79", width 52½", depth 25⅜".
Mrs. William Nash Beverley.

41. *China Cabinet, London, circa 1765.*
Mahogany primary; spruce secondary.
Height 34½", width 42½", depth 18½".
The Colonial Williamsburg Foundation (1958-478).

40a.

40b.

41a.

"Clothes presses to be made by Scott 4f 6I wide High as a desk and bookcase," wrote Thomas Jefferson sometime in 1773 or 1774. The unusual piece (fig. 42) has a case measuring 4 feet 4⅜ inches wide, is fitted with a double-door bookcase section on its top and certainly appears to be the reality of Jefferson's order. This example, however, was owned by Robert Beverley and still stands at Blandfield with the pair of bookcases just discussed. Jefferson's order and the surviving press present strong evidence to support the Scott attribution and together they record the only evidence of this form in Virginia known to the writer. Neither the extreme width nor the combination of press and bookcase has any known parallel, although both the two-part offset form and the pierced gallery are seen on a similar example (fig. 50). That piece, a dressing chest, differs significantly in construction and bears an attribution to the shop of Williamsburg cabinet-maker Anthony Hay.

This unusual Scott press embodies all the constructional features outlined in other case pieces of the group, but its unique form adds significantly to our knowledge of design and decoration. To accommodate the width of the piece, the feet were made wider and their ogee curve is considerably stronger than the others. The upper case has familiar doors with indented corner panels and the cornice has an elaborate wall of Troy molding. The top, however, differs from the others in several respects. It originally had a fretwork gallery and a central plinth made in two pieces. As the surviving evidence shows (fig. 42a), the front of the plinth was the same depth as the surviving part of the gallery, and the second piece was twice its thickness. Behind these was glued a support block. On the corners of the case the gallery is mitered, and no evidence of corner plinths can be found there.

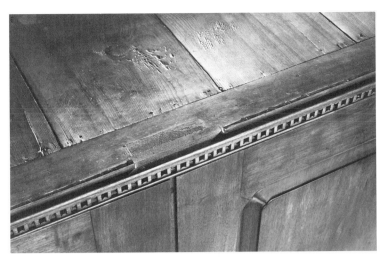

42a.

42. *Clothespress, attributed to the shop of Peter Scott, Williamsburg, circa 1765.*
Walnut primary; yellow pine and walnut secondary.
Height 79″, width 52½″, depth 25⅜″.
Mrs. William Nash Beverley.

In addition to gallery and plinth, this press has a double top. It is normal in Scott construction to glue large support blocks to the top of the upper case and then secure the cornice to these blocks, leaving an open space behind. Here, however, a second top is made of pine boards running from front to back, nailed above the support blocks and sitting flush with the top of the cornice.

A border of finished walnut, parallel to the front, extends behind the fret approximately three inches and then continues (still parallel to the front) along the sides, creating cross banding there. This finished appearance in an otherwise invisible area suggests that the press was made for use in a stair hall, where it could be viewed from above.

In the lower section, tucked beneath the top and accessible only after removal of the upper drawer, are two small secret drawers. Made entirely of walnut and less than an inch in height, they are unusual features by any standard.

Some of the evidence presented by these case pieces offers a rare look beyond techniques of construction, revealing shop practices for which evidence has not often survived. One of these, seldom understood today, is the process of manufacturing ogee bracket feet. A study of the growth ring patterns of the pine lamination backing the walnut primary wood shows very clearly that the feet were formed from long boards. They were first glued together to form the lamination and were then planed into the ogee shape from end to end. This contoured board was then cut into separate brackets and mitered together, a method that insures that the feet are uniform in their ogee profile. In contrast, rural furniture often has feet that were shaped into ogee curves after attachment to the case and that are easily recognized by their naiveté and lack of uniformity.

Further evidence of shop practices is found in the support blocks for the crown molding on a desk-and-bookcase (fig. 35). Made of yellow pine, they have a large bead molding on the top inside corner. The size of these blocks indicates that they were scrap ends from door or window facings and suggest the possibility that Scott was making, or at least utilizing, interior architectural elements. In further support of this hypothesis are beaded-edged boards on the backs of several case pieces. These beaded boards are included at random and are obviously not part of a decorative scheme for the piece.

Close examination of this furniture reveals a great amount of information concerning its makers and their practices. Without question, a concentrated study of the products of other American centers would shed further light on eighteenth-century cabinetmaking and trade practices. The homogeneous nature of chairs and case pieces attributed to Peter Scott is exceptional, and the quantity and scope of circumstantial evidence regarding them is equally unusual. The corpus of evidence is very strong and the attribution of these pieces to Williamsburg is particularly sound. There are a few nagging circumstances, however, that necessitate a note of caution. Such is the case of two corner chairs found near Fredericksburg (figs. 28, 29), as well as a straight-legged corner chair recorded in the MESDA files (no. S-5964), all of which have unusual arches in their crests. In this feature they differ significantly from the Palace corner chair (fig. 33), but all four share a number of other interrelated features that argue for assignment of the group to Scott's shop (see discussion with figs. 28, 29, pp. 36-38).

Unfortunately, the extent to which Williamsburg-trained cabinetmakers migrated is unknown, although the wide distribution of related furniture indicates it was substantial. It was not unusual in eighteenth-century Virginia for apprentices to come from great distances for training, and undoubtedly they often returned home to practice their trades. These individuals must have been instrumental in carrying specific shop techniques into distant areas, thus contributing greatly to the dissemination of style. It is possible that some of the numerous chairs related to the Scott group that descended in families from the Fredericksburg area may represent the work of transplanted journeymen. The separation of pieces made in Fredericksburg by transplanted artisans from those purchased and sent to that area in the eighteenth century, however, is a task beyond the scope of this work.[21] The lack of related case pieces with Fredericksburg histories is revealing, suggesting that the chairs have an origin outside the area. While there were many cabinetmakers working there, wealthy individuals living in that section of Virginia are known to have patronized Williamsburg artisans.

There are other questions regarding this group that remain to be answered. Lack of written documentation for the use of cherry, occasionally found in Scott pieces, is puzzling, although not of great significance. Its absence from Williamsburg newspaper advertisements may well be due to the prestige of owning mahogany and walnut. Many pieces made of cherry clearly fall within other Williamsburg groups. The lack of a document associating Scott with chair production is also troublesome, although it is not substantial evidence to conclude that he did not make them. Few documents regarding Scott are extant in any form,

and although his newspaper ad of 1755 lists nearly every form of furniture except chairs, it ends with "etc." Chairs were certainly more likely to be produced on custom order than other pieces of furniture. The variable number in a set, a tremendous variety of designs, and an endless degree of quality are good reasons for their being made to order rather than for direct sale from the shop.

Two of the chairs here assigned to the Scott group were tentatively attributed to the cabinetmaker Mardun V. Eventon by Helen Comstock in 1952 and 1954.[22] Miss Comstock's attribution was based upon the existence of the chairs at Mount Vernon (fig. 27) and Shirley Plantation (fig. 18) that closely coincided geographically with Eventon's *Virginia Gazette* advertisements from Dumfries and Chesterfield. The case pieces in the Scott group, however, are completely different from the signed Eventon desk (fig. 113) and thus remove him as the possible maker of the chairs.

While little is known about Peter Scott's early background, the large group of furniture discussed here certainly indicates a strong familiarity with urban British style and technology of the early eighteenth century. The wording of his 1755 advertisement, in which he stated his intention "to go for Great Britain," may provide a clue to his past. His use of this phrase rather than the more common "England" or "London," suggests that he could have had a Scottish origin. James Hamilton, a Scottish carver who worked in Williamsburg and who used the ambiguous "Great Britain," was one of many who preferred that designation. Whatever his background, there is no indication of a Virginia ancestry for Peter Scott, and various features of his furniture cause one to conclude that he might have been trained abroad.

The form of the ball-and-claw foot and knee carving on the earliest group of Scott chairs is quite closely related to London work of the 1730 period (see fig. 17). While an affinity with the English chair is obvious, there are significant differences. The Scott carving is a muted version, having lost a great deal of the sharpness and detail, and the carving of the knee and foot, particularly the latter, are watered-down versions of the London style. This same comparison can also be made between the Scott desk-and-bookcase and a London example in the Metropolitan Museum of Art (fig. 38). Again, a tremendous likeness is apparent in the squat cabriole legs, flattened ball, and extended claws of the feet. Virtually identical construction was followed in forming the back foot on both pieces, although again the Scott example is a muted version that possesses less sculptural detail. Another feature seen on London pieces and consistent in Scott's work is the ogee bracket foot laminated to a secondary wood. A fine example is seen on a London china cabinet that also has composite or built-up foot blocks which are typical of this and other Williamsburg groups (fig. 41a). The method of securing raised panels in doors, with a small nailed-in molding, is another early Georgian feature seen on English cabinetwork of the period, and is identical to pieces attributed to Giles Grendey of London.

Other English construction can also be seen in chairs of this group, with their integral rear seat rail and shoe, knee blocks that overlap the seat rails, and rather stiff cabriole legs—all of which are seen on English pieces of the 1720s and 1730s. The use of beech and oak for slip seats and as secondary woods in upholstered furniture is also a continuation of English cabinetmaking tradition that was practiced by Scott and others in Williamsburg. Little solid evidence of such an extensive use of beech for upholstered furniture can be found elsewhere in America.

The conclusion that these pieces of furniture were made by a tradesman trained in a British urban center, possibly even London, is somewhat startling considering their provincial character. Yet this group unquestionably exhibits an understanding and familiarity with the most advanced urban cabinetmaking technology of its time, while falling short of urban style. No other shop group in America is known to the writer in which such close affinity with English technology is present.

While the presence of urban technology combined with provincial style may seem contradictory, circumstances did exist in the transition from a large center to a small one that could have produced these results. Urban furniture-making was made up of a series of specialized trades consisting primarily of cabinetmaking, chair-making, carving and gilding, and upholstering. Technical evidence presented by this group suggests that Scott was trained as a cabinetmaker or chairmaker and that he had exposure to both. Working through an apprenticeship in a large city shop would have taught him construction and exposed him to high-style carving, although it did not necessarily teach him the techniques of carving and designing. If a person with such a background then migrated to a small city like Williamsburg, where it is doubtful that he could depend upon finding specialists, he would have been forced to handle these skills himself.

While such a tradesman might not have had sufficient skill or business ability to achieve prominence in a large city, his success in Williamsburg would have been understandable had he arrived around 1720 with a sound knowledge of current fashion. Such an introduction, when styles in America often embodied turn-of-the-century features, could have met with extreme success. In Virginia, where the leaders of society were continually seeking the latest but not always conveniently available English styles, it is easy to hypothesize why Scott was so popular.

Twenty-two pieces within the Scott group have been examined in this study. While all the known cases pieces are included, numerous chairs, mostly very plain ones, are omitted. Some of these simpler chairs display different proportions, designs, and quality, indicating that they represent the formation of a regional style. This is easily understood since the group has an early origin and its production spanned five decades. The number of journeymen and apprentices working over this time span must have been great, and when one considers that these men traveled in all directions and trained others, the development of a strong regional style is understandable.

As stated earlier, the consistency in this group is remarkable. The quality and design in the early examples are outstanding, although in later pieces the workmanship declined and attempts to change and adapt to the rococo style were generally not as successful. When looking at the Scott group with a critical eye, most collectors and furniture historians will attempt to compare their baroque forms with later, more rococo examples. The early Scott chair certainly is nothing like a Philadelphia or London chair of 1770—nor should one expect it to be. In evaluating the group, one must consider that its baroque George II style was founded upon a completely different set of aesthetic values than those of the later rococo taste.

If the dates assigned by this study are correct, the earlier pieces are pioneer examples for their time and are certainly among the purest examples of the George II style produced in America. This group shows its origin to be British urban cabinetmaking that, transplanted to colonial Virginia, developed into a provincial city style unique in American furniture.

FOOTNOTES

1. Information courtesy of Harold B. Gill, Jr., historian at Colonial Williamsburg. From his forthcoming book *Arts and Crafts in Virginia.*
2. *The Virginia Gazette,* ed. William Hunter, September 12, 1755, p. 3.
3. Ivor Noël Hume, *Williamsburg Cabinetmakers: The Archaeological Evidence* (Williamsburg: Colonial Williamsburg Foundation, 1971), pp. 15-19; *Virginia Gazette,* ed. Alexander Purdie, June 26, 1776, p. 3.
4. *The Virginia Gazette,* ed. John Dixon and William Hunter, December 2, 1775, p. 3.
5. *The Virginia Gazette,* ed. Alexander Purdie, January 5, 1776, supplement p. 1.
6. Ibid., January 26, 1776, p. 3.
7. Hume, *Williamsburg Cabinetmakers,* p. 14.
8. John Custis Papers, 1711-1764, Virginia Historical Society, Richmond, Virginia. Information courtesy of Harold B. Gill, Jr.
9. *The Virginia Gazette,* ed. Alexander Purdie and John Dixon, April 18, 1776, p. 3.
10. All Jefferson accounts courtesy of Charles Granquist, assistant director, Thomas Jefferson Memorial Foundation, Monticello, Virginia.
11. Col. William Bassett Manuscripts Account Book (1730-1748), Virginia Historical Society, Richmond, Virginia. Information courtesy of Harold B. Gill, Jr. (See page 42 for full quote.)
12. John Mercer Manuscripts Ledger (1725-1750) Bucks County Historical Society, Doylestown, Pennsylvania. Information courtesy of Harold B. Gill, Jr.
13. Robert Carter Manuscripts Day Book, Manuscripts Division, Duke University Library, Durham, North Carolina, Vol. 14 (1776-1778), p. 146.
14. Robert Carter Manuscripts Letter Book, Manuscript Division, Duke University Library, Durham, North Carolina, Vol. 6 (1784-1785) pp. 134-135.
15. Information courtesy of Charles Granquist.
16. Ibid.
17. Ibid.
18. Letter from John Kirk to Graham Hood, April 24, 1972, Accession File No. 1972-230, Department of Collections, Colonial Williamsburg Foundation, Williamsburg, Virginia.
19. *Report of the Curator 1975* (Monticello, Virginia: Thomas Jefferson Memorial Foundation, 1975) p. 11.
20. Bassett Account Book.
21. See Ann W. Dibble, "Fredericksburg-Falmouth Chairs in the Chippendale Style," *Journal of Early Southern Decorative Arts* 5 (May 1978): 1-24. In this article, Ms. Dibble attributes many of the chairs illustrated, as well as others that share similar features, to the Fredericksburg area. All of the chairs covered by her article are clearly within the Scott group designation used in this work. Ms. Dibble further divides these examples into three sub-groups. Her attribution to the Fredericksburg-Falmouth area is based on the fact that numerous chairs survive with histories there. While it is entirely possible, if not probable, that some production of these chairs occurred in that area, evidence is very strong for the origin of this group in Williamsburg. Several important pieces not covered by Ms. Dibble's article include examples from three sets of chairs with Williamsburg histories (figs. 22, 30, 32, 34, 58, and 62), and all six of the case pieces (figs. 35, 36, 37, 39, 40, and 42). The case pieces are firmly linked to the chairs through their use of identical ball-and-claw feet and the inclusion of beech as a secondary wood—features that are otherwise rare in eastern Virginia. If these provenances are added to Ms. Dibble's map, they create an entirely different picture. They also add important provenances, many of them distant from Fredericksburg. In addition, some have document correlations with Williamsburg, and specifically with the shop of Peter Scott.
A surprising number of chairs in this group have association with the Washington and Custis families. Six are known: one is shown in Ms. Dibble's article, three are cited in her footnotes, and two others are discussed here (figs. 21, 27). These examples have intriguing connotations when it is realized that Peter Scott rented both his shop and his home from the Custis family and their heirs for forty-three years. When George Washington married Martha Dandridge Custis in 1759, he took over management of the property, and Scott continued to rent it from him for the following sixteen years. While not conclusive, the longstanding association the cabinetmaker had with these two families could explain their ownership of so many related chairs. This interpretation gains further credence if considered in light of the evidence that associates the group with Scott.

Ms. Dibble uses techniques of pegging as the criteria for dividing these chairs into three groups. This raises some important questions. Inconsistencies of pegging have caused this author to conclude that much, if not all, of the evidence has resulted from repairs that occurred over the years. It was a standard practice to tighten loose joints by clamping and pegging—thus avoiding the necessity of completely dismantling a chair in order to glue it properly. Inconsistencies occur not only from chair to chair but also within a single example, where some joints are pegged and others are not. Occasionally, in more elaborate pieces they are crudely placed in the midst of the knee carving (see figs. 20a, 28a). Other pegs almost miss the tenons entirely.

Vertically grained, two-part support blocking is also used by Ms. Dibble to segregate one of these groups. Again, there are discrepancies, since it is probable that most chairs originally had blocking, though many have lost it. However, there are examples with this blocking that fall within her other groups, which by her designation, should not have them, and thereby prove division by this feature unreliable. These include the Benjamin Waller chair (fig. 62), the Washington chair (fig. 27), the Virginia Historial Society chair (fig. 19), and the Lodge IV chair (fig. 59e). In addition, the horizontally grained poplar blocks of the Shirley chairs (fig. 18) cited by Ms. Dibble, are without question old replacements and are crude in execution when compared with others in the group. This conclusion is reinforced by the original vertical-grained cherry blocking of the matching Virginia Historical Society chairs. These double vertical blocks are cut with a slightly convex surface on the interior, giving them a triangular cross section that conforms to many cited here. Unfortunately, it appears that the support blocking of the entire group has suffered loss at a rate comparable to the knee brackets on the cabriole leg chairs. While it may seem unusual that such a large percentage of the original vertically grained blocking has been lost, evidence for knee bracket blocking used on cabriole leg chairs is even more fragmentary. An almost intact example can be seen on the Lodge IV chair (fig. 59f), where large horizontally grained blocks back up the knee bracket beneath the seat rail. Here the support on the right is intact while that behind the left knee bracket is missing. One side chair in the Scott group (fig. 20) has a very small splinter from its original yellow pine horizontal block, and was identical in construction to those of figure 59f. This strongly suggests that all were originally made this way, even though all have been lost except the example cited here. (These horizontally grained blocks form a parallel to the principle of the composite foot found on case pieces attributed to Scott, where horizontally grained blocks are also used (fig. 40b). These unusual knee blocks, together with the vertically grained support blocks, form another strong tie between the chairs in this group and point to their common origin. Sub-groups within the larger group do exist, as Ms. Dibble has noted, yet for the reasons pointed out in the foregoing discussion, her attempts to separate them are not valid. One of the sub-groups includes the Lodge IV chair. The relationship of this chair to the Scott group is more fully examined under the Edmund Dickinson section of the chapter that deals with the Anthony Hay Shop.

One further argument used by Ms. Dibble to tie these chairs to the Fredericksburg area is found on an armchair that descended in the Green family there (see Dibble footnote no. 17). This chair has construction details found throughout the group: the integral rear rail and shoe with horizontal shaping; parallel stiles; serpentine arm supports; and arms dovetailed into the sides (Ms. Dibble describes them as notched). The basis of her argument relies upon the similarity of its splat to those found on earlier style chairs from the northern Tidewater area. However, the splat on the Green chair is a replacement. Removed from a taller piece, its addition to the Green family example necessitated reshaping of the shoe and the underside of the crest rail. The added splat is the only tie between these groups, and consequently there appears to be no valid basis for relating the two.

A Fredericksburg association for one chair of this group is presented by Conover Hunt-Jones in *Dolley and "the great little Madison"* (Washington, D. C.: American Institute of Architects Foundation, 1977), p. 96, fig. 96. Ms. Hunt-Jones states that this chair, together with several others surviving from the same set, was purchased in 1773 by James Madison from an unidentified cabinetmaker in the Fredericksburg area. This cabinetmaker's account book, which records the transaction, is in the Joseph Downs Manuscript Library, Henry Francis duPont Winterthur Museum, Winterthur, Delaware. If the chair illustrated by Ms. Hunt-Jones is in fact part of the set noted in the account book, it will mark an important beginning in isolating Fredericksburg area production of Scott types. There is, however, some question in identifying this chair as part of the set and Ms. Hunt-Jones does not discuss how this was determined. She shows another chair having Scott group characteristics with the same family tradition. Still another very different example in the Colonial Williamsburg Collection (acc. no. L1977-307) has an inscription indicating that it, too, belonged to James Madison. Admittedly the reference in the account book is to walnut, and it is true that the second Scott example shown by Ms. Hunt-Jones is cherry, while the Williamsburg example is mahogany. Yet the crucial point that remains unaddressed is the validity of matching a specific example to the account without further support. Traditions often have accuracy problems and the Madison family obviously owned a large quantity of furniture in the eighteenth century. The inexpensive price of the set is also disturbing since the Madison family chair has a splat with piercing. The account book entry to Col. James Madison notes that on Sept. 2, 1773 the cabinetmaker "finsht 12 Marlborgh chairs walnut £6-6-o," meaning that each chair cost 10½ shillings each. This low price is particularly disturbing if compared to the cost of the Windsor chairs at 15 shillings each, that were purchased by Frances Jerdone of Yorktown from a carpenter in 1769. The price and materials of other forms recorded in the account book confirm a level of modest production. The lack of mahogany also indicates inexpensive production, and makes any close association with the finest carved Scott chairs very unlikely.

In reference to this account book, Ms. Dibble cites an entry for a "pillar and claw" table as evidence that this shop was producing examples bearing ball-and-claw feet ("Fredericksburg-Falmouth Chairs in the Chippendale Style," see footnote 3). However, pillar and claw does not refer to ball-and-claw feet—a fact that is clearly shown on page 38 of the London Society of Upholsterer's *Genteel HousHold Furniture*. Three tables having tripod bases are illustrated there in a plate entitled "claw tables," and all of them have scroll feet. This is firm evidence that the term "claw," when applied to this form, referred to its three legs and not to ball-and-claw feet.

22. Helen Comstock, "Discoveries in Southern Antiques," *The Magazine Antiques* 65 (February 1954): 131-133.

Figure 44

The Anthony Hay Shop

MASTERS OF THE HAY SHOP

Unquestionably the most important cabinet shop in Williamsburg, and one of the most important in America, the Anthony Hay Shop on Nicholson Street was in use for over twenty years and was operated by at least four masters. From this shop came the most extraordinary group of ceremonial chairs produced in colonial America.[1]

It appears as though Anthony Hay founded the shop and served as its first master. He, in turn, was followed by Benjamin Bucktrout, William Kennedy, and Edmund Dickinson. Two professional carvers, James Wilson and George Hamilton, were also employed there, and numerous appeals for journeymen cabinetmakers, chairmakers, and apprentices indicate that there were many others whose names are unrecorded. Only in several instances has the record of an apprentice survived, and the extent to which black cabinetmakers were employed is even more obscure. It is known that Hay owned one black cabinetmaker, but that lone reference comes from his inactive period in the trade.[2]

While documented evidence indicates that Hay was the founder of this shop, it should be noted that details of Williamsburg furniture dating from the 1730s and 1740s show a close relationship to his work. These suggest that Hay may have been apprenticed in Williamsburg, or that such details appear on his products as a result of the employment of locally-trained workmen. Interestingly enough, long after Hay had left his Nicholson Street location it continued to be known as "the Shop formerly occupied by Mr. Anthony Hay" and "the shop formerly kept by Mr. Hay."[3] This, together with archaeological evidence that dates portions of the building to the time of Hay's ownership of the property, is strong evidence that he was its founder and is the reason for treating this group of furniture under his name.

Before discussing and examining the large production attributed to the Hay shop, it is important to study documentary evidence pertaining to its various masters, as well as the series of events and circumstances that affected them. This study, chronologically arranged, is followed by a parallel study of the furniture.

Figure 48

1751-1766: Anthony Hay

The earliest document concerning Anthony Hay in Williamsburg is found in the *Virginia Gazette* daybook of 1750-52. On July 27, 1751, Hay purchased a copy of *Compleate Housewife* and in the following month he bought stationery, a slate, and pencils. From that point on, Hay kept a running account for similar items and books. He often sent family members and shop employees to pick up these articles, all of whom are noted in the daybooks.[4] They included his sons "Joe" and "Thomas," Edmund Dickinson, Benjamin Bucktrout, and "Wiltshire," the latter a slave.

On November 7, 1751, Hay placed his first advertisement in the *Gazette:* "Wanted. A cabinet or chair-maker, who understands his business. May such man hear of Employment on applying to the Printer."[5] Although this advertisement does not give Hay's name, the *Gazette* Daybook contains an entry for that date noting his payment for an "advertisment for journeymen." Three weeks later, essentially the same notice appeared but with an added offer to pay for the remaining time of a servant qualified in the cabinet or chair-making business.[6]

The success of Hay's appeals for journeymen is unknown, but it appears that he may have taken two apprentices shortly thereafter. On December 31, 1751, he bought "Blanks For a pair of Indentures" from the *Virginia Gazette*, and five months later made an identical purchase.[7] As he was buying only a pair of indentures at a time, and since they follow his known advertisements, they may indicate individual instances of apprenticeship. The possibility exists, however, that they were intended for deeds, slaves, or servants.

In 1756 Hay paid £200 for the two lots on Nicholson Street where his shop and home were located.[8] Their excavation in 1960 established that the main building was constructed sometime between 1740 and 1755. A westward extension, built on brick pillars and spanning a small stream, was added no earlier than 1755, but before 1770.[9] A small bridge that had crossed the stream prior to the completion of this addition was discovered to have footings of mahogany, and a long narrow building behind the shop, possibly used as a drying kiln, had foundations laid on planks that also included mahogany. This wood was used, no doubt, because the builders were aware of its resistance to decay. (See "Hay Shop Excavation" for a discussion of artifacts recovered at the site.)

It is possible that the expansion of the shop dates to the approximate time of Hay's purchase of the lot.

The main portion of the building already existed at that point, and it is reasonable to surmise that Hay had rented it prior to the purchase. Supporting this conclusion is an advertisement placed in 1755 by James Wilson, a London carver working with Hay, indicating that he was already established in a well-known location.[10] Some of the pieces attributed to Hay's shop appear to date from the 1740s, and although he is not documented as being in town until 1751, he may have been working at the Nicholson Street location during the earlier decade.

Like most tradesmen of this period, Hay is difficult to research. Few records concerning him exist, although he is known to have been associated with Christopher Ford, Jr., a Williamsburg carpenter and joiner, during March of 1755. At that time they advertised in the *Virginia Gazette:*

Just Imported, and to be SOLD, by the Subscribers in

WILLIAMSBURG

A Large Assortment of Carpenters, Joiners, and Cabinet-Makers Tools, consisting of White's Steel Plate Saws of all Sorts, Glue Jointers, long Planes, Bench Planes, Tooth and Smoothing ditto, Moulding Planes of all Sorts, Plane Irons, Chisels, Formers, Scribing Gouges, Rasps, Files, Turkey Oil-Stones, German Slates, and Variety of other things.

Christopher Ford, Jun.
Anthony Hay[11]

Neither the duration nor extent of their partnership is clear, and no further mention is made of a joint venture by the two. A short time thereafter Hay was working with another artisan, a professional carver, who advertised from his shop in June of 1755:

JAMES WILSON, Carver, from LONDON, MAKES all kinds of Ornaments in Stuco, human Figures and Flowers, &c. &c. Stuco Cornishes in Plaster, carved or plain, after the best Manner; likewise Stone finishing on Walls; he likewise carves in Wood, cuts Seals in Gold or Silver; and is to be spoke with at Mr. Anthony Hay's, Cabinet-Maker, in Williamsburg.[12]

It is worth noting at this point that an important ceremonial armchair attributed to the combined talents of Anthony Hay and James Wilson will be discussed in depth in a later portion of the text (see fig. 46).

While pieces attributed to Hay have wide geographic provenances, documentation establishing corresponding patronage is lacking. A few accounts of work he did for Williamsburg residents survive, however, including those of six chairs at fifteen shillings each for William Hunter, editor of the *Virginia Gazette*, in 1752. Between 1755 and 1762 he charged William Lightfoot, burgess from Charles City County, £18 for a dozen chairs, £3 for two small tables, and £4 for a writing table. Hay also made a coffin for his father-in-law, Thomas Penman, and a desk-and-bookcase costing £10 for Alexander Craig.[13]

Anthony Hay's active employment in the cabinetmaking trade ended late in 1766. An important notice, one of two that sheds light on his move from the cabinet shop and on his sucessor, appeared early in the following year:

WILLIAMSBURG, JAN. 8, 1767
MR. ANTHONY HAY having lately
removed to the RAWLEIGH tavern, the subscriber has taken his shop, where the business will be carried on in all its branches. He hoped that those Gentlemen who were Mr. Hay's customers will favour him with their orders, which shall be executed in the best and most expeditious manner. He likewise makes all sorts of Chinese and Gothick PALING for gardens and summer houses.
N.G. SPINET and HARPSICORDS made and repaired.
BENJAMIN BUCKTROUT[14]

Hay's new business as proprietor of the Raleigh Tavern was an important move and reflects the tendency of successful eighteenth-century artisans to step into the realm of the business and mercantile community. An interesting analysis of Hay's new venture and of its dependence upon his previous success has been made by Mills Brown in 1959 when he was historian at Colonial Williamsburg, in a research report entitled *Cabinetmaking in the Eighteenth Century*:

> That Hay abandoned his craft and turned to tavern-keeping as a livelihood might be interpreted to mean that he had not done well in the former occupation—but, in fact, quite the opposite seems to have been the case. Buying the Raleigh and readying it for business involved financial obligations in the neighborhood of £4,000—the Raleigh and some additional land, apparently pasture, cost £2,000; the furnishings, to judge from the appraisal of Hay's estate, another £1,000; and the Negro help, close to £1,000 more.
>
> Hay did not lay out this £4,000 in cash, of course; at the time of his death he still owed William Trebell, from whom he had purchased the Raleigh, more than £2,000. He had other debts, also, some of which were probably contracted while he was furnishing and stocking the Raleigh. No doubt Hay did hope to do better with the Raleigh than he had as a cabinetmaker—but this is not the point. The significant fact that emerges from his purchase of the Raleigh is this; after sixteen or more years as a Williamsburg cabinetmaker, and with no other assets than those he had developed during that period—no hidden assets appeared in his will or in the settlement of his estate—Hay's financial standing

was good enough to permit him to undertake obligations in the vicinity of £4,000—no small sum then, or now.[15]

Brown's analysis seems essentially sound, although the statement that Hay "abandoned his craft" appears far too strong in the light of the facts supplied by the documents. After Hay's death in 1770, his estate was offered for sale in accordance with his will. Two of the items advertised in the *Virginia Gazette* at that point deserve attention: "a very good Dwellinghouse on the back Street, where Mr. Hay formerly lived, with a large Cabinet Maker's Shop and Timber Yard" and "nineteen Negroes belonging to the said Estate, among them a very good Cabinet Maker."[16] Hay's continued ownership of the shop, timber yard, and black cabinetmaker even after his purchase of the Raleigh Tavern suggests that he was still involved in the trade as a business venture. These circumstances strongly indicate that he probably rented the shop to Benjamin Bucktrout, leasing the black cabinetmaker along with the shop, and evidence is strong that Edmund Dickinson (possibly an apprentice at that time) also went with it. Apparently Hay maintained control of the timber yard and its accompanying business during his ownership of the Raleigh and continued to purchase and import wood for his shop and possibly for sale to other local craftsmen as well.

The financial and social potential of the Raleigh Tavern might have been a major inducement to Hay's move from the active cabinetmaking craft, but another possibility exists. After a long illness, Hay died of cancer of the lip and face on the 4th of December, 1770.

WILLIAMSBURG, Dec. 13

On the 4th instant died, of that painful and lingering disorder a cancer, Mr. ANTHONY HAY, master of the Raleigh tavern in this city. He underwent several severe operations, in his lip and face, for the disorder, at home; and at length went (unhappily too late) to Prince Edward, where he was some time under the care of Mrs. Woodson, famous for the cures she has made. His death is a heavy loss to his large family, to whom he was a tender husband and kind parent; and he is regretted by his acquaintances, as being a good citizen and honest man.[17]

Having long suffered with this cancer, it is possible that Hay's "painful and lingering disorder" forced him from the irritating, dusty atmosphere of the cabinetmaking trade. If this were the case, then his continued ownership of the property and the announcement that he was turning both his business and patronage over to Bucktrout are seen in logical perspective. In this respect, Hay's last advertisement is certainly in an unusual form, one not seen among other cabinetmakers' advertisements in the *Virginia Gazette*. Not only does he give his business location to Bucktrout, but also passes to him all unfinished orders:

WILLIAMSBURG, Jan. 6, 1767

THE Gentlemen who have bespoke
WORK of the subscriber may depend upon having it made in the best manner by Mr. BENJAMIN BUCKTROUT, to whom he has given up his business.——I return the Gentlemen who have favoured me with this custom many thanks and am

Their most humble servant,
ANTHONY HAY.[18]

1767-1770: Benjamin Bucktrout

Benjamin Bucktrout is of extreme importance to the study of Virginia furniture, due largely to his stamped signature on the back of an important Masonic Master's chair (fig. 49). It is currently the only known piece of signed Williamsburg work and is a cornerstone in the study of the Hay shop.

Bucktrout, who referred to himself as a cabinetmaker from London, probably served his apprenticeship in that city and may have come to Williamsburg as a journeyman or identured servant to Anthony Hay.[19] An entry in the *Virginia Gazette* Day Book for September 28, 1765 shows that he paid five shillings toward sundry accounts for Hay, a common practice among shop employees and one that clearly links the two men during Bucktrout's earliest period in America.

By the summer of 1766, however, Bucktrout had established an independent business of his own and had placed an advertisement to advise the public of his new location:

B. BUCKTROUT

CABINET MAKER, from
LONDON, on the main street near the Capitol in Williamsburg, makes all sorts of cabinetwork, either plain or ornamental, in the neatest and newest fashions. He hopes to give statisfaction to all Gentlemen who shall please to favour him with their commands.
N.B. Where likewise may be had the mathematical GOUTY CHAIR.[20]

His stay at the new location was short lived, however, for in 1767 Bucktrout took over Hay's old business.

Some indication of Bucktrout's English background can be gained through a study of the items he made and repaired at his new location. One of the most unusual forms noted in his first *Virginia Gazette* advertisement was a "mathematical gouty chair." It was not the first time that this obscure form had appeared in Williamsburg. According to the *Virginia Gazette* daybook of September 7, 1765, Hay had placed a similar ad in an issue of the paper that no longer survives. When considering the character of Bucktrout's later notices and the fact that he was working in the Hay shop during that period, it becomes apparrent that Bucktrout had introduced the unusual form to Williamsburg.

In 1767, after Bucktrout returned to the Nicholson Street shop as its new master, he advertised the manufacture and repair of spinets and harpsichords. During the Revolution he constructed a manually operated powder mill, and although it appears to have been a successful venture, he encountered considerable difficulty in obtaining payment for his services. John Page, burgess from Gloucester County, wrote to Richard Henry Lee in February of 1776 and complained of the situation:

> I moved too, with like [little] success that the sum of £40 should be paid to Bucktrout, for his ingenuity in constructing; and to defray the expense of erecting a powder mill; and to enable him to prosecute his plan of working up the Salt Petre which may be collected in the neighboring Counties, with his Hand Powder Mill now at work in this City.[21]

Bucktrout was also engaged in the repair of umbrellas, a specialty that required great dexterity and skill with a variety of materials. He repaired an umbrella for Henry Morse in 1775[22] and continued with this sideline for nearly twenty years, as evidenced by a 1794 bill from Bucktrout to Joseph Prentis:

> Decr 16 to putting new walebone in umbrella £-1-3
> New wire for top takeing out fixn Curve 1-3[23]

While accounts exist for many repairs and odd jobs handled by Bucktrout or someone in his employ, the accounts mentioned above are similar in nature: they require special mechanical skills combined with fine workmanship in varied and somewhat unusual media. This combination, rare in colonial Virginia, could have been acquired in London and may reflect Bucktrout's training there in a special branch of the cabinetmaking trade, or as a musical-instrument maker, the latter also requiring skill in varied materials. Bucktrout's one advertisement for spinets and harpsichords supports this conclusion, although a lack of demand for such work could account for the later emphasis on cabinetmaking in his newspaper notices.

Sometime after moving to the Hay shop, Bucktrout entered into partnership with William Kennedy. The venture was of short duration, however, and nothing is known about Kennedy's background. The only records concerning their business are two advertisements in the *Virginia Gazette:*

> WILLIAMSBURG, Feb. 16, 1769
> The partnership between Bucktrout and Kennedy being dissolved, the subscriber now carries on the cabinet making business, as usual, at the shop formerly kept by Mr. Hay, where he hopes for the encouragement of his old customers, and others.
>
> BENJAMIN BUCKTROUT[24]

Apparently communication between the two craftsmen was lacking, since two weeks after Bucktrout had declared the business "dissolved" Kennedy advised the public that it was not yet so:

> WILLIAMSBURG, March 1, 1769
> THE partnership between Bucktrout and Kennedy, though not yet dissolved, will terminate as soon as the work which is already bespoken can be finished, and matters brought to a proper settlement; at which time
>
> WILLIAM KENNEDY
>
> Proposes carrying on the business of cabinet making, at the house where Mr. Pelham now lives. Any of those Gentlemen who have been customers to Bucktrout and Kennedy*, and all other who please to employ him, may rely on his best endeavours to give satisfaction.
>   *He has no intention to rob Mr. Bucktrout of his old customers, nor does he think he can as yet properly call any his own.[25]

The partnership seems to have been completely dissolved by August 31, when Bucktrout advertised for journeymen by himself.[26] He must have remained at the shop throughout 1770, but Hay's death in December of that year appears to have concluded his stay there. In January of 1771, less than a month after Hay's death, Edmund Dickinson advertised from the shop. Lacking further documentation, we must assume that Bucktrout then moved to his Francis Street location, where he advertised in 1775.

William Kennedy also continued to work in Williamsburg for a while, presumably "at the house where Mr. Pelham now lives." He is known to have made "a case for a sett of musical glasses" for Robert Carter in 1770, and appears to have been working with John Crump, an obscure Williamsburg cabinetmaker who was later in partnership with Richard Booker.[27] It was Crump who received payment for unspecified work done by Kennedy for Henry Morse in May of 1770.[28] William Kennedy is documented as working in Richmond by 1775, but Crump's eventual fate is unknown.[29]

It is unfortunate that so little information survives concerning other workmen of Bucktrout's shops. Documentation survives of only one of his apprentices:

> RUN away from the Subscriber, in Williamsburg, David Davis, an Apprentice Lad about twenty Years of Age, about five Feet ten Inches high, walks very straight, wears his own light brown Hair, which is tied, is much marked with the Smallpox, and a Cabinet Maker by Trade; had on, and took with him, a new light coloured Cloth Coat and Breeches, a new Waistcoat of reddish Wilton Cloth, an old brown Coat and waistcoat, a Pair of Breeches of a lighter Colour, new Shoes, and an old Hat. He likewise took with him a brown shagged Dog with a short Tail, that had an Iron Collar. Whoever conveys the said Apprentice to me shall have FORTY SHILLINGS Reward.
>
> BENJAMIN BUCKTROUT

I forewarn all Persons from harbouring him, and Masters of Vessels from carrying him out of the country.[30]

Bucktrout, like Hay, expanded his business beyond his craft. After moving from the Hay shop, he operated a retail store where he offered upholstery services and materials, and sold general merchandise. Like Hay's venture at the Raleigh Tavern, it was apparently quite successful, although Bucktrout actively continued cabinetmaking and upholstering. In 1775, having firmly established his second business, he advertised to the public that he "still" carried on the cabinetmaking trade and ended with a note that reinforced his intention to continue doing so:

> I should be glad to take one or two apprentices of bright Genius, and of good Dispositions, and such whose Friends are willing to find them in Clothes.[31]

The most informative documents regarding Bucktrout's furniture are the accounts of Robert Carter, for whom he made a desk and bookcase in 1769, at a cost of £16.[32] In 1772 Carter moved from Williamsburg back to his Westmoreland County plantation, Nomini Hall. Bucktrout not only assisted in packing for the trip but also made new articles for the large country home:

To Benjn Bucktrout

1772
June 18 To mending a Music stand	0 .. 1 ..6
Octobr 26 Mahogy Chares Stufed over the Rails with Brass nails @ £25 per doz	16 ..13 ..8
To 4 Elbow Chares @ 55/	11 .. 0 ..0
Decemr 29 To 65 feet of pine @ 1 1/2 d	0 .. 8 ..3 1/2
To 150 8d nails for a packing Case for Harpsicord 3/ makeing and packing Do 10/	0 ..12 ..0
	£28 ..15 ..5 1/2

Wmsburg June 14th 1774 then received of Robert (Carter) the above account in full I say received.

Benjn Bucktrout.[33]

The pricing of the chairs per dozen brings up an intriguing question. Did Carter purchase eight chairs out of a set of twelve that Bucktrout had on hand for direct sale, or does this represent Bucktrout's usual practice of pricing side chairs? It would seem that if only eight chairs were custom ordered, the price would be per chair rather than per dozen.

Consistent with eighteenth-century cabinetmaking in both America and England, Bucktrout also made coffins and directed funerals. He served in this latter capacity when Virginia's Royal Governor, Lord Botetourt, died in 1770. Bucktrout billed the Botetourt estate "to the Hearse and fiting up to carrey his Lordship's Corps in 6-0-0" and "to four days attendance 2-0-0." Bucktrout did not make Lord Botetourt's elaborate triple-case coffin, which was constructed by Joshua Kendall, a Williamsburg carpenter-joiner.[34] But that same year he did bill Robert Carter for a coffin, and a year later, for a second. These were not simple pine boxes, as often imagined, but well constructed, expensive products with great ceremonial significance. One of the Carter coffins, which cost £5, was described as "a neat coffin covered with superfine Black Cloth with wite nails lined with flannel".[35] Lord Botetourt's coffin was embellished with silver fittings by William Waddill, a Williamsburg silversmith. It is of particular interest here to note that Bucktrout's employment as an undertaker long outlasted his cabinet trade, surviving to the present day as Bucktrout Funeral Service, one of the oldest such businesses in continuous operation in America.

In addition to his undertaking, retailing, and cabinetmaking businesses, Bucktrout also served as purveyor of public hospitals for the new State of Virginia. He acted in this capacity from 1777 until the fall of 1779, when he offered his house and lots in Williamsburg for sale. The sale also included a large group of household furniture, "a chest of cabinet makers and house joiners tools," and "a quantity of very fine broad one, two, and three inch mahogany plank, which has been cut this five years." He concluded the notice by stating his plans to leave the colony the following October and by clarifying his intention to rent his house had it not been sold by that time.[36]

Bucktrout's destination is unknown; if he left at all, it was for only a short time. He was certainly in Williamsburg by November of 1781, when he was included in a list of local people alleged to have joined the British army but who had returned after Cornwallis's defeat at Yorktown.[37] Considering Bucktrout's London background, the accusation is understandable, but the evidence against the charge is very strong. His construction of the powder mill and his public service for the hospitals during the Revolution could hardly be claimed as pro-British. In further support is the announcement of his intention to leave Williamsburg in 1779, when he claimed that his house would be rented if not sold—a highly unlikely proposition for a Tory. Finally, Bucktrout continued to reside in Williamsburg until his death in 1813. He was appointed to public office as town surveyor in 1804, and apparently he prospered, for in Williamsburg's tax list of 1812 he is listed as the owner of eight and one half lots.[38]

1771-1776: Edmund Dickinson

Edmund Dickinson is first associated with the Hay shop in a *Gazette* daybook entry of August 7, 1764; on that date he picked up miscellaneous items for Hay at the newspaper office. Dickinson's exact position in the shop at that time is unclear, but the long-held assumption that he was an apprentice, based upon the fact that he ran the same type of errands as Hay's sons, is not valid.[39] Benjamin Bucktrout appears in the same daybook performing essentially the same task, and his status as journeyman at that time seems relatively secure.

Dickinson does not appear in records between 1766, when he served under Hay, and 1771. It seems that he remained in the shop and worked with Bucktrout through that period, however, for when Bucktrout left to open his own business in 1770 (probably on Francis Street) it was Edmund Dickinson who remained as new master of the Hay shop:

EDMUND DICKINSON:

CABINETMAKER, WILLIAMSBURG, INFORMS the public that he has lately opened the SHOP formerly occupied by Mr. Anthony Hay, where may be had all sorts of CABINET WORK. Those Gentlemen who please to favour him with their Orders may depend on their Work being well and punctually executed. *** He has for SALE two Hundred and fifty ACRES of WOODLAND, within seven Miles of Petersburg, which he will sell for Cash, or short Credit.[40]

Dickinson's business seems to have grown rapidly. In November of 1771 he advertised for "Journeymen—Cabinet Makers who understand their business well." In August of the following year James Tyrie was apprenticed for five years to learn "the art of a Cabinet Maker."[41] Dickinson again advertised for journeymen in September of 1773, and by 1774 he had acquired the services of a professional carver and gilder:

WILLIAMSBURG, July 28, 1774
GEORGE HAMILTON, CARVER and GILDER, just from Britain, and now in this City, hereby informs the Publick that he intends carrying on his Business in all its Branches, viz. Looking-Glass Frames in Burnish or Oil Gilding, Girandoles, Ornaments and Decorations for Gentlemens Houses, Chimney Pieces, Door and Window Cornices, Mouldings and Enrichments, Hall and Staircase Lanthorns, Picture Frames black and gilded, Ladies Toilet and Dressing Glasses; all the above after the new Palmyrian Taste. ——Any Gentlemen wanting Designs of the above Articles may be furnished either at their respective Houses in Town or Country, or at Mr. Edmund Dickinson's Cabinet Maker; where old Frames may be re gilded, and Glasses new silvered, History and Portrait Paintings (though much defaced) cleaned and renewed to their former Lustre, also Chairs and Chariots gilded.[42]

Hamilton, of Scottish origin, had left England in April of 1774 bound for Virginia.[43] It is not known exactly where he worked in Great Britain, but he apparently came from a style-conscious urban area, if this advertisement is any indication. It contains the first indisputable reference to the neo-classic style in Virginia and is one of the earliest in America. The "new Palmyrian Taste" had already arrived in Williamsburg with the Buzaglo stove in 1770 and the Botetourt statue in 1773, as already discussed in the introduction.

How long Hamilton worked with Dickinson is not known, but he may have remained in Williamsburg through 1776, when a local merchant was dissatisfied with prices in Dickinson's shop: "I am at least overcharged for gilding of Picture Frames," complained Robert Prentis in his notebooks of accounts.[44] If Hamilton did the gilding, and it is probable that he did, he was working for Dickinson in this case and not contracting independently.

Numerous accounts survive that concern Edmund Dickinson, but unfortunately few give specific details. The estate of John Prentis maintained a running account with him from 1773 to 1775, and numerous small jobs—from cleaning chairs to putting locks on doors—are included. Charges for two coffins are also listed, one for Prentis's son William costing £2/15/0 and another "lined throughout for himself," for which Dickinson also served as attendant and charged £5/15/0. Dickinson had an extensive account with Robert Prentis, Williamsburg merchant, from 1772 to 1776, but, except for the gilded frames cited, the only piece of furniture is a card table, and that is scratched out in the account. Thomas Jefferson also patronized Dickinson, as indicated by a single entry from his accounts: "Dec. 18, 1777 gave Robert Nicholson my bond for 160-4-11 note; this included £25/5 due from me to Peter Scott's estate +26/due from me to Edmond Dickesson the joyner."[45]

In February of 1776 Lord Dunmore paid Dickinson £30 for unspecified articles, and on August 19 of the same year, shortly after Patrick Henry became governor, the State of Virginia paid him £92 "for furniture furnished the Pallace."[46] Judging from these few accounts, it appears as though Dickinson had both wide patronage and a successful business, particularly if we consider the short time span covered by these documents.

At the outbreak of the Revolution Edmund Dickinson enlisted in the service, was comissioned a captain in the 1st Virginia Regiment, and by October of 1777 had been promoted to major. He was killed in the Battle of Monmouth on June 28 of the following year, and as a ranking American officer his death was reported in the *London Gentlemen's Magazine*. Never married, most of his estate was left to his two single sisters, and £60 to a third sister's son.[47]

Dickinson's inventory is the most complete example for a Williamsburg cabinetmaker to survive from the pre-Revolutionary period, and it is of considerable importance in understanding his business and his life (see Appendix). Among the more interesting objects listed is a book described as "Chippendales Designs." Valued at £6, it is one of the few instances in America that documents the shop use of Chippendale's *Director*. It is quite possible that Anthony Hay originally owned this same book, since some of Dickinson's books are the same titles bought by Hay from the *Virginia Gazette* some years earlier. Perhaps this is not the case, but since Dickinson appears to have been in the shop continuously after Hay's departure from the business the possibility seems convincing. Further support of this theory is found in the Masonic chair signed by Bucktrout that has features directly relating to the *Director* illustrations; yet the possibility exists that Bucktrout, having come directly from London, also may have also owned a copy of the *Director*.

Less than a year after Dickinson's death, the Hay shop was rented to the state and served as part of the Public Armory during the Revolutionary War. Muskets and other arms were repaired there under the direction of James Anderson, "Public Armourer," but it must have been destroyed two or three years later.[48] The "Frenchman's Map" of Williamsburg, drawn around 1782 and considered to be one of the more accurate renderings of the town, indicates no building on the site where, for at least twenty-five years, Williamsburg's finest cabinetwork had been produced.

PRODUCTS OF
THE HAY SHOP

Furniture Attributed to Hay

As with Peter Scott's work, no signed or labeled furniture made by Hay is known. Significant evidence concerning his shop's production, however, is garnered from important pieces with Williamsburg histories, from archaeological excavation of the Hay shop site, and from the physical evidence presented by Bucktrout's signed Masonic chair (fig. 49).

Having noted the fairly homogenous nature of early Williamsburg pieces and the extremely consolidated approach in the Scott group, it should be stated that products attributed to the Hay shop are far more varied in design and construction. This produces a much more complex picture to reconstruct, and a typological study is by necessity more fragmented, due largely to the steady stream of craftsmen that passed through the shop. These problems are overcome by very good documentation and by pieces with longstanding historical traditions.

The earliest pieces attributed to the Hay shop are tables, which are closely related to the latest examples from the early Williamsburg group. The separation of these pieces is, in fact, very difficult, particularly in the case of several early dining tables (see figs. 11, 12).

A marble-top side table made of cherry (fig. 43)

is the earliest piece firmly attributed to the Hay shop. The blue-gray marble top is the only example from Williamsburg, but the trumpet-shaped section of its lower pad feet (similar to detail 57b) is seen on an unfinished easy chair leg that was excavated at the Hay site (fig. 65). In addition to the foot, the knee carving and flanking blocks of this table are virtually identical to those on two card tables (figs. 44, 45) that are also related constructionally to a later example associated with Hay shop production (fig. 48). The undercut skirt detail (fig. 43b) is unusual and its execution is identical to a similar detail on a tea table in the early Williamsburg group (fig. 8). This table descended in the Irby family and is thought to have first belonged to William Irby of Sussex (1752-1811) and to have been passed on to his son Edmund (1781-1829) of Nottoway. The table then went to Edmund's son Richard (1825-1902), and from him to Miss Nellie Irby who gave it to her niece, Dorothy Fitzgerald, its present owner, in 1930.[49]

Two virtually identical card tables relate closely to the design of the preceding example (figs. 44, 45). Both exhibit excellent workmanship, are constructed of mahogany, and have shaped tops that correspond to their shaped skirts. These examples also have knee carving that associates them with the preceding side table, and they once had small drawers hidden in their skirts behind the swing leg, though they are now missing. Both tables have an unusual skirt construction in which the tops of the rear legs are neatly concealed behind the sides of the table. This causes an unusual swing-leg arrangement

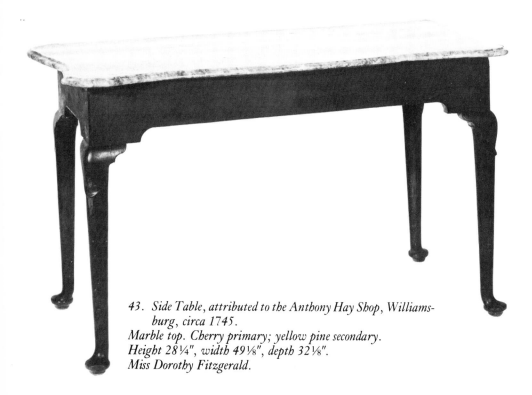

43. *Side Table, attributed to the Anthony Hay Shop, Williamsburg, circa 1745.*
Marble top. Cherry primary; yellow pine secondary.
Height 28¼", width 49⅛", depth 32⅛".
Miss Dorothy Fitzgerald.

43b.

43a.

in which the table's side skirt overlaps the top of the gate leg when closed (fig. 45a). Another example of this type of leg construction is seen on a later table from this same group (fig. 48c). It should be noted that this arrangement is conceptually related to the applied skirt found on the early Williamsburg tea table (fig. 8), where the continuous skirt also hides the vertical leg joints.[50] While these Virginia card tables are the only known examples of this construction made in America, they are clearly derived from English prototypes. Another feature, one that is common in England but equally rare here, is the interesting knee carving found on these three early Hay tables (figs. 43, 44, 45).

The first of these two card tables (fig. 44) descended in the Semple family. Its first known owner was Parson James Semple of St. Peter's Church in New Kent County, who served as pastor there from 1767 until his death twenty years later. The table has remained in the family until the present day.[51]

The second card table (fig. 45) is one of a surviving pair with a history of ownership on the Eastern Shore of Virginia. Its pad feet represent a slight variation of the trumpet shape discussed earlier. Like the preceding example, it appears to date from the 1740s, though a date as late as the 1750s is possible. This dating is based upon their relationship to the early Williamsburg group and the next phase of development in the Hay shop, which is considerably more advanced in style.

44. *Card Table, attributed to the Anthony Hay Shop,*
Williamsburg, circa 1745.
Mahogany primary; yellow pine and oak secondary.
Height 29⅜", width 34", depth 16¼".
Mr. J. McKenzie Semple.

45. *Card Table, attributed to the Anthony Hay Shop,*
Williamsburg, circa 1745.
Mahogany primary; yellow pine, oak and poplar secondary.
Height 29⅜", width 34", depth 16¼".
Private collection.

45a.

This new phase of production in the Hay shop reflects the rococo fashion that was dominating taste in western society by the middle of the eighteenth century. Understandably, the earliest Hay shop examples in this style have rococo ornamentation applied to earlier George II forms. The premier Williamsburg example of this period, and also the earliest, is a magnificent ceremonial armchair made for the Capitol in Williamsburg (fig. 46). It was taken to Richmond when the capital was moved there in 1780. It was eventually consigned to the attic, and early in the twentieth century was given to a custodian now known only as Mr. Dillard. It was sold by Dillard to Hugh Proctor Gresham, an antique dealer from Richmond who in turn sold it to J. F. Biggs, also of that city. In 1928, Dr. W. A. R. Goodwin purchased the chair from the Biggs Antique Company for Colonial Williamsburg.[52] Appearing to date from the 1750s, this piece most likely served as the Governor's chair in the General Court, and a set of similar chairs of regular height may have originally accompanied it. Its imposing stance and height would necessitate the use of a stool, and though the form may appear awkward to the twentieth-century eye, it was often used for elaborate ceremonial purposes two centuries ago. The throne of George III, similarly proportioned, survives today with the original footstool intact. The majestic effect that such a suite is intended to project is readily apparent in John Singleton Copley's London portrait of Henry Laurens, colonial Governor of South Carolina (fig. 46f). The elaborate canopy shown, undoubtedly representing the manner in which the Capitol chair was displayed, is further intended to reinforce the status and power of the individual seated in it.

Colonial Governors represented an extension of the King's authority, and the lavish elegance of these chairs is certainly in accord with their royal connotation. They contrast with the austere formality of the Speaker's chair of the Virginia House of Burgesses (fig. 7) and the British House of Commons, both bodies of elected legislators.[53]

The primary wood of the Capitol chair is mahogany, and beech is found in secondary usage. The front seat rail and two diagonal braces are yellow pine. Displaying poorer workmanship than the other elements, they appear to be eighteenth-century repairs. The upholstery is new, although it now displays the correct contours, with brass tacks in the original holes. Several of the carved knee brackets are also replaced, as are the tips of the rear feet.

Because of the superb carving and the use of beech, this chair has had an English attribution since

46. *Capitol Chair, attributed to the Anthony Hay Shop,*
    carving attributed to James Wilson, Williamsburg, circa 1755.
Mahogany primary; beech secondary with yellow pine repairs.
Height 49", width 21½", depth 24½".
The Colonial Williamsburg Foundation (acc. no. 1930-215).

46a.

47. *Williamsburg Masonic Lodge Six Master's Chair, attributed to the Anthony Hay Shop, Williamsburg, circa 1760.*
Mahogany primary.
Height 52¼", width 29½", depth 26¼".
Williamsburg Masonic Lodge Six.

47a.

its acquisition by Colonial Williamsburg in 1928. There is now sufficient evidence to disprove this attribution and to indicate that the piece was actually made in the Hay shop. This evidence is interwoven in the chair's carved details, as well as in the details found on three pieces that follow (figs. 47, 48, 49). Their study will proceed individually, emphasizing interrelated features.

The carving and sculptural quality of the Capitol chair is the finest of its time, and the anatomical qualities of its paw feet and lion's heads have no contemporary parallel in America. The knee carving is an English formula that also occurs in Massachusetts and New York furniture (fig. 46e), although the execution in this piece has a delicacy and a flowing quality superior to them. This delicate quality is consistent in the carving of all four legs, and the arm supports are equally well executed. Inside the arm supports is unusual geometric carving similar to that found on gilded English looking glasses. The elements include concave-sided diamonds, a cabochon, and a complex circle, all located within a chip-cut border (fig. 46c).

An impressive Masonic Master's chair (fig. 47) shares interrelated features with the Capitol chair. Traditionally, it is said to have been given to Williamsburg's Lodge Number Six by Lord Botetourt, Royal Governor of Virginia from 1768 to 1770. Its arm supports, carved in designs almost identical to those of the Capitol chair, are nearly square in cross section from the seat rails to the arms (fig. 46b, 47c). The outside corner on each arm forms the central vein of the long acanthus, which begins as two scrolls flanking the bottom corner at the level of the seat rail. The effective curled tip of the acanthus, found on the Capitol chair arm supports (fig. 46b, 46c), has been omitted on the Masonic example, although the inside surfaces of the latter arm supports have the same geometric designs, in the same order, as those on the Capitol chair. Both have rounded bottoms on the lower sections of the arm supports where they join the seat rails. The acanthus carving of the arm supports is very good, although well below the highest order seen on the Capitol chair. There is also a noticeable decline in the curvature of the arm supports, but the greatest decline in quality and in understanding of design is evident in the carving of the lion's head (figs. 46b, 46c, and 47c, 47d). Those on the Capitol chair display exceptional modeling, with subtle wrinkles and a complexity of shape, indicating that the carver not only had studied anatomy but also had understood it well. The lion on the Lodge Six chair shows a closely related anatomical approach, one that is particularly meaningful since English examples

71

exhibit enormous variation.[54] It has lost both subtlety and complexity of shape, however, and a major departure can be seen in the modeling of the eyes and eye sockets. Those of the Capitol chairs are anatomically correct, with lids pointed down toward the nose in the front and, on the sides, toward the lower part of the ear. This essentially repeats the position of the eyes of an actual lion, although some stylization of the skull proportion has occurred. On the Masonic chair the eyes and eye sockets have been given a humanoid configuration. This loss of anatomical knowledge is even more dramatically evident in the mane carving.[55]

The well-formed cabriole legs of the Lodge Six chair are also related to those of the Capitol chair, with knee carving that is a variation of the asymmetrical design that is used on the Capitol chair. Again, the quality is not as high, although it is equal or superior to the variations of this design seen in New York and Massachusetts furniture. The smooth animal-paw foot, a London alternative to the hairy paw (fig. 47e), relate to those on the Capitol chair and represent the only known production of this type in eighteenth-century America. The back legs are similar to numerous examples illustrated in Chippendale's *Director*, and the crest rail, with its volutes, is similar to those of the Scott group, although here the volutes are more attenuated.

The massive back of the Lodge Six chair, carved from a solid block of mahogany, undoubtedly serves as an intentional demonstration of the carver's art. An easier method would have been to fashion it from separate pieces, which was a far more common technique for such construction. To better understand this laborious departure from tradition one must understand that eighteenth-century freemasonry emphasized craftsmanship, and in that respect the piece is a symbolic representation of the principles of their organization. (For a further understanding of this chair and its Masonic significance, see related material under "Ceremonial Chairs.")

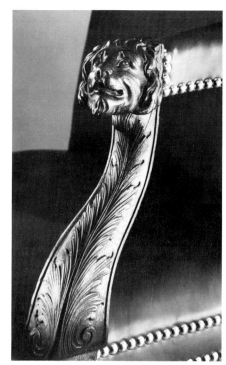

46b.

46c.

46f. Henry Laurens *by John Singleton Copley, 1782.*
Oil on canvas.
Height 54¼", width 40⅝".
National Portrait Gallery, Smithsonian Institution,
  Washington D.C., Gift of Andrew Mellon, 1942.

47c.

47d.

47b.

46d.

46e.

47e.

48. *Card Table, attributed to the Anthony Hay Shop,*
    Williamsburg, circa 1760.
Mahogany primary; yellow pine and mahogany secondary.
Height 27⅝", width 33⅜", depth 16½" closed, 33" open.
The Colonial Williamsburg Foundation (acc. no. 1932-12).

A fine mahogany card table is closely related to these two ceremonial chairs (fig. 48). Its knee carving (fig. 48a), while much simplified, is a variation of the same formula, including the asymmetrical fronds and tilted C-scroll that point to the center of the table. The acanthus flows from the top volute of the tilted C-scroll on the card table and Capitol chair (fig. 46e), although the former does not have the ruffled shell attached to the scroll like the Capitol and Lodge Six chairs. The simpler design may have resulted from economic considerations, but the naive quality reflects the carver's lack of skill and understanding. Other aspects of this table relate to Hay shop production as well. The shape of the top, with its recessed square and oval pockets, is identical to two earlier card tables in this group (figs. 44, 45), as is the hidden drawer and the continuous side skirts that overlap the swing-leg when closed (fig. 48c). The sinuous legs also have a quality and proportion similar to those of the early Williamsburg tea table (fig. 8) and a later side table (fig. 53).

This table is the most attractive surviving Virginia card table known to the writer. It is of extreme importance to the study of the Hay shop since it consolidates the early Hay production with the second phase represented by the Capitol and Masonic chairs.

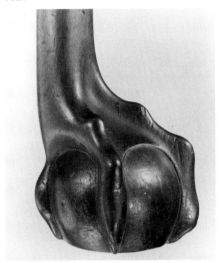

48a.

48b.

48c.

Furniture Attributed to Bucktrout

A Masonic Master's chair (fig. 49) signed by Benjamin Bucktrout gives an undisputed look at high quality carved furniture produced in the Hay shop.[56] Details of this signed chair have an affinity to those of the preceding three pieces, not an unexpected development considering Bucktrout's association with Hay and his eventual ownership of the business.

The Bucktrout chair was taken to the Edenton, North Carolina Unanimity Lodge No. Seven in 1778, according to an entry in the minute books there. Further information on the piece is found in their library, where a letter from Norfolk Lodge No. One, dated 1811, claims the chair and states that it was taken to Edenton to save it from destruction by the British. Unfortunately it does not clarify which lodge in Virginia originally owned the chair before it was taken there for safekeeping. Another letter from the Norfolk Lodge, this one dated 1815, again claimed the chair, as did one in 1876 from the Alexandria Lodge. This latter claim was without validity, however, since the lodge was not in existence when the chair was taken to Edenton. On October 6, 1877, the *Raleigh Observer* featured an article on the piece, noting its signature and establishing its maker's position in early Williamsburg: "On the back of the chair is the odd name Benjamin Bucktrout. Capt. [Octavious] Coke [North Carolina Secretary of State], who came from Williamsburg, says that Bucktrout is an 'immemorial patronymic of cabinetmakers in that old town.' "[57]

The overall design of this piece, which was created entirely for ceremonial purposes, is by far the most ambitious of all American Masonic chairs. Its elements have been scaled in proportion to the abnormal size, and the exceptional architectural quality of the back gives it a distinction not encountered in other American Masonic chairs.

The crest of the chair simulates a cut stone arch (fig. 49a), with a gilded scroll on its keystone and a book on top. Capping the central column is a magnificent bust of Matthew Prior (1664-1721) (fig. 49b), a rendering after a marble sculpture carved by the Frenchman Antoine Coysevox about 1700. The origin of the chair's wooden bust has been questioned, and Philadelphia has been suggested as its source,[58] but close study reveals that the features of the masks on the moon and the sun that flank the bust are executed in the same style and appear to be by the same carver. The sculpting of the lips and the areas around the corner of the mouth show the same approach and techniques of modeling as do the eyes,

49. *Masonic Master's Chair, attributed to the Anthony Hay Shop, stamped signature of Benjamin Bucktrout, Williamsburg, 1767-1770.*
Mahogany primary; walnut secondary, original black leather upholstery.
Height 65½", width 31¼", depth 29½".
The Unanimity Lodge No. 7, Edenton, North Carolina.

49a.

49b.

with their exaggerated lids extending over the sides of the eyeballs. In addition to this sculptural affinity, these three elements—sun, moon, and bust—are critically linked with the scale and design of the curved arch and flanking columns. This evidence indicates that the chair was conceived as a total unit and produced by Bucktrout, or under his supervision. The existence of another chair from this shop, with sculptural carving equal to that of the bust, is further support for this conclusion (fig. 46).

While the exact design source for the bust is unknown, the dolphin legs (figs. 49g, 49h) derive from plate XXI of Chippendale's *Director*, possibly from the same copy that appeared in Edmund Dickinson's inventory several years later. In contrast, the design for the arm supports is from Hay shop examples of a decade or more earlier. The acanthus originates at the outside base of the supports, then runs upward and folds back upon itself (fig. 49d), modified from the heavily curled acanthus found on the Capitol chair support (figs. 46b, 46c). The acanthus found on the Capitol chair arm support and on the closely related Lodge Six chair (fig. 47c), however, flow from a pair of small volutes that flank the lower corner of the support. This configuration allows the acanthus to flow upon both outside faces. In the Bucktrout example a different support was used, featuring a piercing through its lower outer edge.[59] The carver, unable to adjust to this change, attempted to execute the acanthus from the side, as in the two earlier chairs, even though the stem of the acanthus conflicted with the position of the piercing. With no area to complete the stem as a volute, it was cut off squarely, and results in an awkwardly finished product. The veining of this acanthus also shows a degenerate relationship compared with those of the Capitol and Lodge Six chairs. The delicate, flowing character on the Capitol chair is executed with a fine gouge that was skillfully handled and produced a surface of parallel and converging flutes. This same technique was used on the Lodge Six chair (fig. 47), although executed with less skill. With deeper veining and a greater accent on the flutes, the carving of the Lodge Six chair does not show the flowing quality of the Capitol example. This rigid contrast is more accented on the Bucktrout acanthus; the carving has deep, wide, concave flutes separated by high, narrow ridges. In a naive attempt to achieve the delicacy of the earlier work, the carver has added small veins to his harshly modeled foliage. An early stage of this decline from academic design can be seen in veined foliage on the Lodge Six chair back (fig. 47b). This loss of style and skill parallels that previously discussed regarding the lion's heads of the Capitol and Lodge Six chairs.

49c.

49e.

49d.

49f.

49g.

49h. *"French Chairs," detail, Plate 21, Thomas Chippendale's* Gentleman and Cabinet-Maker's Director, *third edition, 1762.*

Other close relationships to the Lodge Six chair are found in the endings of two large acanthus leaves which flank the central "ruffled shell" pendant of the skirt on the Bucktrout chair (fig. 49f). These two fronds end very abruptly, leaving a space between their tips and the shell ornament. This same abrupt ending is seen on the arm support of the Lodge Six chair (fig. 47c, 47d). In both examples the addition of an extended point, or of a curled overlap, would balance the weight of the overall design. Another similarity between these two chairs is seen in the crisp C-scrolls above the dolphin's head (fig. 49g) and on the central skirt, and those of the knee carving of the Lodge Six chair (fig. 47e).

In view of the foregoing discussion, the Bucktrout chair appears to be the product of at least two tradesmen, perhaps even more. The bust and the Masonic symbols exhibit extremely high quality carving, while the arm supports are poorly executed in comparison. The skirt carving has hollowed-out features and a harshness of outline seen in the arm supports, although it displays better workmanship. The involvement of several carvers in such an extensive effort is certainly understandable, and it is quite likely if considered in light of what is known about the Hay shop and the practice of craft specialization in the eighteenth century.

The collective study of these three chairs and the ball-and-claw-foot card table provides firm evidence for several very important conclusions. The interrelationship of their designs and their carved elements show the Capitol chair to be a product of the Hay shop and not an English piece, as it was assumed to be in the past. The various design elements that unite this group are not imitations of a single prototype, but examples of a firmly developed style that evolved over a period of two decades— precisely the case seen in the arm supports of these chairs. Likewise, the Lodge Six animal feet and knee carving are not copies from the Capitol chair. They are variations within the George II style, with enough individual characterization to make their affinity to each other clear, yet distinguishable from examples produced elsewhere.

The signed Bucktrout chair and the ball-and-claw-foot card table establish Hay's shop as the origin of the Capitol chair. Its mid-century style coincides with the rebuilding of the Capitol in the early 1750s, thus providing strong circumstantial evidence to attribute the carving to James Wilson, the London-trained artisan who was working for Hay in 1755. Certainly the quality and style of this carving supports a London association.

The Lodge Six chair represents an intermediate stage between the Capitol and the Bucktrout examples. It also appears to have been made after the uncertain date of departure of James Wilson, the London carver who worked with Hay. The carving, although fine, would be hard to accept as having been executed by the same hand that executed the Capitol chair, and it probably represents the impact of Wilson's style and training on Hay shop products (see footnote 55).

The signed Bucktrout chair was probably made during his ownership of the Hay business (1767-70). Its numerous designs, which relate to earlier Hay production, have already been pointed out. It is also known that elements were taken from Chippendale's *Director*, a copy of which is documented in the shop during Edmund Dickinson's time and which possibly had been there since Hay's active practice of the craft. We have also seen that Dickinson and "Wiltshire" probably remained with the Hay business when Bucktrout returned in 1767, which means they would have retained a knowledge of earlier Hay shop design and technique. While none of these reasons alone is indisputable proof, collectively they point to the Bucktrout chair as a product of the Hay shop between 1767 and 1770.

50. *Dressing Chest, attributed to the Anthony Hay Shop,
    probably Benjamin Bucktrout, circa 1770.*
Cherry primary; yellow pine and cherry secondary.
Height 72", width 40", depth 21".
Mr. and Mrs. Malcolm Jamieson.

50a.

50b.

The next three pieces of furniture are attributed to Bucktrout on somewhat tenuous grounds, and their separation from other Hay shop production is difficult. The first example is a dressing chest made of cherry, with yellow pine and cherry secondary woods (fig. 50).[60] The Bucktrout attribution is based on the fret design in its cornice. Before a discussion of this fret, however, there are several features of the chest that should be noted since they are associated with the Scott group and are otherwise unknown in Virginia furniture. The chest is breakfront in form (the bottom section is deeper than the top and therefore forms an offset at their juncture) and the top had a cut-through gallery above its cornice—two features already seen on a clothespress at Blandfield that clearly falls within the Peter Scott group (fig. 42). The indented corners on the raised panel doors are also similar in design and execution to those of the Scott group.

The fret beneath the cornice of this dressing chest (fig. 50a) features four-petalled flowers with centers formed by a drilled hole. Two "china tables" (Chippendale's definition for the form) also attributed to the Hay shop have a series of identical

flowers in the design of their legs (figs. 51b, 52). In addition, they have a guilloche-like detail that originates from these flowers, with small lobes in matching pairs, that give a floral quality quite unlike the more frequently encountered geometric designs. This same floral guilloche is carved in relief between the pilasters of the Lodge Six chair (fig. 47b), although there it is more complex than on the fretwork tables. This is probably due to the differences in techniques: carving certainly gives more detail, but its employment in a fret might cause problems of execution and strength. Despite these differences, the basic designs of these three pieces are the same and thereby further emphasize their relationship.

In addition to this fret design, the overall plan of the skirt on the china table (fig. 51) is closely associated with that on the Bucktrout chair (fig. 49f). Both have a pronounced central element, with scalloping that is similarly handled: they have a harshness of outline and modeling that, in the Bucktrout chair, is most pronounced in the carved ruffled shells that flank the knees and that surround the C-scrolls in the center skirt. In these examples the outline of the shells is symmetrically composed, with an edge that repeats a cove followed by a projecting astragal. This is quite unusual in rococo design, where shells generally display a flowing form and are most often very asymmetrical. The Capitol chair knee carving (fig. 46e) features a flowing ruffled shell that drapes naturally over the knee, while that of the Lodge Six chair (fig. 47e) is stiffer and lacks a spontaneity of line. The splashing convex teardrops in the Capitol chair's tattered shell projects great movement in contrast to those of the Lodge Six chair; here, they have lost their effective motion and are executed in a much coarser manner. The ruffled shells of the Bucktrout chair display an even greater loss and have an extremely simplistic approach, showing yet another way in which it relates to the Capitol chair, with the Lodge Six chair of a quality between the two. Since the dolphin-legged chair in Chippendale's *Director* has a standard, flowing, asymmetrical shell quite unlike that of Bucktrout's, it is thus likely that these chairs are related by similar design and conception. The scalloped skirt of the Byrd china table (fig. 51) is also harshly designed in the Bucktrout style and contrasts vividly with the representative flowing character seen on the central skirt of an English china cabinet (fig. 41).

The cherry dressing chest (fig. 50), the only known example from Virginia, has a fully developed dressing drawer in the top of the lower section (fig. 50b). The drawer is cherry throughout, and in its center is a reversible platform with a looking glass on

one side and on the other a writing surface originally covered with leather or felt. This platform is raised and lowered on a ratchet and is flanked by numerous compartments and small drawers. The cover of one compartment on the right has a block-like handle that is slotted for holding rings. The design of this drawer is similar to one in plate LII of Chippendale's *Director*, which is described as having "a Glass made to rise, and hung with Hinges . . . Places for Combs, Rings, Bottles, Boxes, &c. . . ."[61] Originally, two long horizontal strips were attached to the back of this drawer. They extended beyond its sides and slid into slots cut in the insides of the case. They served as "stops" to prevent the drawer from pulling too far out.

This chest has three regular drawers beneath the fitted one. Each is constructed with a bottom having a slight bevel around three faces and is fit into grooved sides. Three long blocks, approximately one inch apart and mitered at the corners, are glued to the bottom against the front edge. The side blocks that formed the drawer runners are missing, and it is not clear if they were continuous or segmented. The bottoms are secured to the back with several small L- or T-head nails.

The lower case has dust partitions between the drawers. The partitions are as thick as the drawer blades and continue the full depth of the case. This form of dustboard is termed "full bottom" by the English furniture historian R. W. Symonds, and is seen in a number of other Williamsburg pieces.[62] These dust partitions fit into grooves that are cut in the sides of the case and are sporadically wedged with narrow pieces of cherry approximately one inch wide; the wedges are driven in from below to tighten them. The feet and base molding are replacements.

The interior of the upper section was constructed with numerous drawers—some of which are now missing—and central shelves. The section's well-designed door has pilasters that flank a large, well-proportioned, raised panel. The pilasters are attached by wood screws, which enter from the back; their stop fluting may be associated with that on the signed Bucktrout and Lodge Six chairs (figs. 49, 47b). The cornice is detachable, separating just below the fret, and although the gallery at the top is a replacement, the lower section of the original survives. These suggest that it had a guilloche design similar to that seen on the following table.

This china table (fig. 51) is made completely of mahogany, and has a bold quality that distinguishes it from British examples. Each leg is cut from a solid piece of wood, as is the gallery—which in English pieces is often triple-laminated. The table originally stood slightly higher and probably had molded block

51. *China Table, attributed to the Anthony Hay Shop, probably Benjamin Bucktrout, Williamsburg, circa 1770. Mahogany primary. Height 30⅛", width 36⅜", depth 23¼". Private collection.*

52. *China Table, attributed to the Anthony Hay Shop, Williamsburg, circa 1770. Cherry and curly maple primary; oak, maple and poplar secondary. Height 31", width 35", depth 21". Diplomatic Reception Rooms, Department of State, Washington, D.C.*

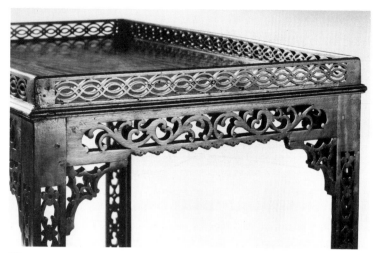

51a.

51b.

feet as well as columns inside each leg (see fig. 52 for comparison). It was made without secondary wood but now has several white pine blocks beneath the top, possibly put there during the late nineteenth century when the piece was in Baltimore. These blocks, clearly not original, contain nail holes from previous usage. The glue smears that accompany them are of a much later date than the table's original construction.

An oral tradition associated with this table reveals that it descended through the Lewis family of Gloucester County, Virginia. Susan Lewis married William Powell Byrd, son of William Byrd III of Westover. The bird featured in the skirt (carved only on one side) may well be an indication of the latter family's connection.[63]

Closely related to this table is a similar but more elaborate piece with skirt and legs of cherry and a top of curly maple (fig. 52). The fret of the legs is a slight variation of the type of the Byrd table, strengthening their association with carving on the Lodge Six chair back. The floral guilloche has double lobes in each segment, and at the top of each leg the last piercings develop into confronting lobate leaves—variations closer to the Lodge Six chair carving than the Byrd table.

Unfortunately, several of the leg brackets and the pierced gallery are replacements, and it is not known if the gallery is a copy of the original. The original gallery may have had a complex guilloche design similar to that on the Byrd table, which would better complement the overall design than the replacement. The quality of this gallery is vastly inferior to the piercing in the skirt and leg, where the masterful use of the fret saw can be seen. Every portion is cut with assurance and sharpness, creating fine lines that produce a flowing quality in the foliage. The replacement fret is crudely executed and displays a tremendous misunderstanding of the design.

Several other details on this table are also seen on the Byrd table. One that is particularly distinguishable is a small shoot that ends in three bulbous lobes; it is found on the lower corners of the front skirt. This detail is also present on the skirt of the Byrd table, located just in front of, and touching, the bird's beak. Also, this example, like the Byrd table, is symmetrical, with only a small element establishing a "front." Here the two front legs have a very small bead carved down their corners, a feature that is omitted on the back. Likewise, the Byrd table has only one bird carved, while the other is simply cut in profile.

The top of this table is curly maple, a wood that is rare in southern furniture and even more so in the products of eastern Virginia. Seen here, quarter-sawn and book-matched, it is certainly indicative of the traditional approach to the construction of a fiddle back, further reinforcing the possibility that Bucktrout was a musical instrument maker.

There is a third china table in this group that relates to the previous piece through its well-executed piercings, but this example has the addition of a delicately cut cross-stretcher. Like the preceding table, it was among the collection formed by Lewis G. Myers, the great furniture connoisseur of the early twentieth century, but its location is currently unknown. The catalogue for the sale of his collection notes that this table ". . . stood in a Virginia home one hundred and fifty years, and was doubtless the work of an American craftsman."[64] These three pieces are the most fully developed American fret-work china tables known. Their fine proportions, superb piercings, and free-standing columns distinguish them from other American examples of the same form.

Another piece with mixed primary woods is a dressing table of delicate scale (fig. 53). Principally of cherry, but having drawer fronts of mahogany, it has a top with indented corners like those on a tea table in this group (fig. 57). The bead molding on the skirt is related to those in the following examples, and the chamfered and fluted corners of the case are an effective refinement. Its long, graceful legs are quite similar to those of a much earlier tea table (fig. 8) and a card table (fig. 48), the latter having beading on the knees that also relates to this piece. The volutes, which are relatively weak in design, overlap the rails of the skirt as seen in the Bucktrout chair and later examples from the Hay shop. The ball-and-claw feet are essentially of the Scott group type, with flattened ball and concave rear toe. Their finely knuckled front toes, though somewhat unusual, seem to be a combination of the Scott foot and the type on the Hay shop card table (fig. 48b).

53. Side Table, attributed to the Anthony Hay Shop,
*   probably Benjamin Bucktrout, Williamsburg, circa 1770.*
Cherry and mahogany primary; poplar secondary.
Height 27½", width 31¼", depth 20½".
Museum of Early Southern Decorative Arts.

A small side table (fig. 54) is characteristic of much furniture from eastern Virginia in its simplicity. It is an original furnishing at the College of William and Mary, although the date it entered the collection is unknown. It is made of walnut with yellow pine and has the original brass. The Williamsburg provenance, together with drawer construction resembling the large dressing chest (fig. 50), are reasons for including it in the Bucktrout group. Across the bottom of the skirt is a small bead that continues down the outside edges of each leg. This bead is also found on the finished skirt of the walnut back, although the molded edge of the top does not continue there, indicating that the table was intended for use against a wall. The top is glued to the frame with small pine blocks that are spaced a few inches apart.

54. *Side Table, attributed to the Anthony Hay Shop,
    Williamsburg, circa 1770.*
Walnut primary; yellow pine secondary.
Height 28½", width 30¼", depth 20¼".
The College of William and Mary.

55. *Side Table, attributed to the Anthony Hay Shop,
    Williamsburg, circa 1770.*
Cherry primary; poplar secondary.
Height 34⅞", width 52⅝", depth 27¾".
The Colonial Williamsburg Foundation (acc. no. 1975-84).

A cherry side table closely related to the preceding example has an identical attachment for the top and the same fine bead on the legs and skirt (fig. 55). The rear skirt is also completely finished, and the top is molded across the back. Again, the intent was to place the table against a wall, for despite considerable work in finishing all four sides, the rear brackets are not pierced. The unusual feature of the finished back with unfinished brackets presents an important tie between the two china tables (figs. 51, 52) and these side tables (figs. 54, 55). The top is attached with a number of small blocks, which also relates to the preceding example. This table descended in a family of Westmoreland County, Virginia.

55a.

A magnificent clothespress, once owned by the Haxall family of "Strawberry Hill" in Petersburg, shares many features with Williamsburg cabinet-work, some of which relate it to Bucktrout (fig. 56). The lower case, constructed with full-bottom dustboards, is virtually identical to that of the cherry dressing chest (fig. 50). As in the dressing chest, the dustboards are tightened with an occasional narrow wedge driven from beneath. The feet are replacements, although the original base molding and some of the support blocks survive—enough in fact, to determine that the original feet were ogee brackets. The partially surviving blocks indicate that the foot construction was of the composite type, which is also seen on Scott examples and is common in other Williamsburg groups. The molding at the base and at the top of the lower case has rounded corners, which conform to the previous pieces. The drawer construction also relates this press to the dressing chest: the bottoms are set in grooves with short blocks glued to support them, although the blocks are not mitered at the corners and are more numerous.

The top section of this clothespress is fitted with five sliding trays and two small drawers; all the bottoms are constructed like those of the lower case drawers. A difference in construction, however, is found in the single dust partition above the two drawers. Made of very thin red cedar, it is held in place by a strip of yellow pine running from front to back—the same method employed in all the Scott group case pieces (fig. 37d).

The sliding trays for storing clothing have mahogany fronts and red cedar linings. Cedar was undoubtedly used because of its qualities as an insect repellent. It is also found in the fitted desk interior of the lower section; the drawer fronts here are covered with a one-eighth inch veneer of crotch mahogany (fig. 56b).

This piece also has yellow pine tops and bottoms on each case, some small elements of poplar, and backs of tongue-and-groove black walnut. The walnut provides another association with Bucktrout, who employed it for secondary usage on his signed Masonic Master's chair.

In certain details, this clothespress resembles the cherry dressing chest recently discussed (fig. 50): both have fitted drawers in the lower sections and cupboards in the tops. The doors of this piece are English in construction with joints similar to those on drop-leaf tables, stopping them at a right angle when they are opened. The press is also unusual for having a desk interior combined with a cupboard and for using sliding trays for clothing storage, a design also closely related to English chest-on-chests. One

basic difference between these two chests is the construction of the cornice. On the clothespress it is glued directly to the case, and on the dressing chest it is detachable.

Several features of this piece might suggest a rather late date. Some of those features, in fact, are usually considered to be indications of federal period production. The flat panels of the doors and the fitted desk drawer with hinged front are usually associated with cabinetmaking in the late eighteenth or early nineteenth century. Flat panels appear on English pieces from the 1760s, however, and the Norfolk clothespress dated 1775 is a definite example of their use in pre-Revolutionary Virginia (fig. 105). Another early example from Williamsburg also exists (fig. 77), and like this one it has ogee spandrels in the upper corners of its flat panels, a trait that appears to indicate their early date. Fitted desk drawers, like flat panels, are also most commonly seen on federal furniture; however, they clearly appear before that date, and the form is known to have been used in Charleston, South Carolina during the 1770s.[65] This fitted drawer (fig. 56b) differs from later ones by the use of a brass hook-and-eye latch to keep the drawer front closed, instead of the later push-button mechanism, thus suggesting that this form is an earlier stage in its development.

As stated earlier, the attribution of these six pieces to Bucktrout is very tentative (figs. 50-56). The case is stronger with the earlier examples and they may actually precede Bucktrout and represent Anthony Hay production. Collectively, this furniture exhibits strong evidence of Williamsburg origin in light of its interrelationship with the signed Bucktrout chair and with other Williamsburg groups.

56a.

56b.

56. *Clothespress, attributed to the Anthony Hay Shop, Williamsburg, circa 1775.*
Mahogany primary; yellow pine, red cedar, poplar, and walnut secondary.
Height 81¾", width 47⅜", depth 25⅜".
The Colonial Williamsburg Foundation (acc. no. G1977-228), gift of Miss Martha B. D. Spotswood.

57. *Tea Table, attributed to the Anthony Hay Shop,*
   Williamsburg, circa 1771-75.
Mahogany primary.
Height 28³/₁₆", width 34½", depth 22".
Mrs. William F. Low, Sr.

57a.

57b.

Furniture Attributed to Dickinson

Edmund Dickinson operated the Hay shop from 1771 until 1776, and if written documentation is any indication, he ran a very successful business. Unfortunately, no indisputably documented furniture by him is known, and again a group of furniture is attributed to the Hay shop on circumstantial evidence. Only in one instance can Dickinson possibly be associated with furniture that corresponds to a written document: a tea table (fig. 57) reputedly sold from the Governor's Palace in the eighteenth century, and a chair with a history indicating that it was among the property abandoned by Lord Dunmore and sold in 1776. This chair was purchased by a member of the Galt family of Williamsburg who continued to own it until it was acquired recently by the Colonial Williamsburg Foundation. In addition, it was among the few colonial furnishings shown in Norfolk's Art Loan Exhibition of 1879, which is the earliest documentation of its Dunmore-Palace tradition.[66] The chair may be associated with Dickinson on the basis of Dunmore's £30 account with him (see footnote 46).

Attribution of the tea table to the Hay shop depends principally on the use of the trumpet foot (fig. 57), which corresponds to an unfinished leg excavated at the Hay site in the context of objects dating from 1765-75 (fig. 65). The top of this table was originally attached to the base by a series of small, evenly spaced blocks, a method similar to the two side tables attributed to the Bucktrout period of the Hay shop (figs. 54, 55).

Another feature associated with the Hay shop is the method of forming the top by gluing a molding into the rabbeted edge, although in this example the added pieces have long since disappeared (fig. 57a). The indented corners are another Williamsburg feature, and each was originally fitted with two small sections of raised molding, mitered at the corner and butted against the longer portions of the side. This method of construction is remarkably similar to the indented corners of door panels in the Scott group (fig. 36b) and the Williamsburg case-piece group (fig. 77b).

The "Dunmore" chair (fig. 58) is made of walnut with a yellow pine and oak slip seat; it retains the original black leather upholstery beneath a later covering. The upholstery technique is consistent with that of the Scott group and another example excavated at the Hay shop (fig. 67). It has an integral rear seat rail and shoe, and although this feature is also consistent with the Scott group, there is a departure: the bottom edge of the rear rail is straight without the usual horizontal shaping. Other variations from the Scott type are the stiles that flare outward, thereby creating a wider crest rail and a narrower stance to the rear legs. While this chair shows some association with those of the Scott group, it also introduces variations, and its relationship to Edmund Dickinson cannot be established until another piece that repeats these variations is examined.

58. *Side Chair, attributed to the Anthony Hay Shop, probably Edmund Dickinson, circa 1771-75.*
Walnut primary; oak and yellow pine slip seat with original black leather upholstery beneath later covering.
Height 36⅜", width 21", depth 17⅛".
The Colonial Williamsburg Foundation (acc. no. 1978-10).

59a.

59. *Fredericksburg Masonic Lodge Four Master's Chair, attributed to the Anthony Hay Shop, probably Edmund Dickinson with carving by George Hamilton, Williamsburg, circa 1775.*
Mahogany primary; walnut blocking.
Height 42½", width 27½", depth 18⅛".
Fredericksburg Masonic Lodge Four.

Displaying some of the finest carving from eastern Virginia, the Master's chair from Masonic Lodge Four in Fredericksburg is the fourth example of ceremonial chair production from the Hay shop (fig. 59).[67] The modified concepts of the Scott group seen in the preceding chair are repeated in this example. Other Scott construction is also present: the arms are dovetailed into the stiles; the knee brackets overlap the seat rail; the gadroon is glued to the front of the seat rail;[68] and the rear legs are contoured to end in a shaped foot. The flaring back, straight rear rail, and the carving, however, differ from that of the Scott group.

To understand the combination of details seen on this chair, one must again study the excavated easy chair leg from the Hay shop (fig. 65). This leg has two features that relate it closely to the Lodge Four chair (figs. 59, 70). First, its long mortises are the Scott type which utilizes a deep seat rail with wide tenons. This arrangement causes the knee brackets to overlap the seat rails. Second, the sharp corner on the leg is carried down the front of the cabriole and is so prominent that a fairly angular finished product is indicated. This is particularly noticeable near the foot, where insufficient wood remains to produce a rounded ankle of the usual type. This relates to the legs of the Lodge Four chair, which have an acute angle down the front to such a degree that the carving is divided into two planes (fig. 70). The relationship between them is very convincing, particularly in light of a major emphasis in the Williamsburg school on rounded legs and rounded corners.

Many other reasons exist to support the attribution of this chair to the Hay shop. One of the most important is the inclusion of animal feet, which are rare in America, the only other Virginia examples being clearly associated with this shop. The superb lion's feet of the Capitol chair, the smooth paw of the Lodge Six chair, and the dolphin's feet of the Bucktrout chair are all attributed to the Hay shop masters. One further example, an unfinished table leg from the Hay site, certainly appears to have been intended as an animal foot (fig. 66) and gives solidity to the attribution of these feet to the Hay shop.

Several important features of the Lodge Four chair link it closely to the Lodge Six chair, and to other Hay shop production as well. The cabriole leg and nearly vertical toes are remarkably similar to the legs and feet of the Lodge Six example (figs. 47, 72). The arm terminal (fig. 59a) features an acanthus that is contained within a relief border that follows the outline of the arm. This arm carving is a modified version of the arm support on the Capitol and Lodge

59b.

59c. *Base Molding of Botetourt Statue (see fig. 4).*

59d.

59e.

Six chairs (figs. 46b, 47c), on which the acanthus is also confined within a border. The punched background in some areas of the carving is another technique linking these chairs. In each example two different types of punch were used: the majority was done with a sharp-pointed tool, while in other areas a tool with a small circular point was employed. The Lodge Four chair uses circular marks to simulate nail heads on the edges of the coffin depicted at the bottom of its splat (fig. 59b), while the Lodge Six has such marks on the area behind the coat of arms, thistle, and rose (fig. 47b).

Certain carved designs on this chair appear to have been inspired by Chippendale's *Director*. The naturalistic stems with flowers and leaves that issue from the volutes on the knees (figs. 59d, 70) are strikingly similar to those on the center chair of plate X. This *Director*-inspired foliage was abbreviated to accommodate the opposing C-scrolls that form the basis of the central knee carving. This design was also adapted to the knee bracket on a Scott chair (fig. 20). The same Chippendale plate also appears to have influenced the shoe carving (fig. 59b), but instead of the continuous vertical flutes shown in the *Director*, the carver interspersed four flowers.[69]

Although overwhelmingly rococo, the carving on the Lodge Four chair does have several departures from this style. The center of the arm supports has a running husk design typical of neo-classic taste. An example of this design is found on the Buzaglo stove, ordered from London for the Capitol and delivered to Williamsburg in 1770 (fig. 3). Two other details, both of them carved moldings, are indisputably neo-classic (fig. 59b). On top of the shoe is a row of flat leaves, each with a simple vein in its center; below these is a repeat carving of three vertical flutes alternating with incised circles, containing five-petalled rosettes (fig. 59b). The location of this carving appears to have been inspired by the central chair in plate X of Chippendale's *Director*, although the design of this example is neo-classic. A virtually identical carved border appears on the top of an English commode, ca. 1772, which is attributed to John Cobb, upholsterer to George III.[70] A variation of the same design is found on a base molding of the statue of Lord Botetourt, which was ordered from sculptor Richard Hayward of London in 1771 and arrived in Williamsburg during June of 1773 (figs. 4, 59c).

A summation of the findings regarding this chair show it to be a product of the Williamsburg school, with a revealing combination of features:

—The construction is tied to that of the Scott group.

—The style is definitely related to Hay shop products and is firmly linked to excavated material from that site.

—While portions of the design are related to earlier Hay shop examples, the carving is quite different from that of Hay, Bucktrout, or Scott, and indicates the work of a different artisan.

—It has details taken from Chippendale's *Director*.

—It incorporates several elements of neo-classic design.

With the Hay shop established as the origin of the Lodge Four chair, the Palace chair (fig. 58) associated with it may be more firmly linked to the Dickinson account with Dunmore. The Governor's presence in Virginia between 1771 and 1775 provides a bracket date for the chair and also corresponds to Dickinson's operation of the shop. Further corroborating this time bracket are the neo-classic details, which represent developments of the early 1770s.

Attribution of these chairs to Dickinson thus established, it is possible to examine other aspects of the Lodge Four chair. Its relationship to Chippendale's *Director* is not unexpected since Dickinson owned a copy of that book. The high quality of both the design and the execution are directly related to London taste, confirming the work to be that of a professional carver with a sound knowledge of urban style. The flowers and leaves are well sculptured and have a character often seen on rococo looking glasses. The gadroon with the overlapping acanthus, fre-quently seen on English chairs, is the only such work known in America. This carving, which differs from earlier Hay shop production and incorporates neo-classic detail, is explained by the presence in Dickinson's shop of George Hamilton, the professional carver and gilder from Scotland. His advertisement mentioning the "Palmyrian taste" is concrete proof that he worked in the neo-classical style and is one of the earliest such references of its kind in America. This combined evidence indicates that this chair is the product of Dickinson and Hamilton, and it can be considered among the earliest furniture produced in America to show an impact of the neo-classical style. Interestingly, oral tradition states that this chair was given to the Fredericksburg Lodge by the Grand Lodge of Scotland—a claim that is incorrect unless the Grand Lodge commissioned it to be made in America. It is possible, however, that Hamilton's Scottish origin was the cause of this belief.

All the pieces in the Hay group dating before the signed Bucktrout chair have knee brackets nailed and glued, or just glued, to the underside of the rails. Oddly enough, the signed Bucktrout chair is the Scott type in this respect. This holds true for the easy chair leg excavated at the Hay shop, as well as for the Dickinson Lodge Four chair. Such a mixture of construction undoubtedly resulted from the frequent use of journeymen, for whom pay-by-the-month, or pay-by-the-piece allowed a great deal of latitude. A journeyman trained in the Scott approach might produce this type in a shop that had previously employed other methods of construction.

There are two other Williamsburg chairs in the Fredericksburg Masonic Lodge. The Senior Warden's chair (fig. 60), obviously made en suite with the Master's, has a splat that is essentially the same, although considerably weaker in execution. The stiles appear to be very old replacements, and are rougher in workmanship than the rest of the elements. They also have an unusually straight angle from the seat to the floor. This piece, like its more sophisticated mate, may be considered a product of Dickinson's shop. A third chair owned by the Lodge (fig. 61) is very simple and also shows peculiarities of Scott construction. Its rear seat rail is numbered "XIII," indicating the original existence of a large set. The set may have been made for Lodge use, or perhaps it was originally intended for a household and then brought to the Lodge.

60. *Senior Warden's Chair, attributed to the Anthony Hay Shop, possibly Edmund Dickinson, Williamsburg, circa 1775.*
Mahogany primary; walnut secondary.
Height 43", width 28¾", depth 18⅞".
Fredericksburg Masonic Lodge Four.

60a.

61. *Junior Warden's Chair (?), attributed to the Anthony Hay Shop, Williamsburg, circa 1775.*
Mahogany primary.
Height 39⅛", width 26½", depth 16⅞".
Fredericksburg Masonic Lodge Four.

62a.

62. *Side Chair, attributed to the Anthony Hay Shop,*
probably Edmund Dickinson with carving by George
Hamilton, Williamsburg, circa 1775.
Cherry primary; oak slip seat.
Height 38⅞", width 21", depth 20".
The Colonial Williamsburg Foundation (acc. no. 1965-184).

One of the finest side chairs produced in Williamsburg descended in the Benjamin Waller family there (fig. 62). Made of cherry, it has carving with a crispness of quality equal to that of the Lodge Four chair. The crest rails are also quite similar, with three C-scrolls across the top and large ears at the sides. These rails are stylistic variations of a Scott type (fig. 27). The molded stiles are also related and both share Scott group construction as well. The Waller chair's rear seat rail is not straight, however, but has horizontal shaping identical to the Scott group.

Two elements of the carving in this piece are of special interest. The lower center of the splat has a tied ribbon (fig. 62d) that is virtually identical to one shown on the left chair in plate XV of Chippendale's *Director* (fig. 62e). Above this ribbon, in the center of the crest, is a well-carved anthemion (fig. 62b). Here the design, like that of the Lodge Four chair, combines details from the *Director* and early neo-classic elements. The anthemion, with husk and pendant, is remarkably similar to the one on the Buzaglo stove (fig. 62c)—enough so, in fact, to suggest it as a possible source for the design. This is emphasized by the fact that other anthemia found on the stove and on the Botetourt statue lack the husk and pendant detail.

62b.

62c. *The Buzaglo Stove (see fig. 3).*

62d.

62e. *Plate 15, detail, Thomas Chippendale's* Gentleman and Cabinet-Maker's Director, *third edition, 1762.*

The carving of this chair is further related to other pieces in the Hay group. Stippling or punch work is found within the carved ribbon and, likewise, on the inside areas of the anthemion. This is precisely the practice seen on the knee carving of the Lodge Four chair (fig. 70) and repeated on its seat rails. It is also utilized on the Lodge Six chair back (fig. 47b) and on the capitals of the Bucktrout chair (fig. 49b). Certainly stippling was used elsewhere in this manner, but examples from New England and Philadelphia usually show the use of punch work outside the area encompassed by the carving. Considering the scarcity of carved Virginia furniture and the localized provenance of these pieces, this restricted use is significant.

The C-scrolls of the ears on the Waller chair (fig. 62a) end with a heavily lobed acanthus that curls from the back of the scroll. This is also seen on the Lodge Four chair, where it is most obvious in the large acanthus on the front of the knee (fig. 70). The C-scrolls, like the acanthus, are also similar, with a cove on the inside surface and a slightly convex surface on the back. In contrast the scrolls of the Bucktrout and Lodge Six chairs are quite different, since their backs are not contoured and stand out harshly. Another feature common to the Lodge Four and Waller chairs is the practice of shading, achieved by using a small gouge to cut small parallel lines at right angles to the main direction of the ornament. This can be seen on the petals of the flowers of the

Lodge Four chair (fig. 59d) and in numerous places on the ribbon of the Waller chair (fig. 62d).

Another example is a high post bed with Marlboro legs and molded block feet that descended in the Galt family of Williamsburg (fig. 63). Although the carving on its foot posts is somewhat coarser than that of the preceding chairs, it is related to them. A strikingly similar bed illustrated in *The Magazine Antiques* has carving with wheat grain, flat palm leaves, and reeds that simulate clustered columns on its top section—features that are found in a simplified version on the Galt bed.[71] It also has wheat sheaves held by a tied ribbon that is very closely related to the ribbon on the Waller chair. The execution of these ribbons and of the grains of wheat of the beds are so nearly identical that their origin appears to be the same—in all probability the Hay shop during Dickinson's period there.

63a.

63. *Bed, detail, attributed to the Anthony Hay Shop,*
   Williamsburg, circa 1775.
Mahogany primary; poplar secondary.
Post size: height 84¼", width 3⅜", depth 3¼".
The Colonial Williamsburg Foundation (acc. no. 1978-14).

64. Side Chair, attributed to the Anthony Hay Shop,
Williamsburg, circa 1770.
Mahogany primary; beech slip seat.
Height 38⅛", width 21¾", depth 17⅞".
The Kenmore Association, Inc.

Two side chairs at Kenmore in Fredericksburg can also be tentatively attributed to the Dickinson period (fig. 64). They have an integral shoe and a rear seat rail that is straight in profile—a feature consistent with the Palace and the Lodge Four chairs (figs. 58, 59). The simple crest rail can be seen on several other Williamsburg pieces, and molded stiles also occur on the Lodge Four and Waller chairs (fig. 62), although all three moldings are different. The splat has chip carving around the piercing in its base —a technique used extensively on the Capitol and Lodge Six arm supports (figs. 46c, 47d). The beaded edge and the small volute on the splat of the Kenmore chairs are related to those on the Lodge Four chair. Only the narrow seat rails of this piece differ from most others of local origin, and they alone constitute the greatest doubt for an attribution to Dickinson. However, they are also found on a chair originally at Blandfield, that has a simple ribbon in its splat and that appears to be related to figure 62.[72]

The twenty-one pieces of furniture that have been studied closely in this section share many interrelated constructional and stylistic features. Of the Williamsburg group that follows, some contain pieces with evidence that suggest they, too, may be from the Hay shop. These will be clearly pointed out, and the evidence they present will be discussed in corresponding portions of the text. Before proceeding to these groups, however, discussion of a number of objects excavated from the Hay site will help shed further light on the cabinetmaking trade in early Williamsburg.

64a.

THE HAY SHOP EXCAVATION

The excavation of the Anthony Hay shop by Ivor Noël Hume, Colonial Williamsburg's resident archaeologist, was the most successful of several cabinetmaking sites examined in Williamsburg. Many artifacts were recovered, yielding a remarkable quantity of information regarding the building and its activities, and providing the main thrust of Noël Hume's *Williamsburg Cabinetmakers—the Archaeological Evidence* (see footnote 48). This booklet gives an account of the excavation and illustrates and discusses many of the hundreds of artifacts from that site. The abundance of material contrasts markedly with the lack of evidence yielded by the excavation of the site where Peter Scott's shop stood for over forty years.

Several artifacts excavated at the Hay site provide firm evidence for identifying production there. The most important is an unfinished leg intended for a mahogany easy chair (fig. 65). Corresponding to this is a complete easy chair with identical construction and similar trumpet-shaped pad feet. It was exhibited in the Virginia Museum exhibition *Furniture of the Old South* in 1952.[73] Although that example had rounded knees, it probably represents another version from this same shop. It is unfortunate that the chair's current location is unknown, for closer study would probably be extremely revealing.

Although the leg excavated at the Hay site was originally thought to have been discarded from a repaired daybed, three aspects prove that it was intended for an easy chair and that it was in an unfinished state when thrown away.[74] The side mortise in the excavated leg enters at an acute angle (fig. 65b) and contrasts significantly with those of a daybed, which by necessity are perpendicular and form square corners. The post above the cabriole is shaped parallel to the angled mortise, thus proving it to be a right front leg. The height of thirteen inches indicates that it was made for an easy chair rather than a couch. Furthermore, the leg's intended use on an upholstered piece is verified by the peak at the outer corner of the post, which has been dulled somewhat by decay but is still very apparent. The purpose of the peak was to help maintain a straight, neat upholstery line on the corner of the chair where its covering was pulled over the rails. The outline of this shaped point is still visible on top of the original seat of the signed Bucktrout chair (fig. 49c).

With the angled mortise indicating that the leg is from a chair, and the point on its top proving that it was intended to be upholstered, the lack of tacks and tack holes is then substantial evidence to show that

65a.

65b. *Easy Chair Leg, top and mortise.*

65. *Easy Chair Leg, excavated at the Anthony Hay site, Williamsburg, 1755-1775.*
Mahogany.
Height 13¼", width 2⅞", depth 2¾".
The Colonial Williamsburg Foundation (acc. no. 6099 E.R. 748B-28.D).

the leg was never used on a finished chair. Despite the fact that decay has eroded the piece somewhat, there is sufficient surface remaining without evidence of nails to determine, without question, that this leg was neither finished nor had upholstery nailed to it. There are obvious signs of damage as well, most notably the loss of wood above the lathe-turned foot, on the back of the ankle. This may have been split off during the shaping and, if so, would have been sufficient reason for discarding the piece.

The mortises of the leg are cut 1¼ inches below the top of the knee, a feature that causes the knee brackets in the finished piece to overlap the front face of the seat rails. This construction can be seen on two surviving chairs attributed to the Hay shop (figs. 49, 59), on the signed Bucktrout chair (fig. 49), on the Speaker's chair (fig. 7), and on all the cabriole-leg chairs in the Peter Scott group.

Another leg from the excavation (fig. 66) is in a better state of preservation and appears to have been cut from similar, fine quality mahogany. The dimensions suggest that it was intended for either a dining or dressing table, although the heaviness of the top section would seem to rule out the latter. It was in an earlier stage of production than the easy chair leg when it was ruined by the loss of a long section from the center. The evidence of this mishap is well preserved, and clearly shows an area of curly wood where the workman's draw knife caught in the cross-grain and lifted out a long splinter.

Although this leg does not provide the constructional information found on the easy chair example, it does provide one of the rarest extant documents of cabinetmaking techniques in the eighteenth century. Originally interpreted as representing an early stage in the formation of a ball-and-claw foot, it actually appears to be an unfinished animal or hairy-paw foot.[75] This is somewhat unexpected since the leg is the straight type, and animal feet are normally associated with cabriole legs. Its extreme mass, however, precludes the only other possibility: a pad or a trifid foot.

The identification of this foot's intended form rests jointly on a knowledge of the production of the paw foot and on the physical evidence of this surviving example. To fully understand the design of a paw foot, however, it is first necessary to discuss the process of creating a ball-and-claw.

A ball-and-claw foot is carved from a squared block (fig. 66e). The bottom of the block is laid out for carving by designating the center and by marking the circumference of the ball with dividers or a compass. The four claws are then marked at the extreme corners of the square where they would be formed from the projecting wood. After the toes are marked, a second compass circle is inscribed within the previous one to designate the base of the ball. With the outlines thus marked, the carver proceeds to cut away the area between the claws and forms the contour of the ball along the compass lines. After this stage is complete, the contours are continued up and over the top, forming the remainder of the ball and the claws.

Animal feet are characterized by five toes, in contrast to the four of ball-and-claw feet. In most examples they have four toes crowded together on the front, with a fifth, the fetlock, on the back. Since the animal paw does not utilize all four corners of the roughed-out block, the front and side corners are removed completely in carving (figs. 66a, 66d), thereby necessitating a larger piece of wood than required for a ball-and-claw foot of comparable size. A paw foot could not be effectively carved from a

66. Table Leg, excavated at the Anthony Hay site,
    Williamsburg, circa 1760.
Mahogany.
Height 30¾", foot 2⅞" square, top 2⁹/₁₆" square.
The Colonial Williamsburg Foundation (acc. no. 2562 E.R. 243A-28D).

103

66a. *Table Leg, base of unfinished animal foot.*

66c. *Table Leg, back corner of foot with slight shaping of ankle above embryonic fetlock. At the top of the curved section on the left side of the ankle, part of the scratch line from the marking out of the original pattern remains.*

66b. *Table Leg, front right of unfinished paw foot showing first stages of toe carving.*

block of wood designated for a ball-and-claw, for the finished product would be too small and therefore would not project forward from the ankle enough to produce a successful design. The unfinished leg excavated at the Hay site has this extra allowance for the paw foot and is made from a block of wood that was originally 2⅞ inches square. The front corner is removed by two distinctive blade cuts (fig. 66a) and the two side corners have also been removed, leaving the back, from which the fetlock was to be carved, untouched. One side of the roughed-out foot has a series of chisel cuts (fig. 66b), which appear to be the first stage of shaping for one of the large toes. The slight groove formed by these cuts moves up the vertical part of the foot, then turns inward toward the ankle.

Through a comparison of this unfinished Hay foot and those surviving from the eighteenth century, it is possible to reconstruct the geometric system used to lay out construction lines for carving. First, the center of the square block is determined by making diagonal lines from opposite corners. From the center point, the largest circle possible is inscribed within the base. This circle, however, stops short of the back corner, which will eventually form the fetlock. The front and two side corners are then cut away to make the block conform to the arc on the base. The excavated Hay leg clearly represents this state in the process (fig. 66a). At this point it is necessary to inscribe the first full circle on the bottom of the block, which will outline the base of the ball on which the paw rests. Only one is needed, rather than the two found on a ball-and-claw. This difference arises since an animal foot usually grasps only the upper third of a ball. By contrast, the ball under a claw foot is larger and more fully rounded, necessitating two circles in its layout. The outer circle establishes the ball's circumference, which is above the base, and the inner circle indicates the segment that rests on the floor. With the base circle of the animal foot thus marked, the compass (maintaining the same radial setting) is used to mark the centers of the two front toes. These centers are marked by placing the compass point on the intersection of the diagonal lines with the base circle (fig. 66d). The center of the two side toes and the fetlock are at the intersection of the diagonal lines and the base circle, and therefore they are perpendicular to each other.

It should be pointed out that many eighteenth-century feet were not produced by the use of these two geometric systems, and many appear to have been carved from memory. This is particularly true of ball-and-claw feet. Those that were not laid out show a flat-sided configuration that is clearly an echo of the square block from which they were carved. All the ball-and-claw feet in the Scott group reflect this degeneration, while that of the London example (fig. 17) is made by the geometric system, resulting in a foot of bold, high quality. Paw feet were sometimes produced by employing a variation of the ball-and-claw system. In these cases, the side corners of the block were utilized for the two side toes, and only the front corner is completely removed. This procedure produces a paw foot with all of the toes nearly equal in length and lacks the sculptural form of those produced by the geometric system.

Of the paw feet attributed to the Hay shop, those of the Lodge Six chair (figs. 47, 72) were produced by the ball-and-claw method, while the Capitol chair (figs. 46, 68) and Lodge Four chair (figs.

66d. Paw Foot, in various stages of development, illustrating the geometric system and construction lines used to lay it out. This system was used on the table leg from the Hay shop site.

66e. The geometric system for laying out a ball-and-claw foot.

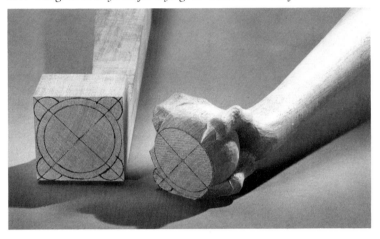

59, 70) represent the geometric plan found on the excavated leg. It appears significant that the two chairs that utilize this system date from periods when professional carvers were employed in the Hay shop. The Lodge Six chair dates in the interim and exhibits a lack of knowledge of the geometric system at a time when no professional carvers are documented there. In light of these circumstances, the excavated leg would seem to date from the period of one of the carvers; either the mid 1750s or between 1774 and 1776. The form of the top of the leg indicates the 1750s, since its massive upper section is quite similar to tables shown in the early Williamsburg group. The association of these legs with the Hay shop production thus established, the following illustrations provide a good perspective of the relationship Williamsburg paw feet have to others made in America and England (figs. 68-74).

Among the other significant artifacts from the Hay site, one of the most intriguing is a portion of a slip seat for a chair (fig. 67). Remarkably, it survives with a three-inch section of original leather upholstery. The complete slip seat shown beside the excavated example comes from a set of chairs made for the Governor's Palace (fig. 32) and is upholstered in identical fashion to the discarded example. The most unusual feature seen here is the long tab of leather pulled over the corner and attached underneath with a single wrought nail. The excavated fragment shows this same upholstery technique, and the outline of the original tab is visible. Beneath the nail is a surviving strip of leather. In addition to utilizing the same upholstery technique, both seat frames are oak.

While the excavated slip seat fragment cannot be firmly attributed to the Hay shop, it is solid documentation for this type in Williamsburg and it further supports a local origin for two sets of chairs that also have this feature. Both of these have histories in the Governor's Palace. The slip seat shown here (fig. 67) is attributed to the Peter Scott shop, and the other (fig. 58) is attributed to Edmund Dickinson. The latter piece further verifies the presence of the corner tab upholstery technique in the Hay shop during Dickinson's time there. Together with Scott details that appear on other furniture attributed to Dickinson, this suggests that the technique may have originated in Scott's shop.

Also recovered from the Hay site is the top section of a chair leg, apparently discarded from a repair. The molding on its top edge compares closely to that on top of the seat rails and legs of the Palace chair attributed to Dickinson (fig. 58). It also occurs in a cruder form on the Jefferson chairs from the Scott group (fig. 30). Although this molding is somewhat standard on chairs from areas outside Virginia, it is rarely encountered on examples from eastern Virginia.

As research continues and other related objects emerge, materials excavated at the Anthony Hay site will undoubtedly continue to furnish important insight into the products of Williamsburg cabinet-makers.

Products of the Hay shop show a diversity of design, quality, and constructional approach that forms a sharp contrast to the consistency of the Scott group. Correspondingly, the various masters of the Hay shop continually advertised for journeymen, while no such advertisements are known from Peter Scott. The conclusion to be reached from this correlation of objects and documents is that the Hay shop was operated by masters who were progressive businessmen, willing to contract with various

67. *Slip Seat fragment excavated at the Anthony Hay Shop. The fragment is here compared to an original slip seat from a chair in the Palace set (fig. 32).*
Oak, leather, iron.
The Colonial Williamsburg Foundation (acc. no. ER 205-28D).

67a. *Slip Seat, fragment. A portion of its leather upholstery survives on the outer edge. Close inspection reveals that a ghost image of the original corner tab remains, showing the technique to be the same as that of the Palace chair. The nail that held the leather tab appears as a roughened triangular lump on the far left. A small portion of leather remains trapped beneath this nail.*

specialists within the trade to produce the finest quality possible. Conversely, the Scott shop exhibits a dogmatic approach indicating a master of fixed, unyielding principles.

The Anthony Hay shop stands unique among colonial cabinetmaking establishments. None other in early Virginia is currently recognized as having produced such quality, and no other workshop in America created such an outstanding group of ceremonial chairs. A number of features—lion's heads, animal feet, and dolphin's legs—are unique to this shop, proving that its masters stood in the vanguard of British colonial furniture production.

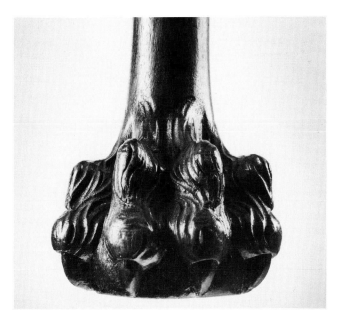

68. *The Capitol Chair (fig. 46), paw foot. This foot is of the highest quality, showing an excellent understanding of anatomy and a masterful control of the medium.*

68a. *The Capitol Chair, side view of paw foot. This foot was produced by the geometric system used on the excavated leg (see fig. 66d).*

69. *Philadelphia Side Chair, leg and foot, circa 1770.*
Mahogany.
The Colonial Williamsburg Foundation (acc. no. 1974-680).

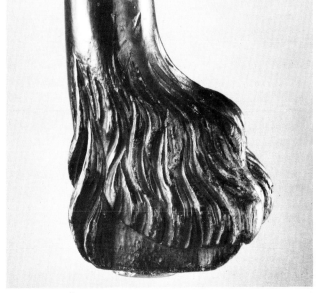

69a. *Philadelphia Side Chair, profile of foot. This example has a somewhat naive modelling of the side toe, and coarse, tassel-like hair.*

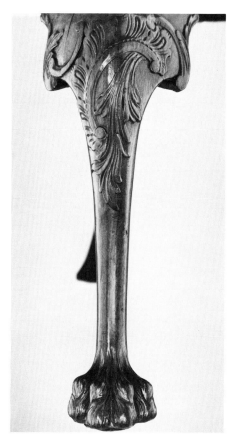

70. *Fredericksburg Masonic Lodge Four Master's Chair (fig. 59), leg and foot.*

71. *English Armchair, leg and foot, circa 1755. This piece represents English work of average quality.*
Mahogany.
The Colonial Williamsburg Foundation (acc. no. G1965-194).

72. *Williamsburg Masonic Lodge Six Master's Chair (fig. 47), leg and smooth paw foot.*

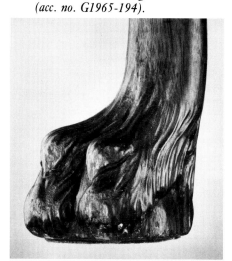

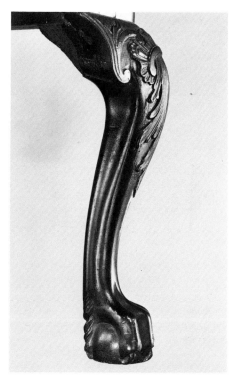

70a. *Lodge Four Master's Chair, profile of foot showing severely vertical toes.*

71a. *English Armchair, profile of foot. The lower portion has been worn sufficiently to remove the claws. It originally stood slightly higher.*

72a. *Lodge Six Master's Chair, profile of leg and smooth paw foot, showing an unusual fetlock ending with a small claw.*

73. *Clothespress, smooth paw foot, attributed*
to the shop of Giles Grendey,
London, circa 1740.
Mahogany.
The Colonial Williamsburg Foundation
(acc. no. 1956-298).

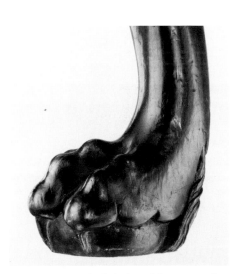

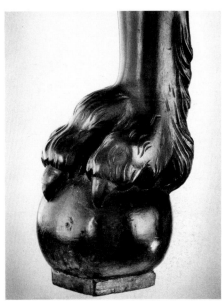

73a. *Between the fetlock and front toes of*
this foot are highly developed pad segments,
often seen on English paw feet. These are rare
on American examples, and those found on
the Capitol chair (fig. 61) are exceptional
in this respect.

74. *Irish Side Table, paw foot, circa 1760.*
With the exception of a smaller ball, some
Massachusetts paw feet relate to this
example, with toes that are noticeably
separated.
Mahogany.
The Colonial Williamsburg Foundation
(acc. no. 1967-461).

74a. *Irish Side Table, side view of foot.*
The exaggerated fetlock shown here is
often seen on English paw feet.

Figure 59, detail.

CEREMONIAL CHAIRS

The five ceremonial chairs shown in this study comprise one of the most important groups made in eighteenth-century America. Two of them (figs. 7, 46) have histories of usage in the Capitol building in Williamsburg. The remaining three are Masonic Master's chairs (figs. 47, 49, 59).

As a rule, furniture from eastern Virginia is stylistically conservative, relatively plain on the exterior, and extremely well constructed. These five chairs represent opposites of this general stylistic trend. They are the most exuberant, fully decorative examples from the colonial Tidewater area. This contrast reflects the society that produced and used them: a society that emphasized elaborate public ceremony, as opposed to a conservative approach to private life.

The Capitol Speaker's chair is known to have influenced the design of a similar chair in the Court House of Chowan County in Edenton, North Carolina.[76] In fact, its extended back and architectural pediment are not even unique in Williamsburg, for a chair with these features was built into the James City County Courthouse when it was constructed in 1770. Although that chair no longer survives, its shadow outline still exists on an interior brick wall of the building. Another impressive example to survive from this early period is the lion's-head armchair made for the Capitol (fig. 46), which may have served as the governor's seat in the General Court or the Council Chamber. Extraordinary proportions, with tall legs and a high seat requiring the use of a footstool, distinguish this piece from others in the group. Ceremonial seating furniture of a commanding height was used in England, the most notable example being the royal throne. Some English Masonic Master's chairs were made with seats of comparable height, but this Williamsburg example is unique in American furniture. With well executed carving and a fully upholstered frame, it ranks as one of the most sophisticated ceremonial chairs produced here or abroad.

Three Masonic Master's chairs attributed to the Hay shop have a wealth of Masonic symbolism that gives insight into the political, stylistic, and philosophical awareness of eastern Virginians. These chairs were used in lodges of accepted (or speculative) Freemasons that developed from older organizations of practicing (or operative) stonemasons. By 1717, when the first Grand Lodge of Free and Accepted Masons was established in London, freemasonry lost all connection with these early groups and had developed into a society of various trades and professions bound together for social and benevolent purposes. It was during these early years that a system of ethical and philosophical teachings evolved, utilizing the tools and emblems of the operative masons as symbols.

The Master's chair of Williamsburg's Lodge Six (fig. 47) is the earliest of these pieces and has been in continuous use since it was made. The top of its back bears the arms of the first Grand Lodge, which were appropriated in 1717. These are flanked by the rose and thistle, representing the union of England and Scotland that formed Great Britain in 1707.[77] This upper section is supported by three stop-fluted pilasters, which, in English examples, would have capitals placed in ascending position of importance, from left to right: doric, ionic, and corinthian. Here, instead, they are corinthian, ionic, and composite. The substitution of the elaborate composite order for the simple doric and the apparent lack of traditional order is also found in another combination in the Bucktrout chair (fig. 49a), with its central composite capital flanked by two corinthian ones. This might suggest that the orders on these chairs were rearranged for aesthetic purposes. But the columns of the Fredericksburg Lodge Four chair (fig. 59) have capitals placed in ascending order, although again the doric has been omitted in favor of the composite. This absence of the doric on all three chairs, and the rearrangement of the sequence on two examples, may well represent a development in Virginia Masonic symbolism that has long since passed into obscurity. It certainly seems to have no other parallel in English or American examples.

Between the pilasters of the Lodge Six chair are carved a number of symbols important to an eighteenth-century mason. Several of these appear to be copied directly from a print published in London in 1754. Entitled *A Free Mason Formed out of the Materials of his Lodge*, it features an abstracted human composed not of flesh and bones but of Masonic emblems.[78]

Elements on this chair back related to the print include a Bible on the left and a "tracing board" on the right, the latter with a chip border composed of triangular segments. This board bears the geometric figure of the 47th proposition of Euclid, better known as proof of the Pythagorean theorem. Initially, this proof was important to practicing masons in truing their squares; it then became an integral symbol of speculative Masonry. The decorative borders on the cover of the Bible are also similar to those shown in the 1754 print, as are several combinations of other symbols.

The Master's chair by Benjamin Bucktrout (fig. 49) bears a number of Masonic emblems that are executed more realistically than those of the other chairs treated here. The Bible is opened to "Kings I: Chapter VII," which contains a description of the building of Solomon's temple. According to tradition, this marked the beginning of all Mason's organizations. The Bible originally had a five-pointed star applied to its center, and it is overlaid with a compass and a square of fine workmanship. The compass is realistically depicted and the square is inscribed with the 47th proposition on its left tip. The trowel at the upper right has a gilded ferrule, and is only one of many elements that are highlighted by gilded decorations.

The chairs of the Master and Senior Warden of Fredericksburg's Lodge Four have several rather unusual Masonic motifs (figs. 59, 60a). The backs were apparently made from the same plan, but they differ in two ways. The first is the relationship of the compass and square that denote the various levels of achievement within Freemasonry.[79] The most intriguing difference, however, is seen in the interpretation of the 47th proposition, which is rendered as three carved blocks sitting upon a scroll. On the simpler example these blocks are shown in their proper relationship. On the master's chair, however, they are disassembled—a feature unknown on any other example in either England or America. It is possible that this unusual version symbolizes the knowledge of assembly which is passed from master to master, but the true meaning may never be known.

Several other unusual symbolic details are found on these chairs. The bases of the splats are formed by ziggurats with nine terraces. These terraces may allude to Zeus' nine daughters, mythological Greek muses who presided over art, poetry, and science. During the early 1770s, several London Masonic lodges were named after these muses, which is not unexpected considering the rise of the neo-classic movement and its pronounced influence on Freemasonry. Certainly the appearance of neo-classic moldings on this chair, which have already been discussed at length, coincides with the documented introduction of the neo-classic style in Williamsburg in the 1770s.

Over the terraces on the splats are traditional emblems of mortality—the coffin with skull and crossbones. Above these are a Bible, a compass, and a square, flanked by crossed pens (the jewels of the secretary) and crossed keys (the jewels of the treasurer). On top of the lectern is a sundial, a somewhat unusual feature since the hourglass is more commonly used in English Masonic iconography to denote the passage of time. The sundial of the senior warden's chair has the incised numeral "XII," while the Master's chair lacks this feature (fig. 60).

Since the origin of Freemasonry is rooted in craft, it is not surprising to see that these chairs exhibit the highest level of skill. They codify the basic principles of the organization by illustrating the tools of the operative mason. Through this emphasis on the virtues of workmanship, Freemasonry emphasized and promoted the integrity of craftsmanship. Masonic lodges were the only craft-oriented organizations in many communities of colonial America. They must have had a tremendous influence upon the trades, although to what extent is unknown. The subject merits further study. In Williamsburg, it appears accurate to conclude that Freemasonry stimulated chair-making of the highest order and, along with patronage by the government, provided an opportunity for the artisan to excel beyond the limits of conventional forms. In a society that held ceremony in high regard, these extraordinary chairs must have received great attention, thereby gaining recognition for their makers and influencing both style and taste in colonial Virginia.

FOOTNOTES

1. The Hay Shop's prominence in American cabinetmaking is established by its production of elaborate forms not seen elsewhere in America. These include lion's-head arm terminals, dolphin feet, smooth-paw animal feet, and the group of exceptional ceremonial chairs. The documented use of Thomas Chippendale's *The Gentleman and Cabinet-Maker's Director* also distinguishes this shop from most others in colonial America.
2. *The Virginia Gazette*, ed. Alexander Purdie and John Dixon, January 17, 1771, p. 3.
3. Ibid., January 3, 1771, p. 3; and March 9, 1769, p. 3.
4. *The Virginia Gazette* Day Book, Alderman Library, University of Virginia, Charlottesville, July 27, 1751.
5. *The Virginia Gazette*, ed. William Hunter, November 7, 1751, p. 2; *The Virginia Gazette* Day Book, November 7, 1751.
6. *The Virginia Gazette*, November 28, 1751, p. 4.
7. *The Virginia Gazette* Day Book. Entries of December 31, 1751, and May 28, 1752.
8. York County Deeds, No. 6, 1755-1763, p. 65. Cited by Mills Brown, "Cabinetmaking in the Eighteenth Century" (unpublished research report, Williamsburg: Colonial Williamsburg Foundation, 1959) p. 123, footnote 18.
9. Personal communication from Ivor Noël Hume.
10. *The Virginia Gazette*, ed. William Hunter, June 20, 1755, p. 3.
11. Ibid., March 21, 1755, p. 4.
12. Ibid., June 20, 1755, p. 3.
13. Brown, "Cabinetmaking," p. 127.
14. *The Virginia Gazette*, January 8, 1767, p. 3.
15. Brown, "Cabinetmaking," p. 127.
16. *The Virginia Gazette*, ed. Purdie and Dixon, January 17, 1771, p. 3.
17. Ibid., December 13, 1770, p. 2.
18. Ibid., January 8, 1767, p. 3.
19. Bucktrout was probably a journeyman when he worked for Hay. This assumption is based on the fact that he bought a large number of tools and unfinished chairs from the estate of John Ormeston, a Williamsburg cabinetmaker who died in 1766, and shortly thereafter advertised his new business near the Capitol, quite possibly at Ormeston's old location. Since Bucktrout apparently took advantage of opportunities presented him upon Ormeston's death, it is likely that he was a journeyman able to leave Hay's employment when he pleased. Had he been a servant, on the other hand, he would not have had the freedom to move until his indenture was completed. Ormeston sale information courtesy of Harold B. Gill, Jr., historian, Colonial Williamsburg Foundation, Williamsburg, Virginia.
20. *The Virginia Gazette*, ed. Purdie and Dixon, July 25, 1765, p. 3.
21. Brown, "Cabinetmaking," p. 143.
22. Ibid., p. 141.
23. Ibid., p. 146.
24. *The Virginia Gazette*, ed. Purdie and Dixon, March 9, 1769, p. 3.
25. Ibid.
26. Ibid., September 7, 1769, p. 4.
27. Robert Carter Papers, Virginia Historical Society, Richmond, Virginia. M-82-8. Reference courtesy of Harold B. Gill, Jr.
28. Ibid.
29. Ibid.
30. *The Virginia Gazette*, ed. Purdie and Dixon, April 4, 1771, p. 3.
31. *The Virginia Gazette*, ed. John Dixon, February 4, 1775, p. 3.
32. Carter Papers.
33. Ibid.
34. Brown, "Cabinetmaking," p. 142.
35. Ibid., p. 141.
36. *The Virginia Gazette*, ed. John Dixon, August 28, 1779, p. 3; Brown, "Cabinetmaking," p. 144.
37. "Cabinetmaking," p. 145.
38. Ibid., pp. 146 and 148.
39. Ibid., p. 131.
40. *The Virginia Gazette*, ed. Purdie and Dixon, January 3, 1771, p. 3.
41. Ibid., November 14, 1771, p. 2; Brown, "Cabinetmaking," p. 108-109; date of Tyree apprenticeship courtesy of Harold B. Gill, Jr.
42. *The Virginia Gazette*, ed. Purdie and Dixon, July 28, 1774, p. 3.
43. Information courtesy of Harold B. Gill, Jr.
44. Brown, "Cabinetmaking," p. 134.
45. Ibid., pp. 133-134; Thomas Jefferson Bill courtesy of Charles Granquist.
46. Brown, "Cabinetmaking," p. 133.
47. Ibid., p. 135; *London Gentlemen's Magazine* 48 (September 1778): 420. Reference courtesy of Harold B. Gill, Jr.
48. Ivor Noel Hume, *Williamsburg Cabinetmakers: The Archaeological*

Evidence (Williamsburg: Colonial Williamsburg Foundation, 1971), pp. 39-40.

49. The history of this table was related to the author by Miss Dorothy Fitzgerald in the summer of 1977. Additional information on the Irby family came from Virginia Fitzgerald Jordon, *The Captain Remembers: The Papers of Captain Richard Irby* (Blackstone, Virginia: Nottoway County Historical Association, 1975).

50. These constructions clearly relate to Chinese examples that have miters at their skirt and leg joints. See Gustav Ecke, *Chinese Domestic Furniture* (Rutland, Vermont, and Tokyo, Japan: Charles E. Tuttle, 1962).

51. The history of this table is thoroughly discussed in an article by J. McKenzie Semple, "Loo Table Much Traveled Piece," *Antique Monthly* 8 (October 1975) section A, p. 13.

52. The earliest documentation on the use of this chair in the Capitol at Williamsburg is recorded in the June 16, 1866 issue of *Frank Leslie's Illustrated Newspaper*, a copy of which is deposited in the Department of Collections, Colonial Williamsburg Foundation, Williamsburg, Virginia. Engravings of it and the Speaker's Chair (fig. 7) are accompanied by a short article that states that they were moved to Richmond from Williamsburg, and had been in constant use since the move. At that time this chair (fig. 46) served the Senate, while the Speaker's Chair (fig. 7) served the House of Representatives [Delegates]. The twentieth-century history of this chair is recorded in file folder no. 1930-215, the Department of Collections, Colonial Williamsburg Foundation.

53. Engravings of the House of Lords and the House of Commons are illustrated in H. M. Colvin, *History of the King's Works*, (London: Her Majesty's Stationery Office, 1976), Vol. 5 (1660-1782), plates 51 and 53. The chairs shown in these prints are nearly identical in form to those of the Virginia Capitol.

54. R. W. Symonds, *English Furniture from Charles II to George II* (New York: International Studies, Inc., 1929), figs. 16 and 17, p. 38; figs. 19 and 20, p. 41.

55. Despite all these differences in quality and design, one very puzzling feature ties the carving of these two chairs closely together. On each chair the lion's head on the right arm has a more pointed face and is looking up at a higher angle than the lion on the left. The latter has a flatter, broader face and appears less sculptural, with a more box-like shape. Their size difference indicates that they were not cut from the same patterns (patterns that could have transmitted this difference from right to left). Therefore, the fact that both chairs have great difference in proportion from right lion to left lion, appears to be a very personal trait of the carver. This unusual characteristic strongly indicates that both chairs were carved by the same hand. Perhaps a decade or more separates their production, which accounts for the diminished quality.

56. This chair was illustrated and discussed in Thomas C. Parramore, *Launching the Craft: The First Half-Century of Freemasonary in North Carolina* (Raleigh: Litho Industries, 1975), pp. 71-72. It was extensively examined and illustrated by Bradford L. Rauschenberg in "Two Outstanding Virginia Chairs," *Journal of Early Southern Decorative Arts* 2 (November 1976): 11-20.

57. Rauschenberg, "Chairs," pp. 19-20.

58. Ibid., pp. 15-16.

59. A similar arm piercing is shown in plate 17 of the first edition of the *Director*. This is the first of four plates that illustrate French chairs, and from the last plate in this series Bucktrout used the dolphin leg design. Since plate 17 is not in later editions of the *Director*, and since other Hay Shop ornament derived from the *Director* does not occur in later plates, it appears that the copy in use in the Hay Shop was a first edition, published in 1754. All further references to the *Director* in this study will be cited from the third edition, 1762, reprinted by Dover Publications (New York, 1966).

60. "Dressing chest and bookcase" is the term used to describe this form in Chippendale's *Director* (cf. plates 114, 115).

61. Ibid., p. 7.

62. Symonds, *English Furniture*, pp. 100-101, diagrams 4a, 4b.

63. Will of Mrs. Mary Wilting Byrd of Westover, 1813, with a list of Westover portraits, *Virginia Magazine of History and Biography* 6 (1899): 356, note 28.

64. *Illustrated Catalogue of the Rare and Extremely Choice Collection of Early American and English Furniture formed by Louis C. Myers* (New York: American Art Association, 1921), entry no. 668.

65. E. Milby Burton, *Charleston Furniture, 1700-1825* (Charleston, South Carolina: Charleston Museum, 1955), p. 43.

66. Catalogue, "Art Loan Exhibition for the Benefit of the Ladies Parish Aid Society of St. Paul's Church, Norfolk, Va., at Mechanics Hall, May 27, 1879," (Norfolk: no publisher) entry no. 302. Research Library, Colonial Williamsburg Foundation, Williamsburg, Virginia.

67. Rauschenberg, "Chairs," pp. 1-11. In this article Mr. Rauschen-berg attributes this chair to an unidentified cabinetmaker in Fredericksburg.

68. Ibid., pp. 6-8. Mr. Rauschenberg states that the gadrooning of this chair is nailed to the bottom of the seat rail, and that the front knee-blocks are also attached underneath. These statements are not correct; the gadrooning and knee-brackets are glued to the face of the seat rail (see figs. 59e, 59f). This construction conforms to that of the Scott group, and is the same group treated by Harold B. Gill, Jr. and the author in "Some Virginia Chairs: A Preliminary Study," *The Magazine Antiques* 101 (April 1972):716-721.

69. Chippendale's *Director*, plate 10.

70. Desmond Fitz-Gerald, ed., *Georgian Furniture* (London: Her Majesty's Stationery Office, 1969), entry no. 103.

71. Helen Comstock, "Discoveries in Southern Antiques," *The Magazine Antiques* 65 (February 1954):131-133.

72. Helen Comstock, *American Furniture* (New York: Viking Press, 1962), no. 278.

73. Helen Comstock, "Furniture of Virginia, North Carolina, Georgia, and Kentucky," *The Magazine Antiques* 61 (January 1952): 68, plate 62.

74. Noël Hume, *Williamsburg Cabinetmakers*, p. 27, fig. 20.

75. Ibid., fig. 19.

76. Johnston and Waterman, *Early Architecture*, p. 249, plates p. 268.

77. Identification of the arms on this chair, and a research report on the Masonic aspects of these chairs, were forwarded to the author by T. O. Haunch, librarian and curator, United Grand Lodge of England, on March 26, 1977. The report is now in the research files of the Archives and Records, and in the Department of Collections, at Colonial Williamsburg. Without the considerate help of Mr. Haunch, it would have been impossible to write this section on Masonic symbolism.

78. A photostatic copy of this print was supplied by Mr. Haunch in the report cited in footnote 77.

79. Because of the relationship between the squares and compasses, Fredericksburg Lodge IV today uses the elaborate Master's Chair as the Senior Warden's, and the simpler Warden's Chair as the Master's. Apparently this is the result of a stricter interpretation of these symbols than that practiced in the eighteenth century. The most elaborate and grandest chair in the set was always the Master's. The purpose of the degree of decoration was to designate rank and order. This held true for government as well as for royal chairs. It is not known when the reversed usage of these Lodge IV chairs first occurred; apparently it is a fairly old tradition predating the present generation.

Williamsburg Case Pieces

Several groups of case furniture survive that can be identified as Williamsburg production, although attribution to specific shops is tenuous at this time. The first and largest of these may represent the Anthony Hay Shop, although evidence is not yet conclusive.

This "Hay" group consists primarily of desks, desk-and-bookcases, and clothespresses. They are made of mahogany or walnut, with yellow pine secondary wood, and have an amazing degree of consistency in construction. The cases invariably have dustboards that are equal in thickness to the drawer blades and that extend the full depth of the case—a type that has been termed "full bottom" by one of the leading British furniture historians, R. W. Symonds. These cases are supported by composite feet and the base molding is a simple quarter round similar to those illustrated in Chippendale's *Director*.

Two desks in this group (figs. 75, 76) have interior writing cabinets with a design seen on many Williamsburg examples. The design is characterized by a long central drawer with a nearly square prospect door above. The interiors have straight drawer fronts and they are strikingly similar to a large group from Piedmont Virginia and suggest a connection between the two areas.[1] Like the Williamsburg examples, the Piedmont interiors feature the long central drawer and square prospect door, but they are significantly different in having their lower drawers advanced, giving a stepped effect. In most examples, several drawer fronts are "blocked" in serpentine or double ogee shapes. Stylistically, these stepped and blocked Piedmont interiors are earlier than their related Williamsburg examples, but it is possible that they represent an early stage of design in the colonial capital, transplanted into the Piedmont by artisans trained in that city. If this is the case, then the form must have had a fairly brief popularity in Williamsburg, although in the Piedmont it persisted into the nineteenth century.

The first of these Williamsburg desks has a Richmond area history of ownership and is dated 1758 on the bottom of a drawer (fig. 75). It is constructed of walnut with yellow pine. Its drawer blades are thin and, like all examples in this group, it has full-bottom dustboards. The drawers of the main case have runners like those of the Scott group (fig. 37g) but do not have the large glue blocks across the front. It is also similar to the Scott desk (fig. 37) in the layout of the main case drawers. The feet have been replaced, although the originals had composite blocking.

One example from this group (fig. 76) has a desk section nearly identical to that of the 1758 example. Made of black walnut and yellow pine, it has a

76. Desk-and-Bookcase, Williamsburg, circa 1760.
Walnut primary; yellow pine secondary.
Height 84", width 39½", depth 22¼".
The Colonial Williamsburg Foundation (acc. no. 1950-349).

75. *Desk, Williamsburg, dated 1758.*
Black walnut primary; yellow pine secondary.
Height 41½", width 37⅝", depth 21¾".
Mr. and Mrs. Arthur L. Murray.

tradition of ownership in Williamsburg by John Minson Galt, whose apothecary shop was located on the Duke of Gloucester Street. Slight variations in the partitions between the lower drawers of the writing interior and the design of the pigeonhole brackets are the only departures from the preceding desk. The case is identically constructed. It also has original bracket feet, although only one of these retains its composite blocking. The bookcase section does not sit directly on the top as in most American examples but, like other Williamsburg pieces, fits within a frame attached to the desk section. The shaped molding at the top of the frame is attached to the bookcase section, forming a strong "interlock joint." (This term will be used throughout the rest of this book to describe this construction, which is a major characteristic of the group.) Several variations were employed, and these too will be illustrated and discussed as this study proceeds. Its origin is

suggested by plate CIX of Chippendale's *Director*, which shows a bookcase having a fret-decorated frame in the same location. A similar desk-and-bookcase (not illustrated), which remains in the Galt family, has an interlock joint into which two slides for candles are fitted. The cornice of each piece is detachable.

Another desk-and-bookcase from the Galt Family has suffered some damage over the years (fig. 77). In this piece, only the upper portion of the composite blocking survives, and the short bracket feet are complete replacements. The interlock joint has lost the top molding, which was glued into a shallow rabbet on the bookcase, and the broken scroll pediment has been severely altered (fig. 77c). The re-cutting of the pediment has virtually destroyed all traces of the original form; it is an unfortunate loss. (The condition of the pediment is so disruptive that it was not included in the photograph.) It appears that

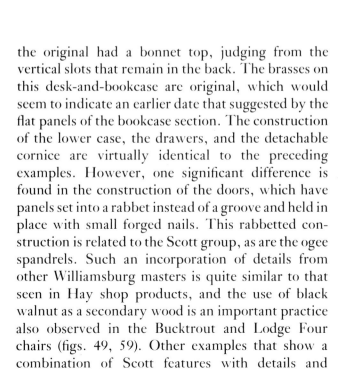

77. *Desk-and-Bookcase, Williamsburg, circa 1765.*
Mahogany primary; yellow pine and walnut secondary.
Height 80", width 40⅜", depth 23⅝".
The Anne Galt Black Collection.

77a.

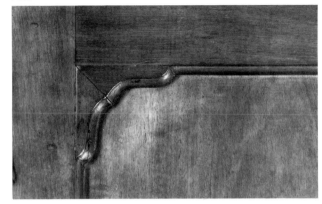

77b.

77c.

the original had a bonnet top, judging from the vertical slots that remain in the back. The brasses on this desk-and-bookcase are original, which would seem to indicate an earlier date that suggested by the flat panels of the bookcase section. The construction of the lower case, the drawers, and the detachable cornice are virtually identical to the preceding examples. However, one significant difference is found in the construction of the doors, which have panels set into a rabbet instead of a groove and held in place with small forged nails. This rabbetted construction is related to the Scott group, as are the ogee spandrels. Such an incorporation of details from other Williamsburg masters is quite similar to that seen in Hay shop products, and the use of black walnut as a secondary wood is an important practice also observed in the Bucktrout and Lodge Four chairs (figs. 49, 59). Other examples that show a combination of Scott features with details and

techniques of the early Hay shop include a side table (fig. 53) and three chairs (figs. 58, 59, 60). Case pieces yet to be discussed reveal additional interrelationships between these two groups.

A mahogany desk-and-bookcase closely related to the preceding example is pictured in the files of the Museum of Early Southern Decorative Arts (S-3888). It has flat panels, is currently lacking its spandrels, and has an interlock joint identical in construction to those just discussed (figs. 76, 77). The writing interior is nearly identical to figure 76, as are the base moldings and bracket feet. The primary wood is mahogany, seen in other Williamsburg examples, and contains the sporadic groups of burls also found in the unfinished table leg from the Hay shop (fig. 66).

78a.

78. *Desk-and-Bookcase, Williamsburg, 1771-1775.*
Mahogany primary; yellow pine secondary.
Height 74¼", width 39¼", depth 23¼".
The Colonial Williamsburg Foundation (acc. no. 1951-489).

Two pieces in this group, a desk-and-bookcase and a chest of drawers (figs. 78, 79), are made of fine curly mahogany. An oral tradition relates that the desk was purchased by William Trebell from the Governor's Palace, and written documentation dating to the 1880s indicates that the chest of drawers was purchased at the sale of Lord Dunmore's possessions in 1776.[2] Unfortunately, there is no record of Trebell among the debtors at the sale, but this does not negate the tradition since he may have acquired one or both of these pieces from another purchaser, or possibly had someone else bid for him. To confuse the issue, Trebell is known to have purchased items from the sale of Lord Botetourt's estate in 1770, and it is possible that by the 1880s this fact had become obscured. Nonetheless, they appear to have come from the same shop, since they exhibit the same construction, and were probably made en suite.

Although this Palace desk-and-bookcase essentially repeats a familiar pattern, it has one major departure from the others: the usual interlock joint has been replaced by a low molding attached to the bookcase sides. It is unusual to attach the molding in this location, but the greatest variation here is in the omission of the supporting frame between the upper and lower case. To achieve stability, four pegs project from the bottom of the bookcase and engage corresponding holes in the top of the desk. Such construction might suggest that the two portions were made at different times, but close comparison of the fine curly mahogany, the secondary woods, and the workmanship indicates contemporaneous production. This piece shares an integral relationship with other examples in the group, and a variation of its peg construction, used in conjunction with a full frame attachment, is found on a desk-and-bookcase with a history in Amelia County (fig. 116).

The cases of this desk-and-bookcase and its accompanying chest are very well constructed. Both have full-bottom dustboards. The desk has simple bracket feet, which have now been restored; only one original bracket and its composite blocking survive. The brackets on the chest are totally replaced, but evidence of their composite blocking remains. The base molding is original, as are the brass pulls and plates, although the escutcheons appear to be replacements. The pierced examples of the desk are replaced, based on outlines left by the originals.

The drawer construction of these two examples closely coincides. The quarter-round "lip" molding is cut from the solid edge of the drawer face and does not overlap the case. The drawer bottoms are nailed into a rabbet and are covered by strips of pine on the

79. *Chest of Drawers, Williamsburg, 1771-1775. Mahogany primary; yellow pine secondary. Height 30⁵/₁₆″, width 36″, depth 19⅛″. Private Collection.*

front and sides. On the desk-and-bookcase these strips are mitered at the front corners, but on the chest the side strips abut the drawer front, conforming to those found on earlier desks in this group.

The high quality material and excellent workmanship of these two pieces are representative of case furniture made in Williamsburg. Their severe lines characterize the period of transition from the rococo to the neo-classic, and are good representatives of the plain style that dominated cabinet design during the 1760s and 1770s.

Even though all the preceding examples have suffered some losses to their feet and composite blocking, two clothespresses owned in the Galt family of Williamsburg have survived in virtually unaltered condition. One of these is made of walnut and yellow pine and has a paneled back (fig. 80a).

Attached to the bottom are long strips of yellow pine which support the base molding (fig. 80b). A close look reveals that these strips have saw kerfs cut through them (fig. 80c). The bottom of the base molding is also kerfed (visible at the top right and left in the illustration), but they do not continue through the front of the molding. These kerfs serve the purpose of allowing expansion and contraction of the wood as it responds to humidity changes, thus alleviating the strain on the glue joints and on the case. Examples without these constructional allowances are often damaged by humidity changes that cause their sides or bases to split, or that break their glued joints. The paneled back serves the same purpose and also prevents gaps from developing between the boards when extreme shrinkage occurs. The composite blocking of the feet (fig. 80d) also has this advantage, and the fact that the grain runs in the same plane as that of the brackets gives them a compatible ratio of expansion and contraction. This foot construction provides more strength than the single vertical block more commonly used in cabinetwork from other areas. These refined construction techniques, virtually unknown in New England and Philadelphia, are also seen in Norfolk examples and are found on urban English products.

The second clothespress (fig. 81), somewhat more elaborate, has an additional raised panel in each door and two drawers within. The base and feet are almost identical in construction to the preceding example, but it does not have a paneled back, a feature that is seen often but is not uniform in this group.

80. Clothespress, Williamsburg, circa 1770.
Walnut primary; yellow pine and walnut secondary.
Height 56⅝", width 49½", depth 23".
The Colonial Williamsburg Foundation (acc. no. 1950-351).

80a.

120

81. Clothespress, Williamsburg, circa 1770.
Walnut primary; yellow pine secondary.
Height 55¼", width 49⅜", depth 22⅝".
The Colonial Williamsburg Foundation (acc. no. 1950-350).

80b.

80d.

80c.

121

An outstanding desk-and-bookcase that descended in the Galt family of Williamsburg is more impressively detailed than others of this group, but its affinity to them is nonetheless evident (fig. 82). The interlock joint, molded drawer edges, thin drawer blades, and full-bottom dustboards are all features seen on previous examples. The large drawers have bottoms nailed into a rabbet on the sides and front. A series of small blocks forms unbroken runners on the sides and a continuous series across the front. This type of blocking is different from the continuous strips seen on pieces already discussed, although they are somewhat related to drawers in the Scott group.

Another departure from the usual construction of this group is the addition of a horizontal batten inside the back of the case. Dovetailed into the sides, it runs parallel to, and behind, the second drawer. This batten provides strong support for the sides at the back, an area of weakness in most case furniture where nailed backboards alone furnish stability.

The interior of this desk (fig. 82a) is significantly different from others examined here, although another unidentified Williamsburg shop produced similar examples.[3] The sources of the design appear to be a combination of the desk interior shown in plate CVII of Chippendale's *Director* and that shown in plate 55 of *HousHold Furniture* (fig. 82e).[4] The fretwork designs, as well as the frame that joins the two sections, appear to combine elements from both of these works. The use of the frame interlock joint may be derived from plate CIX of the *Director*, while the design of its fret is a slight variation of one shown in plate 72 of *HousHold Furniture* (fig. 82f).

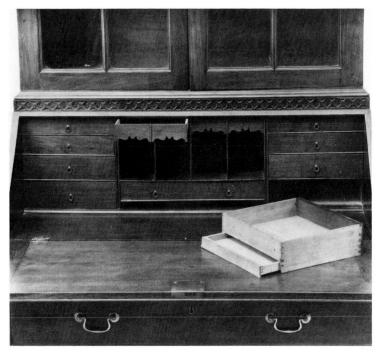

82a.

82b.

82. Desk-and-Bookcase, Williamsburg, circa 1770.
Walnut primary; yellow pine and walnut secondary.
Height 95½", width 39⅛", depth 21⅜".
The Colonial Williamsburg Foundation (acc. no. 1978-9).

The broken-pitch pediment of this desk-and-bookcase is the finest to survive from Williamsburg (fig. 82b). Its most noteworthy feature is the molding, which is designed in perspective, indicating a maker with exceptional skill and an understanding of design (fig. 82c). The fretwork pattern that was used on the frame interlock joint has been reincorporated in the frieze of the pediment, but it is somewhat unusual to see a larger version of this same pattern repeated in the tympanum. The dentil work found here is exceptionally fine, and that of the central plinth is scaled in proportion to the smaller molding.

Some minor alterations have been made to this pediment, including the restoration of the walnut, triple-fluted cylinder that supports the finial. The original had been cut in half and reapplied to the pediment of a mahogany desk-and-bookcase that descended in the same household (fig. 77c). It should also be noted that the spiral decorated finial has lost a pointed tip that extended above its flattened ball, as well as its flaring base moldings. A fretwork design was originally applied to the lower portion of the plinth.

The bookcase section of this example has a finely paneled back (fig. 82d). The interior contains three shelves with seven slots for adjustment. The inside of the doors shows evidence of tack holes that originally held fabric or curtain rods. Many eighteenth-century prints show curtains on the insides of bookcases with glazed doors.

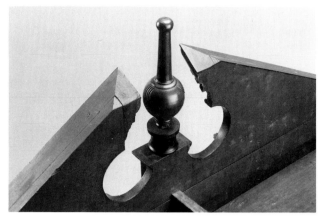

82c.

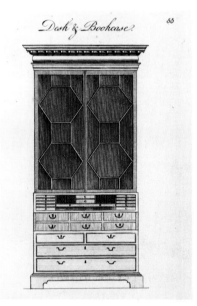

82e. *Plate 55, London Society of Upholsterers, Genteel HousHold Furniture, second edition, circa 1760-63.*

82d.

82f. *Plate* 72, Genteel HousHold Furniture.

A pair of mahogany candlestands with a tradition of ownership by George Washington at Mount Vernon is related to the preceding desk-and-bookcase. Like it, the designs are taken from *Hous-Hold Furniture* (fig. 82f) and are virtual copies of the design book illustrations with only the slightest departures. Yet the execution of the detailed carving is substantially individualistic, and much of it indicates Hay shop production.

The most prominent feature is the large acanthus in the base with its central cabochon (fig. 83b). While this vaguely resembles the foliage of the pattern book illustration, it is more closely related to an acanthus found on the knee of the Lodge Four chair (fig. 70). This knee carving is a somewhat extruded version of that found on the stands, with opposing C-scrolls occupying the approximate position of the cabochon. The elements of both carvings are extremely close, with bulbous scroll or leaf endings that have a tucked-under, concave leaf on the inside curves. The convex, bulbous ends of the candlestand leaves have either one or two additional gouge veins than those of the Lodge Four chair. This heavier veining, although much better executed, appears to be a survival of the earlier technique used on the foliage surrounding the coat of arms on the Lodge Six chair (fig. 47b). Likewise, the acanthus drapes from two C-scrolls just under the top (fig. 83a) and has a central stem and harshly fluted leaves that are quite similar to those found on the arm supports and knee carving of the Lodge Six chair.

83. Candlestand, one of a pair, Williamsburg, 1774-1776.
Mahogany.
Height 48", width of top 10".
Courtesy the Mount Vernon Ladies' Association.

83a.

83b.

Other features exhibiting finer workmanship but bearing a relationship to the Bucktrout chair are the asymmetrical, curled-back acanthus leaves that terminate the base carving (top of fig. 83b). Of these, the last small leaf at the top, which rises and curls to the side, is strikingly similar to those on the triple acanthus rising from the C-scrolls in the middle of the Bucktrout chair dolphin leg (fig. 49g). On the stands these acanthus details represent the individual designs and techniques of the carver and they are similar to those in the design book in only a very general way. Thus, the origin of the candlestands is associated with the Hay shop, and reflects a decade of technique and design development there.

While many of George Washington's furniture orders are extant, none is known that can be associated with these candlestands. Because of the extremely sophisticated form, the lack of secondary wood, and the triple-laminated fret gallery, they had previously been considered English. These elements alone, however, are no longer acceptable for making such a judgment. The existence of documented examples of highly sophisticated Virginia furniture, together with the knowledge that skilled cabinet-makers and professional English carvers are known to have worked in the colonial Tidewater, have disproved many old maxims.

One extremely sophisticated example related to this group is a mahogany tall case clock (fig. 84). Its movement is by Thomas Walker of Fredericksburg, but there is every indication that the case was made in Williamsburg. It has yellow pine, poplar, oak, and cherry as secondary woods—a combination similar to pieces in the Hay group. The rosettes of the pediment are carved in perspective, and they provide an important link with the pitch pediment of the preceding Williamsburg desk-and-bookcase (fig. 84). The rosettes, which have a series of fine gouge cuts to indicate shading, are quite similar in carving technique to the fronds of the Washington candle-stands (fig. 83). The dentil molding has small half-circles between the teeth, a design feature seen in the Scott group, and the quarter-columns are similar to those of the Hay shop clothespress (fig. 56). The shaped door is remarkably close to that of the dressing chest (fig. 50) also attributed to the Hay shop. These last three details are by no means conclusive evidence for relating these pieces, since they appear as somewhat standard details in furniture made elsewhere. They are mentioned, nonetheless, since they are supported by other interrelated features of a more reliable, individual nature.

For a number of reasons, the previous attribution of this clock to Philadelphia has been rejected. Importantly, the entire construction is extremely light in weight, thus showing an affinity to English examples and contrasting with those of Philadelphia, where clock cases were usually quite heavy. A further affinity to English cabinetmaking techniques that is also representative of Williamsburg production is found in the construction of the pediment, which is composed of yellow pine with a thick veneer of mahogany. This now has three slightly recessed panels which were originally filled with pierced fretwork installed from behind. A band of fretwork was also applied around the case, between the astragal molding above the door, although only faint evidence survives. It is important to note that this area of the case was rabbetted to receive the fret-work. This is related to the practice of rabbetting the sides of the case to receive molding for the upper half of interlock joints of desk-and-bookcases (fig. 77). This technique is also consistent with Williamsburg tea tables that have moldings glued into rabbets to form tray tops (fig. 57).

84a.

84. *Tall-Case Clock, Williamsburg, circa 1770; movement*
  by Thomas Walker of Fredericksburg.
Mahogany and mahogany veneer primary; yellow pine,
  poplar, cherry, and oak secondary.
Height 106", width (mid-case) 14⅜", depth (mid-case) 6⅞".
Museum of Fine Arts, Boston.

85. *Bookcase on Stand, Williamsburg, circa 1770.*
Walnut primary; yellow pine, popular, and walnut secondary.
Height 67⅝", width 44⅞", depth 14³/₁₆".
Dr. Janet C. Kimbrough.

85a.

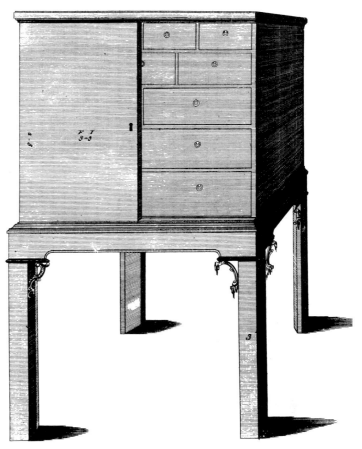

85b. Plate 120, Thomas Chippendale's Gentleman and Cabinet-Maker's Director, *third edition, 1762.*

One of the most unusual pieces in this Williamsburg group is a bookcase-on-stand, which is closely related to designs shown in plate CXX of Chippendale's *Director* (fig. 85). Its cornice blocking and waist moldings are related to those of Scott (figs. 37f, 42), and the paneled back and drawer construction are like those of the elaborate desk-and-bookcase in this group (fig. 82). This piece, which descended in the St. George Tucker family of Williamsburg, is further support for the attribution of these two groups to that city.

While the concept of this bookcase-on-stand seems to have been inspired by Chippendale's *Director*, the maker did not follow this plan exactly, but rather utilized his standard bookcase pattern and then designed a stand to accommodate it. The use of the standard pattern alone may cause one to question the piece, but it is entirely original, with matching woods and a combination of shop details that are consistently repeated in both sections—indicating they were conceived together. This is not the case for two other examples that survive in Williamsburg families. Their frames were made at later dates (one ca. 1800, the other ca. 1880) to accommodate bookcases that had been separated from desks. Nonetheless, they provide additional support for the popularity of this form in Williamsburg—a type unknown to the writer elsewhere in Virginia.

86. *Chest of Drawers, Williamsburg, circa 1770.*
Walnut primary; yellow pine secondary.
Height 38¹³/₁₆", width 43¾", depth 20¼".
Private Collection.

86a.

86b. *Chest of Drawers, front composite foot.*

86c. *Chest of Drawers, rear composite foot. The two bottom layers of blocking are missing.*

Presenting the same problem of shop identification as the bookcase-on-stand is a walnut chest of drawers that descended in the Galt family of Williamsburg (fig. 86).[5] It has full-bottom dustboards, bracket feet, and chamfered corners with flutes, as well as rounded corners on the top. All of these features are seen in pieces attributed to the Hay shop, and they can also be found in other examples from this group. The composite blocking is executed like that of Scott examples and is finished in the front feet (fig. 86b) while left at random at the back (fig. 86c). The drawer bottoms are nailed into shallow rabbets and have no runners, allowing the drawers to run on the flush surfaces of their bases. This type is also seen on an early Williamsburg dressing table (fig. 13). Incredibly, the sides of this piece are dovetailed into the solid top—a rare feature that indicates the quality of construction. The top forms both overhang and molding, which in normal construction consists of a separate applied piece. This complicated the fitting of the concealed dovetail joint that held the case together and totally eliminated the use of the dovetail saw in making the top. The dovetail mortises had to be blind cut using only chisels, although the pins were formed on the case sides with a saw and chisel in the usual manner. While many of the top lips of the drawers have been repaired, one survives intact. This provides still another variation of construction in Williamsburg, and it is the single example in which only the top of each drawer overlaps the case. The lip molding of the other three sides of the drawer have been cut on the solid edge like those of the desk-and-bookcase and chest from the Palace (figs. 78-79).

Two chests of drawers inspired by Chinese cabinets are also associated with Williamsburg shops (figs. 87, 88). Familiar features found here include the bracket foot design, quarter-round base molding, full-bottom dustboards, and drawer construction relating to three other Williamsburg desks (figs. 75, 76, 77). The feet are also related to Williamsburg composite examples, with a triangular block spanning the brackets of each foot, and in this respect they are virtually identical to the simplest clothespress in the group (fig. 80d). In the chests, however, the horizontal composite supports were replaced by large, quarter-round blocks composed of two laminated pieces with a vertical joint. This same foot construction is found on a desk in the Virginia Historical Society collection which, according to tradition, was owned by Peter Jones (1691-1758) of Amelia County. The interior of the Jones desk is identical to that of figure 75. Other features, including full-bottom dustboards, bracket feet, and quarter-round base molding, place it firmly in this group. Perhaps such foot construction separates these chests and desk into yet another Williamsburg shop group.

The first chest (fig. 87) is made of high quality mahogany with yellow pine secondary wood. It has a history of ownership in the Michael family of Brodnax, Mecklenburg County, Virginia. The second example (fig. 85) is constructed of walnut with yellow pine and poplar. It belongs to the College of William and Mary. Like other examples of this form, both of these chests have large secret (not visible) dovetails attaching the tops, while the latter example incorporates this feature in the joining of its bracket feet. It is nearly identical to an example acquired by Colonial Williamsburg in 1938 from Charles Navis Antiques in Richmond (no. 1938-144, not pictured).

87. *Chest of Drawers, Williamsburg, circa 1770.*
Mahogany primary; yellow pine secondary.
Height 36¼", width 42¼", depth 20½".
The Colonial Williamsburg Foundation (acc. no. 1967-99).

88. *Chest of Drawers, Williamsburg, circa 1770.*
Walnut primary; yellow pine secondary.
Height 35¼", width 41¹¹/₁₆", depth 22½".
The College of William and Mary in Virginia.

89. Desk-and-Bookcase, Williamsburg, circa 1775.
Walnut primary; yellow pine secondary.
Height 85", width 44¼", depth 23⅛".
The Colonial Williamsburg Foundation (acc. no. 1930-13).

A desk-and-bookcase with a tradition of owner-ship by President John Tyler (1790-1862) adds considerably to our knowledge of Williamsburg cabinetmaking (fig. 89). Tyler was a native of Williamsburg, and this desk shares many details with pieces from the group, thus forming a strong basis for its attribution. Constructionally it com-bines many details seen in Williamsburg furniture and it may represent another anonymous shop. The case has full-bottom dustboards and the foot block-ing was originally the composite type, although these have been replaced by vertical blocks. The same type of construction of the drawer bottoms is seen in another desk-and-bookcase (fig. 78), and the small drawer on the right of the writing interior has compartments for ink and pens that relate it to similar drawers in two other examples (figs. 77, 78). Although altered at an early date, this desk-and-bookcase originally had an interlock joint uniting its two parts. Evidence of the original joint is clearly visible, including the rabbetted sides of the bookcase section that originally received the upper molding. Inside the top of the bookcase section are two wooden brackets attached to the sides. Used for holding a curtain rod, these provide an interesting parallel to the evidence found in another glazed desk-and-bookcase (fig. 82); together they indicate an eighteenth-century practice that must have been common in Williamsburg. Unfortunately, this piece has sustained several other losses, including two interior drawers and the removable cornice, the form of which remains a mystery. The proportion of the bookcase in relation to the desk and the height of the gothic fret suggest that it was a broken scroll or pitch pediment. The design of the glazed doors and ogee feet are similar to those shown in Chippendale's *Director*.

The following three case pieces (figs. 90, 91, 92) are uncertain in origin and are post-Revolutionary in date. They show a close relationship to cabinetmak-ing in Williamsburg during the colonial period. Stylistically, they combine familiar rococo forms with details that reflect neo-classic influence. The latter style is most apparent in the use of delicately scaled feet and narrow stiles on the doors.

90. Desk-and-Bookcase, origin unknown, dated 1789.
Mahogany and mahogany veneer primary; yellow pine, oak,
walnut, poplar, cherry, and birch secondary.
Height 92½", width 44⅜", depth 21½".
Private Collection.

90a.

90b.

91. *Desk-and-Bookcase, origin unknown, circa 1790.*
Mahogany and mahogany veneer primary; yellow pine and
  poplar secondary.
Height 93½", width 44½", depth 21¾".
Mr. and Mrs. James R. Melchor.

The provenances of these pieces are not helpful at this time in determining their origin. The first desk-and-bookcase (fig. 90) belonged to Dabney Minor of "Wood Lawn" in Orange County, Virginia, and the second (fig. 91) to Branch Tanner of Petersburg, Chesterfield County, and Amelia County.[6] The clothespress (fig. 92) has a Matthews County background. Each desk-and-bookcase has an original inscription: on the first, "Dabney Minor Jan. 24th, 1789" is penciled on top of the desk section; on the second, "B. Tanner" is penciled on the bottom. These appear to be the original owners' names, which were probably inscribed in the cabinet shop to denote the customer. This may have been to prevent confusion with pieces being made there for other patrons, and it is also possible that these markings were used for shipping purposes.

These pieces are related to Williamsburg construction through the method by which the two sections were joined. Figures 90 and 91 show the waist molding attached to the sides of the bookcase but not to the top of the desk as usually seen in other areas. The evolution of this Williamsburg feature is discussed in the text accompanying figures 76, 77, 78, and 82. The Palace desk (fig. 78) shows the latest and simplest phase of this evolution, which is identical with one exception: wooden pegs are used for attachment instead of two screws. The clothespress differs only in the placement of the molding, which has been applied to the lower section and does not form a lip. Like the desk-and-bookcases, the upper section rests directly on the bottom and is secured by two screws.

Both desk pediments had a central plinth, which was composed of a carved rosette with a molded frame. A complete plinth survives on the glazed example (fig. 91b) while the other (fig. 90a) retains only the bottom element of the molded frame. The design of these plinths is unusual. Philadelphia lattice-work pediments are probably the inspiration for these Virginia examples, and these normally have a half-cylindrical plinth with carving, although a few are rectangular with an applied fret. English examples studied by the author do not have the framed plinth with central rosette. In this respect, the Tanner and Minor desks appear to represent a single shop, although they may also reflect a larger regional style.

It is important to note that these desk-and-bookcases relate to another Virginia piece, a Williamsburg clothespress by Peter Scott (fig. 42), where surviving evidence suggests that a square or rectangular plinth was used in the center of the fretwork gallery. While it may not be valid to link these desks to Williamsburg on the basis of their

91a.

91b.

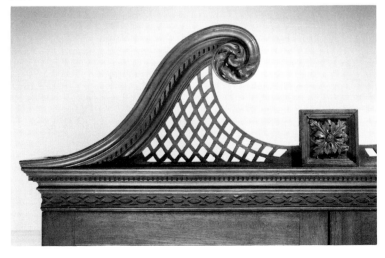

92. *Clothespress, origin unknown, circa 1790.*
Yellow pine.
Height 83¾", width 52¼", depth 26¼".
The Colonial Williamsburg Foundation (acc. no. 1968-279).

plinths, other associations give it more credence. In addition to their relationship to Williamsburg interlock joints, previously discussed, the carving of the acanthus scrolls is quite similar to some of Bucktrout's carving, particularly its concentration on concave elements. The molding of the drawers of figure 90 are cut on the solid fronts and do not overlap the case—a feature seen on several Williamsburg examples (figs. 78, 79, 82). The drawer bottoms are set into grooves and have small glue blocks with spaces between them. This construction method is seen on pieces attributed to Bucktrout, but during the post-Revolutionary period it was becoming quite universal. Thus its value as an archetype is somewhat diminished.

A related desk recorded in the research files of the Museum of Early Southern Decorative Arts (no. S-7652) has further ties to Williamsburg and also shares features with the first five examples in this group. The interior document drawers have fluted pilasters with molded bases and capitals, and they flank an unusual prospect door backed by a mirror. The pilasters are quite similar to those on the Tanner and Minor desk-and-bookcases (figs. 90, 91), thus providing further links with Williamsburg. Even though the desk appears to date circa 1770, it is inscribed "March 9, 1789 J.C." on a document drawer. The inscription might represent the initials of a repairman or owner, but it could also be the mark of the maker and the date of production. The only documented Williamsburg cabinetmaker who could be considered a candidate is John Crump, who is known to have been working between 1770 and 1777, but it is possible that he was practicing his craft over a longer period.

In summary, these three pieces (figs. 90, 91, 92) have a number of characteristics associated with Williamsburg. The exact location of their production is undetermined, and it will understandably remain so until more is known about the production of Norfolk, Petersburg, Richmond, and post-war Williamsburg. The other case pieces in this section have interrelated features and local histories that firmly attribute them to Williamsburg, though the number of shops they represent is difficult to determine. Some evidence certainly suggests that the largest group (figs. 75-84) probably represents production of the Anthony Hay shop.

FOOTNOTES

1. Wallace B. Gusler, "Queen Anne Style Desks from the Virginia Piedmont," *The Magazine Antiques* 104 (October 1973):665-673.

2. A receipt currently owned by Galt descendants records the sale of this chest: "Jan 14th 1888 Received from Mollie J. Galt $30.00 for the Dunmore bureau. Julia E. Lindsay for Susan M. Christian." A copy of this receipt is on file in the Department of Collections, Colonial Williamsburg Foundation, Williamsburg, Virginia.

3. Three examples from this group, or shop, are known. The best is owned by Mr. and Mrs. William Adams of Richmond, Virginia, and has a Gloucester County history. The two others descended in Williamsburg families: one is complete, and another survives only as a bookcase. The latter descended in the Galt family and has an early nineteenth-century stand similar to the one shown here (fig. 85). Numerous features tie these together and distinguish them from other Williamsburg groups. They have an abundance of oak secondary wood, cock beading nailed onto the edges of the drawers, a large double-bead molding on the front of the bookcase shelves, and a flattened astragal arch on the raised panels of the doors.

4. Society of Upholsterers, Cabinet-Makers, Etc., *The IId Edition of Genteel HousHold Furniture in the Present Taste* (London: Robert Sayer, Map and Printseller, ca. 1765), plate 55.

5. Colonial Williamsburg recently acquired a Pembroke table (accession no. 1978-83) that descended in the Prentis family of Williamsburg. Though damaged, it is a remarkable example, and can be compared to tables illustrated in Chippendale's *Director*, having shelves enclosed within fretwork beneath the skirts. The drawer of that table is identical in construction to those on this chest (fig. 86). Since Richard Booker, a Williamsburg cabinetmaker, made a Pembroke table for Colonel John Prentis sometime between 1770 and 1780, it is possible that these examples represent Booker's work. While more documentation is needed to confirm such an attribution, the Scott details (foot construction) of the chest lend some support, since Booker's shop was very near, if not beside, Scott's in the 1770s.

6. According to research conducted by the present owner, this desk apparently remained in Petersburg until Branch Tanner's death in 1793 (Tanner's will is on file in Amelia County). It was then passed (by purchase?) to Tanner's neighbor, Col. Joseph Bragg, and descended in the Bragg family to William, ca. 1825; to his daughter Elizabeth Page Bragg Dunn, ca. 1855; to Lucy Frances Dunn Osborne, ca. 1880; to Mary M. Osborne Bryan, ca. 1921; and to Frances Osborne Bryan Humphreys, ca. 1971. It was then sold to Craig and Tarlton, Inc. and was later purchased by Mr. and Mrs. James R. Melchor.

Figure 101

Other Williamsburg Furniture

There is a large corpus of Williamsburg furniture that cannot be assigned to specific shops based on present knowledge. This includes single items and small groups, some having details or construction that suggest one of the two shops already isolated in this study.

One of the most intriguing pieces in this study is a side table fashioned of black walnut (fig. 93). It has legs carved as three clustered columns and a skirt pierced in abstract rococo designs. The unusual rabbetted edge of the top, which is an old replacement, is identical to the Palace tea table and also incorporates indented corners. This was neither a logical nor an attractive design, and it appears that the restorer was copying the original, which, unknown to him, had lost the applied molding that formed a tray top. This modern rabbet does not continue around the table as it would have on the original. It is unexpected to find that the back skirt is unfinished pine.

In addition to being associated with the Palace tea table (fig. 57), this table is tied stylistically to a large number of Williamsburg pieces. The central piercing immediately beneath the top, and the pair of small vertical piercings in the skirt are quite similar in concept to those in the crest and splat of a chair from the Scott shop (fig. 30). The inverted arches on the tops of the table legs point downward between the columns and therefore are similar to those of the following table (fig. 94).[1] The through-tenoned cross stretcher and the continuous chamfers, which continue to the table top on the inside of the legs, are seen on a number of Williamsburg chairs (figs. 95-97). It is also stylistically related to the china tables attributed to Bucktrout, with their piercing and heavily sculptured legs—features that are otherwise extremely rare in Virginia-made furniture.

Boldly carved gothic style legs distinguish the following breakfast table (fig. 94). This form, known in the eighteenth century as a Pembroke table, is documented in Williamsburg before 1780 when Richard Booker, a local cabinetmaker, made one for Col. John Prentis.[2] The example shown here, which descended in the St. George Tucker family of Williamsburg, is made of dense mahogany with oak and yellow pine. Each leg has a small bead near the skirt that apparently continued onto the original brackets (unfortunately now missing, see fig. 94a) and across the apron. These brackets were relatively large, and evidence suggests that they were higher than they were wide. No Williamsburg parallel to the carved foot is known (fig. 94b), although "shifted square" legs of this type are found on several pieces attributed to northeast North Carolina.[3] Their pre-

93. *Tea Table, Williamsburg, circa 1770.*
Mahogany primary; yellow pine secondary.
Height 27⅞", width 32¹³/₁₆", depth 20".
Mr. and Mrs. William C. Adams, Jr.

94a.

94. *Pembroke Table, Williamsburg, circa 1775.*
Mahogany primary; oak, yellow pine secondary.
Height 28⅝", width 26½", depth 34¼" open, 19½" closed.
Dr. Janet Kimbrough.

94b.

cise origin and their relationship to this table deserve further study.

The next three chairs (figs. 95-97) were undoubtedly made in a single Williamsburg shop and are representative of a large group there. Most are very plain, but the finest example (fig. 97) has a pierced splat and beaded edge on the back. The most characteristic feature of this group is an unusual splat attachment. The splat is not seated in a separate shoe in the usual fashion but was nailed into a large notch on the inside of the rear rail. The notch was then filled with a secondary wood, usually pine (visible on the left rear rail of figure 96a). On corner chairs in this group the notch is normally covered on the right rail with a slip seat support made of pine. The chamfered corners on chair legs run completely to the top of the seat rail rather than stopping just below it in the usual manner.

A simple side chair is one of a set of four that descended in the Galt family (fig. 95). A pair of slipper chairs also belonging to this group were in the same household (not pictured). The ownership of these two sets of chairs in the Galt family of Williamsburg, and the corner chair that descended in the St. George Tucker family there, constitute the nucleus for attributing this group to a Williamsburg shop. Additional support for the attribution to Williamsburg is found in other related pieces—a side table (fig. 93), a corner chair (fig. 28), side chairs (figs. 98-100), and an armchair (fig. 101).

The lone corner chair illustrated from this group (fig. 96) also has a history in the St. George Tucker family. The splat design is related to the type found on a Scott corner chair (fig. 28). Five other corner chairs from this group are pictured in the MESDA files, and three of these have an unusual crest and arm construction related to two Scott corner chairs (see figs. 28, 29 and pp. 36-38 for comparative discussion). One of these five chairs has the same splat design as this one while the other four have extremely simple splats identical to the Galt family slipper chairs (not illustrated). Two have turned columns similar to those shown on this example (fig. 96) and the others have extremely simple columns without molded bases. The turning is abruptly ended at the base leaving sharp corners—a feature also seen on several Scott examples (figs. 28, 29). One of these appears to be considerably later than the others and has heavily tapered legs in the federal style. These five chairs have widely scattered histories in areas to the north, northwest, and west of Williamsburg.

A set of sixteen chairs from this group (fig. 97) are original furnishings of Mount Airy, the fine country house of the Tayloe family. These have the

95. *Side Chair (one of four), Williamsburg, circa 1770. Walnut primary; yellow pine secondary. Height 37¼", width 19¼", depth 16". The Anne Galt Black Collection.*

unusual splat attachment seen throughout the group, but two departures distinguish them: the chamfer on each leg stops just below the seat rail, rather than continuing upward; and they have "H" rather than box stretchers.

In spite of these slight departures from the simpler examples, the Mt. Airy chairs are closely related and probably represent the same shop. Their refinements offer an important opportunity to understand two different levels of quality from a single shop and, by extension, a better understanding of eighteenth-century chair usage. In addition to the H-stretchers, they have more elaborate backs. When compared with others in the group that have less detailed backs combined with box stretchers, they strongly support the conclusion that those with box stretchers were considered a modest form.

96. *Corner Chair, Williamsburg, circa 1770.*
Walnut primary; yellow pine secondary.
Height 30", width (across arms), 29⅝", depth (front leg to back column)
*   26", seat 18⅜" square.*
Dr. Janet C. Kimbrough.

97. *Side Chair (one of sixteen), Williamsburg, circa 1770.*
Walnut primary; yellow pine secondary.
Height 37", width 22", depth 18¼".
Mr. and Mrs. H. Gwynne Tayloe, Jr.

96a.

98. *Side Chair, Williamsburg, circa 1770.*
Walnut primary; yellow pine secondary with yellow pine slip
seat. Original black leather upholstery beneath later
covering.
Height 37⅝", width 21⅛", depth 17½".
Private Collection.

99. *Side Chair (one of a pair), Williamsburg, circa 1770.*
Mahogany primary; yellow pine slip seat.
Height 37¼", width 21⅛", depth 18¼".
The Colonial Williamsburg Foundation (acc. no. 1953-564).

99a.

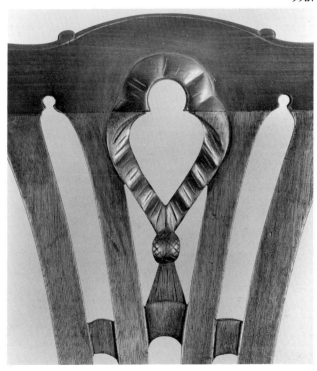

Four chairs that display some consistency of design and construction (figs. 98-101) share features with the last group but clearly come from a different shop. Their splats have normal construction and are mortised into a separate shoe glued to the rear seat rails. The double blocks on the interior corner of the seat frames overlap each other—a construction often thought to come only from Philadelphia, although its origin is actually England. The crossbar of the H-stretchers are half-dovetailed into the sides and enter from beneath, which differs from the preceding group.

One of these side chairs (fig. 98) is a single surviving example from a large set owned by the Galt family. It has a crest rail and delicate bead carving similar to those seen on a chair in the last group (fig. 97). The splat design was popular in England and America, but those made in Williamsburg are distinguished by the addition of trefoil piercing and a tassel. A virtually identical pair of mahogany chairs in the Colonial Williamsburg collection (fig. 99) appear to be products of the same shop, but they are embellished with the addition of carving. All of these examples have yellow pine slip seats and two of them (figs. 98, 100) have the original upholstery. On the black leather of these examples is a fine, hatched design that appears to have been impressed or stamped into the leather. Unfortunately the design is badly worn and remains visible only on the protected underside of the seat.[4]

Quality and construction place another Galt family side chair (fig. 100) with these examples, even though its splat and crest rail are virtually identical to those of the preceding group. In addition to the constructional association, the upholstery technique of this chair is identical to that of figure 98. Significantly, it is upholstered by a completely different method from that employed in the Palace set (fig. 67): it does not utilize a long tab pulled over each corner and the leather was cut so sparingly that it was pulled over the slip seat frame and nailed near the outside edges.

The last piece in this small group is an armchair that bears the deeply impressed marking "VIRG^A" on its rear seat rail and has a tradition of use in the Virginia House of Burgesses (fig. 101). The back is well designed, and, to the knowledge of the author, unique. The crest rail, the carved "loops," and techniques of construction place it firmly in this group. The carved foliage in the splat, like that of the carved ribbon and tassel in figure 99, has a completely different character from products attributed to the Scott and Hay shops. Likewise, the extremely rigid qualities of the narrow scroll borders on the crest, splat, and stiles differ from Hay shop chairs (figs. 59, 62). The lack of molding on the top of the seat rail seems slightly incongruous with its elaborate back, but this feature is seen on pieces made by Peter Scott and on a corner chair in the preceding group (fig. 96). The arms of this chair may be eighteenth-century replacements, since they interrupt the stile molding in a very heavy-handed manner, which is hardly consistent with the character of the back. Examination of the arms resulted in no other evidence of replacement, and the signs of wear are extremely convincing.

The mark "VIRG^A" found on this chair is intriguing and raises several questions. Although the piece has a vague history of usage in the House of Burgesses at the Capitol, why was it stamped when others from there (figs. 7, 46) were not? It seems logical that the circumstances necessitating such marking would have been followed throughout the building and two unmarked examples used in the Capitol seem to remove this chair from consideration as a furnishing there. With the Capitol eliminated,

100. *Side Chair, Williamsburg, circa 1770.*
Walnut primary; yellow pine slip seat with original black
leather upholstery.
Height 37¼", width 19¼", depth 16".
Private Collection.

101. *Armchair, Williamsburg, circa 1770.*
Walnut primary; yellow pine and walnut secondary.
Height 36⅝", width 23¼", depth 18⅝".
The D.A.R. Museum, Washington, D.C.

the most logical building for such a chair would be the Governor's Palace.

Circumstances at the Palace were quite different from those at the Capitol. As a residence, it was not furnished solely by the colony but had a number of items belonging personally to the Governor. Furniture owned by the colony was termed "standing furniture" and in the inventory of Lord Botetourt's estate, taken in 1770, it was listed separately from that owned by the Governor. While it is not known whether standing furniture was marked, the advantages of doing so are obvious, for over 16,500 objects were listed in the Palace at the time of Botetourt's death. Additional support for this conclusion is found in an early order from the Council, specifying that new muskets for the colony be marked "Virginia 1750." This evidence is further reinforced by the lack of identifying marks found on any of the eighteen pieces with a tradition of ownership by Lord Dunmore. Hopefully future research will clarify the history of this chair, but for the moment evidence suggests that it was made as standing furniture for the Palace.

Among the pieces of furniture attributable to Williamsburg are a number of six-legged dining tables, a type that was produced over a wide area of eastern Virginia and northeast North Carolina. The form is apparently English in derivation and dates from the mid-eighteenth century. These tables have three legs at each end when the leaves are down—a stationary one in the center and a movable one on each corner. They are very practical, allowing more adjustment of the legs for seating and providing superior stability. Two six-legged tables of this type are known to have descended in Williamsburg families: a straight-legged example and one with pad feet (fig. 102).

The latter piece is made of mahogany with yellow pine and oak, and it has a variation of the high trumpet-shaped pad feet associated with the Hay shop. Several other mahogany examples that closely correspond to this are known, and many straight-legged pieces are made of walnut. Several with ball-and-claw feet come from northeast North Carolina.

102. Dining Table, Williamsburg, circa 1760.
Mahogany primary; oak, yellow pine and tulip secondary.
Height 28", width 45½", depth 49¾" open, 16½" closed.
The Colonial Williamsburg Foundation (acc. no. 1963-737).

103. *Dining Table, possibly Williamsburg, circa 1770.*
Mahogany and mahogany veneer primary; oak secondary.
Height 28", width 49", depth 69" open, 23" closed.
Mr. and Mrs. H. Gwynne Tayloe, Jr.

103a.

104a.

104. *Card Table, Williamsburg, circa 1775.*
Mahogany and mahogany veneer primary; yellow pine and
poplar secondary.
Height 29", width 35½", depth 17½".
The Colonial Williamsburg Foundation (acc. no. 1977-67).

104b.

One handsome variation of this unusual type is found in a dining table made of mahogany, with oak used as a secondary wood (fig. 103). Here the fixed central leg has been omitted, leaving only a hinged one on each corner. Three such tables were original furnishings of Mt. Airy. Two are still used there and a third from the ensemble, though damaged, survives. It should be noted that these examples may represent English production, since they use oak solely as a secondary wood. Traditionally this has been accepted as indisputable proof of English origin, but many eastern Virginia tables have oak in their gates, although pine or walnut is usually found in the secondary rails. Considering the profusion of English-trained cabinetmakers in eastern Virginia, it would be a mistake at this point to preclude that they represent Williamsburg production.

A serpentine card table is the last Williamsburg example in this study (fig. 104). Found in the Petersburg area about fifty years ago, it is related to several pieces from the Hay group, although it is sufficiently different to make a more specific attribution uncertain at this point. Made of mahogany and mahogany veneer, it has heavy poplar rails while the remainder, including the swing gate, is yellow pine. The egg-and-dart molding around the skirt (fig. 104a) is related to that on the underside of the arms from the Bucktrout chair (fig. 49d). In both examples, the carving is stylized and shows a degeneration of the academic prototype from which it originated. The character of this degeneration is essentially the same in both examples and suggests a connection between them. The misunderstanding occurs principally in the design of the dart element between the eggs: this area is simply cut away, leaving the projections extending beneath the eggs looking very much like flower petals. The well formed block feet are mortised onto the leg with a through tenon that is rounded on the bottom. One block is somewhat loose and cannot be turned, which probably means that the round section projects beneath a square tenon.

With these pieces the study of Williamsburg cabinetmaking is concluded. Five distinct groups have been analyzed, as well as many other pieces that bear a close relationship to them. Unquestionably, the Peter Scott and Anthony Hay shops dominated the volume of production, and many examples dating from the period 1765-75 show stylistic and constructional affinity to their work. By that decade a number of other cabinetmakers had appeared in the area. William Kennedy, John Crump, and Richard Booker have already been mentioned, but others include Archibald Harrocks (1776) and James Honey (1776-84); Matthew Moody (1766- d.1773); Thomas Orton (1768); John Ormeston (1761-1766); James Tyrie (1772-84); and Widdatch & Drummond "Near Williamsburg" (1764). Some of these served apprenticeships under earlier masters, thereby extending the practices and designs of existing Williamsburg shops. Others, aided by the turnover of journeymen, contributed to changes in established styles. The influence of workmen with various training encouraged the combination and re-combination of the old with the new, and they mixed their results with ideas flowing from England or with those drawn from Chippendale's *Director* or *Household Furniture*. This interchange of technology and style, combined with a parallel development of the taste of patrons, is in essence the process by which the Williamsburg "school" was formed.

There are still many questions to be answered and further research is needed to clarify the contributions of cabinetmakers who worked in Williamsburg in the late colonial period. Did cabinetmaking there evaporate abruptly when the capital moved to Richmond in 1780? Or did patronage established in the colonial period keep the shops of Bucktrout and others busy, continuing their production into the neo-classic style? The post-colonial pieces shown in this study have been included to point out the serious need for documentation of Williamsburg and eastern Virginia furniture in the federal period.

In conclusion, cabinetmaking in Williamsburg during the eighteenth century exhibits a tremendous variety, from average or modest examples to the remarkable and unique, from bold or massive pieces to light and delicate ones. The finest achievements of the cabinetmaking trade in Williamsburg, like those of the society in which it flourished, were founded on sound principles and philosophical ideals that enabled cabinetmakers to excel far beyond the limits expected of so small a city.

FOOTNOTES

1. A table recently examined by the author has legs that are nearly identical to those of the Pembroke table depicted in figure 94. It also has pierced cross stretchers, with a design closely related to the heavy piercing on the skirt of the tea table shown in figure 93, thus strengthening its association with both of these pieces. It has a history in Nottoway County.
2. Mills Brown, "Cabinetmaking in the Eighteenth Century" (unpublished research report, Colonial Williamsburg Foundation, Williamsburg, Virginia, 1959), p. 150.
3. Helen Comstock, "Furniture of Virginia, North Carolina, Georgia, and Kentucky," *The Magazine Antiques* 16 (January 1952):97, fig. 155.
4. This stamped black leather is possibly the same material referred to in the account book of Alexander Craig, a Williamsburg harness-maker and tanner. (Craig Account Book, Manuscripts Division, Earl Gregg Swem Library, College of William and Mary, Williamsburg, Va.) Craig is known to have sold "black grained leather" at £1 per hide to a number of Virginia cabinetmakers, including several who lived some distance from Williamsburg. Among them were John Selden of Norfolk and James Allen of Fredericksburg. Since other hides were undoubtedly available from tanneries located much closer to the artisans, those supplied by Craig must have had special qualities, probably their stamped graining. The expense, combined with the fact that these hides were sought by distant patrons who had to pay the additional cost of transporting them, supports this conclusion. Craig Account Book information courtesy of Harold B. Gill, Jr., historian, Colonial Williamsburg Foundation.

PART II

Furniture from Other Areas of Eastern Virginia

Figure 112

Norfolk

On New Year's Day of 1776, Virginia's largest town, Norfolk, was burned to the ground. Unfortunately, most of that area's colonial furniture was destroyed in that fire, but court records for the county of Norfolk that survive from the period are testimony to the existence of a strong community of tradesmen. The lack of notices by these artisans in the *Virginia Gazette* is puzzling, but it may indicate that their market was strong enough to eliminate any need to advertise. With a population of 6,000, this shipping, mercantile, and manufacturing center was the eighth largest urban area in colonial America, and a major focal point of business activity for Virginians south of the James River.[1]

Two signed pieces shown here present a major step in the identification and study of Norfolk furniture: a chest of drawers bearing the chalk signature "John Selden" (fig. 106) and a clothespress inscribed "J.S." and dated "1775" (fig. 105). These are original furnishings of Shirley plantation in Charles City County.

Little is known of John Selden, but he purchased a lot in Norfolk on August 9, 1769, and there are occasional subsequent references to him in the county records. His only newspaper advertisement was placed in July of 1776, after the British had destroyed the city. It was written from Blandford, near Petersburg, where he had moved for refuge:

PRINCE GEORGE, July 15, 1776

THE subscriber, having been one of the unfortunate suffers at Norfolk, has removed to the place lately occupied by mr. John Baird near Blandford where he carries on the CABINET-MAKING business, as formerly, in all its branches. He has also by him, ready made, several dozen of neat mohogany, cherry, and walnut chairs, tables, desks, tea boards, &c. which he will sell on the most reasonable terms, for ready money, and will take in exchange for work some mohogany or seasoned walnut. Those ladies and gentlemen who are pleased to favour him with their custom may depend on being faithfully served, with the greatest despatch and punctuality.

JOHN SELDEN[2]

The clothespress and chest made by John Selden raise some interesting questions regarding patronage patterns in colonial Tidewater. Were the pieces purchased in Norfolk during 1775, or could they have been saved from the fire and taken to Blandford, where they were then sold to the Carters? Is it possible that Selden attempted to peddle his surviving cabinetwork on his move to Petersburg? These questions are difficult to answer. The only known document associated with Selden's cabinetwork indicates that he may have had as wide a patronage as the major Williamsburg artisans: in September of 1776 he sold the state a large quantity of furniture for

105. Clothespress, signed "J. S." for John Selden, Norfolk, dated 1775.
Mahogany primary; yellow pine and mahogany secondary.
Height 74¼″, width 50⅛″, depth 23¾″.
Mr. and Mrs. C. Hill Carter, Jr.

the Governor's Palace, then occupied by Patrick Henry, and charged the sum of £91. He was the only cabinetmaker outside of Williamsburg known to have provided furnishings for the Palace.[3]

These Selden pieces provide important information on Norfolk production and point out a major problem of its separation from Williamsburg. The clothespress has a paneled back, a detachable cornice, and composite feet, all features seen in case pieces made in Williamsburg. The bottom of the drawers on the clothespress and its accompanying chest are nailed into rabbets and are covered on the edges by continuous strips mitered at the corners—characteristics that are also common in Williamsburg examples. It is important to note as well that the press bears a very close relationship to plate CXXIX of Chippendale's *Director* (fig. 105c) and as such is related to other forms and details from this design book that found employment in Williamsburg shops. Nonetheless, these pieces do vary in style from the Chippendale designs, and certain constructional features on the case interiors prove to be helpful in distinguishing Norfolk production.

The most notable variation in Norfolk pieces is found in the design of the feet (fig. 105b). These differ significantly from the straight bracket feet of the *Director* illustrations, and they have a similar but less vigorous outline than ogee brackets found on Scott pieces (figs. 36, 40, 42). The Selden examples flare severely inward at the base (fig. 105b); while Scott's have this detail, they are not as accentuated. In addition, the coved base molding is unknown in Williamsburg examples. It appears that Selden case pieces may be recognized by these features—a possibility that gains further support when it is realized that the clothespress and chest of drawers were not made en suite: the clothespress has a simple quarter-round molding on the edges of the drawers and the chest has an applied cock bead. Another Selden feature that may prove to be a regional characteristic is the exaggerated protrusion of the double ogee spandrels on the doors of the press. It is important that those found on a Williamsburg desk-and-bookcase (fig. 77b) are noticeably softer in profile.

In addition to these artistic variations, one significant constructional detail helps differentiate Norfolk case furniture from that of Williamsburg: the drawer blades are very thin and are backed by three-quarter depth full-bottom dustboards. Occasionally Williamsburg pieces have full-bottom dustboards that fall slightly short of the back, but the separation found on these two Selden pieces is far greater, ranging from one-half to three-quarters of the full case depth.

105a.

105b.

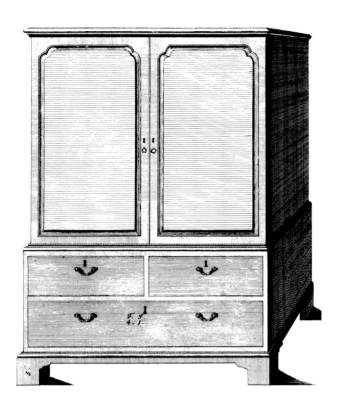

105c. *"Cloaths Press", Plate 129, Thomas Chippendale's*
Gentleman and Cabinet-Maker's Director,
third edition, 1762.

106. *Chest of Drawers, signed "John Selden," Norfolk,*
circa 1775.
Mahogany primary; yellow pine secondary.
Height 32½", width 36¼", depth 20¾".
Mr. and Mrs. C. Hill Carter, Jr.

With features that distinguish these Norfolk case pieces thus isolated, it is now possible to examine several other forms that may reflect production there.

A fine card table with a history of ownership in Norfolk could well have been made in that city (fig. 107). Like other furniture from eastern Virginia its form is derived from English design, but the piece otherwise bears little relationship to furniture from recognized centers in Virginia. It has an abundance of oak secondary wood, and it would undoubtedly be classified English were it not for the poplar drawer sides. The C-scrolls of the knees (fig. 107a) are similar to those of the early Williamsburg group,

which are of higher quality, but the pad feet are different from any others known to have been made there. The bold design and excellent construction of this table show it to be from a well-developed urban center.

Like the preceding example, a tea table that exhibits excellent workmanship and design may also come from Norfolk (fig. 108). It descended in the Barraud family of Norfolk and Williamsburg and on occasion has been attributed to Philadelphia, although its massive scale is quite unlike examples made there. Several other tables from eastern Virginia exhibit this heavy scale, including one with an unspecified provenance (fig. 121).

107. Card Table, Norfolk (?), circa 1750.
Mahogany primary; white oak and poplar secondary.
Height 27¼", width 32⅞", depth 21⅞".
The Colonial Williamsburg Foundation (acc. no. 1962-116).

107a.

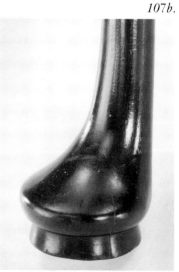

107b.

108. *Tea Table, Norfolk (?), circa 1770.*
Mahogany.
Height 29¾", Diameter of top 37".
The Colonial Williamsburg Foundation (acc. no. 1930-184).

108a.

109. Clothespress, Norfolk, circa 1795.
Mahogany primary; yellow pine and popular secondary.
Height 85¾", width 48⅜", depth 21⅝".
The Moses Myers House of the Chrysler Museum at Norfolk.

Unlike the colonial period, a large quantity of neo-classic furniture made in Norfolk survives; some of it is exceptionally fine. Such production falls outside the scope of this work, but one clothespress (fig. 109) is included here because it retains earlier features. Made of mahogany with yellow pine and poplar, it descended in the Myers family of Norfolk. The ogee feet, with inward flaring bases and unadorned brackets, are an English type of the mid-eighteenth century. A similar example in the Victoria and Albert Museum, signed by David Wright of Lancaster, England, is dated 1751.[4] This same foot is utilized throughout southeast Virginia and into northeast North Carolina from the mid eighteenth century well into the nineteenth and probably reflects the dissemination of a Norfolk style in those areas.

The widespread dissemination of Norfolk style comes as no surprise when one considers the migration of Tidewater Virginians into the Albemarle region of northeast North Carolina. Consider, for example, Thomas Sharrock, who served his apprenticeship in Norfolk, moved to Northampton County, North Carolina and proceeded to train at least six of his sons in the cabinetmaking trade.[5] A large group of case furniture is attributed to the Sharrock family on the basis of a chest signed by George Sharrock, Thomas' son, and these have feet related to the Norfolk federal clothespress, as well as those of a desk-and-bookcase from southeast Virginia (fig. 111). It is also of interest that the dustboards of the Sharrock pieces are related to this Virginia desk, as well as to the Selden chest and clothespress. They also have drawer construction corresponding to Selden pieces. The consistency of such features as these, appearing throughout southeast Virginia and northeast North Carolina, points to the influence of Norfolk over a large region.

As the example of Williamsburg indicates, carved furniture was produced in relatively large quantities in eastern Virginia, so a center as large and active as Norfolk must have made a sizable contribution. Unfortunately, there are no documented carved pieces from that city, and this study can only offer suggestions regarding their identity. One group of carved furniture that may reflect Norfolk production or its influence includes an impressive armchair with ball-and-claw feet (fig. 110). One of a pair, it is the most sophisticated example from a large group with histories in Hertford, North Carolina. A number of related objects, including a pair of card tables and a dressing table, come from North Carolina's Roanoke River Valley, to the west of Hertford and Edenton.[6] All of these have ball-and-claw feet, cabriole legs, and acanthus knee carvings that are interrelated. There is some difference in detail and variance in quality, but the overall artistic approach to the elements is unified and is completely different than in Williamsburg. Several dining tables with ball-and-claw feet also relate to this group. These are the six-legged variety that is common throughout southeast Virginia and northeast North Carolina (fig. 102).

In the past, these tables and chairs have been attributed to Edenton, primarily because they have provenances in the surrounding region, but also because they share some similarities to architectural carving found there. The relationship of the furniture with that of the architectural carving is far from convincing, however, since they embody differing techniques and designs.[7]

110. Armchair, Norfolk (?), circa 1760.
Mahogany primary; yellow pine secondary.
Height 39⅜", width 28¾", depth 23¼".
The Museum of Early Southern Decorative Arts.

The suggestion that this group may represent Norfolk cabinetwork is based largely upon circumstantial evidence. An important clue is that they possess a sophistication far superior to a Masonic chair made in the late 1760s for the Halifax, North Carolina Lodge by a local artisan.[8] Masonic chairs were usually pieces of special commission, committed in every respect to the highest level of artistic achievement in any given region, and they should be a reliable indicator of the prevailing local awareness of style. Admittedly Halifax is some distance from Edenton, but the divergence in style between the awkward Masonic chair and the carved Norfolk [?] group is even greater. It is also somewhat difficult to accept the production of an extremely complicated and stylish George II armchair in the small town of Edenton, where architecture and architectural carving show the strong influence of old-fashioned, baroque design.

In conclusion, it appears that Norfolk cabinetmaking had an influence as far west as Petersburg, and southwest extending well into northeast North Carolina. This is particularly understandable in view of the rural character of the Roanoke River Valley and the isolation of the Albemarle Sound from large ports by the Outer Banks. In an area filled with small towns, it was necessary for wealthy and style-conscious patrons to look to Norfolk as the largest and most accessible urban center.

FOOTNOTES

1. *The Virginia Gazette*, ed. John Dixon, February 10, 1776, p. 12; population statistics courtesy of Harold B. Gill, Jr., historian, Colonial Williamsburg Foundation, Williamsburg, Virginia.
2. *The Virginia Gazette*, ed. Alexander Purdie, July 26, 1776, p. 4.
3. H. R. McIlwaine, *Journal of the Council of the State of Virginia* (Richmond: Virginia State Library, 1931), p. 148. Information courtesy of Harold B. Gill, Jr.
4. Desmond Fitz-Gerald, *Georgian Furniture* (London: Her Majesty's Stationery Office, 1969), entry no. 47.
5. Betty Dahill, "The Sharrock Family, A Newly Discovered School of Cabinetmakers," *Journal of Early Southern Decorative Arts* 2 (November 1976):37-51.
6. Frank L. Horton, "Carved Furniture of the Albemarle, A Tie with Architecture," *Journal of Early Southern Decorative Arts* 1 (May 1975):14-20.
7. While both of these carvings have punched backgrounds and make use of a bead border in some areas, they have quite different approaches to design and divergent techniques of carving. The facia board and stair brackets from the Blair-Pollock House have sinuous entwining vines ending with very small volutes or narrow leaves, and reflect the spirit of baroque design from the late seventeenth century. Many of the leaves and tendrils have busy details formed by gouge cuts, made by driving a gouge at a right angle into the wood. A second cut was made converging with the first, thereby removing a very small plug. The carving on the furniture does not utilize the profuse gouge marks and, with the exception of a few veins in each leaf, is characterized by large, plain rounded surfaces. The leaves are much broader and differ completely from the design of those on the architectural elements of the Blair-Pollock House.
8. Thomas C. Parramore, *Launching the Craft: The First Half-Century of Freemasonry in North Carolina* (Raleigh: Litho Industries, Inc., 1975), p. 82; files of the Museum of Early Southern Decorative Arts, Winston-Salem, North Carolina.

Southeast Virginia

Southeast Virginia is the area bounded by the James River to the north, the Carolinas to the south, and the Piedmont to the west. Colonial furniture produced there is dramatic testimony to the combined influence of Williamsburg and Norfolk on rural cabinetmaking. Styles from these urban centers also extended into the Albemarle Sound and the Roanoke River Valley of North Carolina, and westward into the Virginia Piedmont.

The features found on furniture from this region that are characteristic of Norfolk include half-dustboards and inward flaring ogee feet. However, full dustboards and desk interiors of the Williamsburg type are also seen. Other parallels to Williamsburg are found in furniture from the Roanoke River region—particularly case pieces with five feet, a characteristic that is associated with examples attributed to the shop of Peter Scott (figs. 39, 40).[1]

Much of the furniture produced in southeast Virginia shows the influence of carpentry and house joinery, and indeed some artisans in the area are documented as having practiced these trades. Pieces made under such circumstances would naturally vary from the simple or coarse to the relatively fine and complex. Unlike more sophisticated examples of cabinetwork from Williamsburg and Norfolk, which show a strong reliance upon urban English style, this construction is representative of provincial English furniture. Such construction was also widely used in New England, and it is possible that some of these techniques were introduced into Virginia from that area. Case pieces made under these conditions usually have exposed dovetail joints on the drawer blades. Dustboards usually were not used; instead, strips of wood were nailed to the insides of the cases to support the drawers. Bracket feet commonly have a single vertical block on their interior for support. Such construction methods are easier to execute than those employed in Norfolk and Williamsburg, resulting not only in less expensive furniture but less durable pieces as well. The drawer blades with their exposed dovetails are prone to work their way out the front of the case, and the nailed drawer supports strain the case sides when they shrink, sometimes causing them to split.

An early example of the combined influence of Norfolk and Williamsburg is found in a desk-and-bookcase with a history of ownership south of Petersburg (fig. 111). The ogee feet are quite similar to those of the federal clothespress from Norfolk (fig. 109) and the dustboard construction is found on the examples signed by John Selden (figs. 105, 106). The triple inlays on the document drawers, the method of attaching the crown molding with large blocks, and

111. Desk-and-Bookcase, southeast Virginia, circa 1760.
Walnut primary; yellow pine and oak secondary.
Height 96⅛", width 46", depth 25⅛".
The Colonial Williamsburg Foundation (acc. no. 1975-61).

the wall-of-Troy molding are variations of details on a desk-and-bookcase attributed to Peter Scott (fig. 37). The layout of the drawers in the main case was also popular in Williamsburg (figs. 37, 75), but the drawer construction is an English type that is otherwise unknown in eastern Virginia, although it is found in Charleston, South Carolina. Each drawer bottom is made of two pieces that fit into a rabbet on the front and side and into a grooved batten that divides the drawer in the center.

One feature commonly found in southeast Virginia is the construction of the fallboard, which has a mitered batten attached with through tenons (tenons of this type are easily visible on the next desk, figure 112). The brasses are original, including the lattice-work escutcheons on the doors of the bookcase section.

Two inscriptions are found on the top of the desk section: "Crawfords his desk," appearing to be eighteenth century in origin, and "Jarrett," which may refer to a town in Sussex County and probably dates from the nineteenth century. A simpler desk-and-bookcase now owned by Woodlawn Plantation in Alexandria has a related design and appears to be a product of the same shop. Many details of its design and construction are identical to those of figure 111.

111a.

One of the finest examples from southeast Virginia is a walnut desk-and-bookcase that typifies the robust quality found in rural cabinetmaking (fig. 112). Purchased in Petersburg, it contains the inscription "Comans Well," placing it in Sussex County in the early and mid nineteenth century. Even though it has a pleasing design and is well proportioned, the case construction, with exposed dovetails and no dustboards, is unsophisticated. The scrolled bracket feet and the extremely elaborate raised panels of the top are outstanding features, but the dentil cornice is weak and naive. Such discrepancies are characteristic of cabinetmaking techniques in rural areas. When the provincial tradesman endeavored to produce an elaborate or exceptional example, he often favored one or two elements, developing them extensively while either neglecting or failing to visualize the important relationship of other elements to the overall design. As a result, the finished product lacks the subtle refinement of a sophisticated urban piece and relies on an energetic but simplistic "picking out" of several bold features. One can react to these with only a simple understanding of design, and while this desk-and-bookcase has great aspirations, it falls far short in workmanship and in an understanding of how the materials interact with each other.

Like the preceding desk-and-bookcase, this example also has through-tenoned battens on the fallboard, but here they are mitered at both ends rather than just on the top. Identical construction is also seen on the ends of small table tops made in the area.

112. Desk-and-Bookcase, southeast Virginia, circa 1765.
Walnut primary; yellow pine and oak secondary.
Height 84½", width 40½", depth 21¾".
The Colonial Williamsburg Foundation (acc. no. 1930-109).

Many southeast Virginia features are also found on a desk-and-bookcase that was probably made in Chesterfield County (fig. 113). This piece has exposed dovetails on the drawer blades, and the supports for the drawers have been nailed in since there are no dustboards. Case furniture from the region commonly has drawer supports attached like this particular example: short rosehead nails were used, each of them sunk in a V-notch formed by the removal of wood between two saw cuts.

One of the typical stylistic features of this desk is its writing interior. The outer drawers are stepped, and those that flank the document drawers are serpentine in form. Many desk interiors produced in the Virginia Piedmont have this basic design, although here the interpretation resembles some Boston examples. The bookcase interior has been completely refitted, and while this shows considerable age, the slots for the original are clearly visible on close inspection. The bracket feet are unusually tall and are cut from the same board as the base mold. In this respect they are typical of case pieces from the area.

This piece bears the chalk signature "made by Mardun V. Eventon" inside the back of the desk. Eventon first advertised his cabinet business at Dumfries, in Prince William County, on June 24, 1762, when the *Maryland Gazette* carried his appeal for "Two or Three Journeymen Cabinetmakers" and ". . .two or three thousand feet of good Mahogany plank."[2] These indicate a healthy business, but his advertisements from Chesterfield fifteen years later presented quite another picture. "Wants Employment, and is now at Leisure. . ." he wrote in 1777, perhaps reflecting the economic uncertainty of the war. His advertisements at that point listed cabinetwork in the "Chinese" and "Gothick" taste, and ended by stating his desire to "superintend a number of hands at building."[3] It seems plausible that this desk, which descended in the Gwathmey family of nearby King William County, was made during Eventon's Chesterfield "period."

Mardun Eventon may not have been the only member of the Eventon family to combine the builder's trade with cabinetmaking. In 1769 Maurice "Evington" of Charles City County appealed for four "regular bred" workmen, including "Two to the House Joiners business, one to the Cabinet, and one to the House, chair, and table work."[4] Little more of Maurice is known, and a decade later he offered his household furniture for sale near Four Mile Creek in Henrico County. His other possessions, "sold before Mr. Freeman's door in Richmond Town," included a number of tools and "12 or 15 books of architecture," including works by Swan, Pain, Langley and

113. *Desk-and-Bookcase, signed "Mardun V. Eventon," probably Chesterfield County, circa 1775.*
Height 84", width 41", depth 21¾".
John R. Gwathmey.

113a.

Halfpenny.[5] The exact relationship between Mardun and Maurice is unclear, but the similarity of their occupations, their geographic proximity, and their unusual surname (variously spelled "Eventon" and "Evington" in eighteenth-century documents.) point to a relatively close one.

Despite Mardun Eventon's newspaper advertisements, which state an awareness of current fashion and architectural proportion, this desk-and-bookcase (fig. 113) falls short of his claims. Even if this example were made at Dumfries fifteen years earlier, it would still have to be considered old-fashioned. The brasses are an early style that remained available through English catalogues and could have been ordered in provincial areas where taste was conservative. The style of its stepped and blocked writing interior was popular primarily in the first third of the century, and the applied molding on the fallboard, which forms a writing or reading shelf, also comes from an early style. While it may be unfair to judge Eventon's work from this lone example, it appears that he was producing old-fashioned furniture of somewhat modest character. Such traits are certainly compatible with other production from this section of the state.

The vast area of southeast Virginia could produce a volume on furniture of considerable size. The representative pieces discussed here are a small sampling, but their specific features indicate regional characteristics that typify the area and offer an interesting challenge for further study.

FOOTNOTES

1. Several case pieces with five feet are pictured in the files of the Museum of Early Southern Decorative Arts in Winston-Salem, North Carolina. One signed chest of drawers having this feature is illustrated in Betty Dahill's "The Sharrock Family, A Newly Discovered School of Cabinetmakers," *Journal of Early Southern Decorative Arts* 2 (November 1976):38, fig. 1.
2. *The Maryland Gazette* (Annapolis), June 24, 1762, p. 3. Courtesy of the Museum of Early Southern Decorative Arts, Winston-Salem, North Carolina.
3. *The Virginia Gazette*, ed. John Dixon, August 15, 1777, p. 6.
4. *The Virginia Gazette*, ed. William Rind, February 23, 1769, p. 2.
5. *The Virginia Gazette*, ed. John Dixon, December 11, 1779, p. 3.

Richmond

Richmond did not achieve prominence as an urban center until late in the colonial period, and it was not until the capital was moved from Williamsburg in 1780 that it became the focal point for political activity in Virginia. The city blossomed after that date and, like others during the federal period, attracted a community of craftsmen. There is currently no documented furniture from colonial Richmond, and labeled pieces from the late eighteenth and early nineteenth centuries do not retain features from an earlier style. Some unsigned examples have historical circumstances suggesting an origin there and pre-Revolutionary details found on them may provide some clues for the future identification of its early furniture.

Only two advertisements were placed in the *Virginia Gazette* by Richmond artisans during all of the colonial period—one by the partnership of Clark and Holland in 1774, and another two years later by John Clark. One of the most complete contemporary descriptions of a cabinet shop in colonial Virginia is found in the latter:

RICHMOND TOWN, February 16, 1776

THE Subscriber intends to leave the colony soon, and will sell (or rent) the LOT No. 28 in the lower End of Richmond, fronting the main and cross Streets, with the following Improvements thereon, viz. a Dwelling-House 34 by 24, one Story high, a Brick Cellar of the same size, with a Partition in the Middle, proper for a Cellar and Kitchen, which is floored with Brick, a Chimney with three Fireplaces, the upper Rooms for a Family to live in, and the lower in Order for a Cabinet-Maker's Shop, for which it has of late been used; also a Smokehouse, and a Garden in good Order, well paled in. I will likewise dispose of the Benches and Tools, which are sufficient to employ six Hands, a Quantity of Walnut Plank, Brass Furniture, Locks, Screws and other suitable articles for the above business.

JOHN CLARK

All Persons who have had Dealings with me, being either Debtor or Creditor, are requested to have a Settlement.[1]

Clark's use of his residence as a shop appears to have been a fairly common practice in colonial Virginia, and its size may be typical as well. There were ". . .benches and tools sufficient to employ six Hands. . ." and its two rooms, measuring a total of 24 feet by 34 feet, gave the workmen an average of 136 square feet of floor space apiece. The Anthony Hay shop measured only slightly smaller in its original form, 24 by 32 feet, and when enlarged had an additional wing that measured 12 by 32 feet.

A fall-front desk and a kneehole dressing table that descended in the family of William Geddy, Jr. appear to have been made in Richmond (figs. 114, 115). Geddy's father was a Williamsburg blacksmith

114. Desk, attributed to Richmond, circa 1790.
Mahogany and mahogany veneer primary; yellow pine and
    Spanish cedar secondary.
Height 43", width 38½", depth 20¾".
Mr. and Mrs. Bert Geddy, Jr. of Whitehall, Toano.

and gunsmith whose plantation home, "Whitehall," was twelve miles west of town. After the elder Geddy's death about 1784, his son moved to Richmond, but he returned to Whitehall several decades later.[2] These pieces were probably acquired in Richmond, for not only do their styles coincide with the date of William Geddy's stay there but they differ significantly from any known Williamsburg furniture. In fact, they show a close affinity to the products of southeast Virginia, particularly to the desk-and-bookcase signed by Mardun Eventon of Chesterfield County, near Richmond (fig. 113). Construction details also relate these Geddy pieces with others from the general region, although they are much finer and suggest the production of an urban workshop.

The Geddy slant-top desk (fig. 114) is made of mahogany and has yellow pine as the secondary wood in the lower case. The drawers of the writing interior have Spanish cedar rather than pine as the secondary wood. Found in tropical America, this wood resembles a coarse, open-grained mahogany, and suggests an urban approach to cabinetmaking. It sometimes appears in Boston furniture of the mid eighteenth century, but its principal period of importation was not until the early nineteenth century and later.

The construction of this piece is similar to examples made in southeast Virginia. It lacks dustboards like many pieces made there, but the deep drawer blades are made of pine and run approximately one quarter of the case depth. They are faced

114a.

with a thin strip of mahogany. The drawer supports are replacements, and it is impossible to know if the originals had V-notches for short rosehead nails, as seen on the Eventon desk-and-bookcase and the accompanying dressing table. The drawer fronts are mahogany veneer on yellow pine, and so is the writing surface on the interior. The runners are replaced, but the drawers retain a series of small support blocks across the front, with approximately one-inch gaps between them. The interior drawer-bottoms fit into a canted rabbet, a feature that is also seen on two desk-and-bookcases (figs. 90, 91).

The construction of the Geddy family dressing table (fig. 115) is related to the preceding piece, but it bears an even stronger relationship to the Eventon desk-and-bookcase and to the southeast Virginia group. The case has exposed dovetails on the drawer blades and its drawer supports have V-notches to receive short wrought nails. This piece differs from the Eventon desk-and-bookcase in one major construction feature: the dustboards are one-third the depth of the case and are the full thickness of the drawer blades—a type that is found in other southeast Virginia examples and that can be traced to early Norfolk production. Likewise, the base molding on both the dressing table and desk are like those of Norfolk. The feet have been lost, but there is ample evidence to suggest that they were straight brackets, reinforced by a single vertical block flanked by two horizontal bracket blocks. These support blocks were made of tulip poplar, and small portions survived when they were split from the base.

115. Dressing Table, attributed to Richmond, circa 1790.
Mahogany primary; yellow pine secondary.
Height 30½", width 38½", depth 20¼".
Mr. and Mrs. Bert Geddy Jr. of Whitehall, Toano.

116. Desk-and-Bookcase, Richmond (?), circa 1785.
Walnut primary; yellow pine and oak secondary.
Height 83", width 43¼", depth 22".
The Colonial Williamsburg Foundation (acc. no. 1959-173).

166

New England influence seen in the Eventon desk-and-bookcase is also seen on this dressing table. It has cock-beading cut on the drawer blades and on the sides of the case rather than applied to the drawer. The interrelationship of construction and the combination of stylistic features also indicate influences from the North that could have arrived via migrant cabinetmakers or through exposure to imports. These examples are intriguing evidence of the mixing and blending of technology and style from Norfolk, Williamsburg, and New England.

The last example included in this group is a desk-and-bookcase that may have been produced in the Richmond area (fig. 116). It is filled with genealogical inscriptions indicating that the first owner was Edmond Eggleston of Cumberland County, who married Jane Segar Langton from Amelia in March of 1799. It passed to their son Richard, who lived in Nottoway, and descended through his heirs in Culpeper County. The piece then went to the Cunningham family of Gloucester County and was owned by them for several generations until acquired by the Colonial Williamsburg Foundation in 1959.[3]

Many features on this desk-and-bookcase relate it to cabinetmaking in Williamsburg, but it has several important departures. The coarseness of workmanship and the lack of dustboards point to a source outside the mainstream of that city's production. One Williamsburg feature is the frame attachment of the bookcase section (see text accompanying figs. 76-78 and 90-92 for a discussion). This piece provides a stage in the evolution of the frame attachment that is unknown on Williamsburg examples. The frame is usually joined to the desk section and a separate molding is attached to the bookcase sides to form an interlock joint. Here, both the frame and the molding are joined to the bookcase section, which is secured to the desk by two pegs that project from its base and enter holes in the top of the desk. The Dunmore desk-and-bookcase shows the next stage in this evolution, with the molding attached to the bookcase and with four pegs that fit into holes in the top of the desk for stability (fig. 87). There, however, the frame was eliminated entirely. The Eggleston desk-and-bookcase (fig. 116) thereby represents the missing stage in the Williamsburg evolution from a full interlock joint to a simpler molding attached to the bookcase.

Curiously, the detachable cornice is also held in place by pegs that enter the top of the bookcase. It originally continued into a pediment and could have been either a broken scroll or a pitch form. The flat paneled doors have ogee spandrels of a type seen in Williamsburg (fig. 77) and Norfolk (fig. 105). The

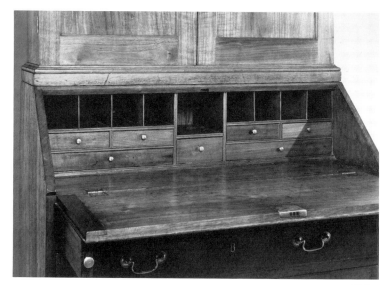

116a.

116b.

ogee feet have unusual concealed dovetail joints (fig. 116b), a feature seen on at least one Williamsburg example (fig. 88). They are rather stiff in contour, but in this respect resemble those of the John Tyler desk-and-bookcase (fig. 89). Both of these pieces also have straight battens in their fallboard.

This desk-and-bookcase shows an affinity to several eastern Virginia groups, but it is quite different from the Geddy family pieces, which present much stronger evidence for a Richmond attribution (figs. 114, 115). Undoubtedly, further research will eventually isolate the colonial furniture of Richmond, but for now an educated guess will have to suffice.

FOOTNOTES

1.   *The Virginia Gazette*, ed. John Dixon, March 9, 1776, p. 2.
2.   Harold B. Gill, Jr., *The Gunsmith in Colonial Virginia* (Williamsburg, Virginia: Colonial Williamsburg Foundation, and Charlottesville, Virginia: University Press of Virginia, 1974), p. 30.
3.   Accession File No. 1959-173, Department of Collections, Colonial Williamsburg Foundation, Williamsburg, Virginia.

Fredericksburg

Fredericksburg, situated on the falls of the Rappahannock River, had become Virginia's leading industrial center by 1770. From the early eighteenth-century settlement of Germanna, and the iron furnace established there by Lieutenant-Governor Alexander Spotswood in 1714, the Rappahannock River basin supported this industry.[1] Fredericksburg's prominence in industrial development is also well documented by two manufactories of firearms, which were established there during the Revolution. One of these was financed by the state while the other, the Rappahannock Forge, was a private venture established by James Hunter.[2]

A large number of Fredericksburg firearms and clock movements from the eighteenth century have survived, although no signed furniture made there is presently known. Circumstances indicate that isolating Fredericksburg's colonial cabinetwork will be difficult, requiring an extensive study of both the documents and of the surviving examples. Intense and conclusive studies of surrounding areas will undoubtedly play a key role in this endeavor.

One of the difficulties of isolating the furniture of Fredericksburg is the large number of chairs found there that have Scott-type construction and ornament. Many of these chairs have been attributed to Fredericksburg because of their conglomerate histories there. While some of these may have been produced in the Fredericksburg area by transplanted cabinetmakers, the evidence of a Williamsburg origin for the group is very strong. The probability that a Williamsburg-trained cabinetmaker worked there is logical in light of the evidence that one prominent Fredericksburg cabinetmaker, James Allen, made repeated purchases of black-grained leather from Alexander Craig, a Williamsburg harnessmaker and tanner.[3] These purchases may indicate a connection between Allen and Williamsburg cabinetmaking, though cabinetmakers in other towns some distance from Williamsburg also made similar purchases. Such patronage, then, may have no greater significance than Craig's ability to produce a refined, sophisticated leather that was unavailable from local tanneries. If this association with Williamsburg is taken at face value, it is certainly another demonstration of the leading role that the capital city played in matters of taste, style, and technology.

James Allen is first documented in Fredericksburg in 1740, and in 1759 he made two mahogany candlestands for George Washington.[4] He is also known to have employed an indentured servant cabinetmaker who ran away in 1752.[5] The practice of employing indentured servants in Fredericksburg —as opposed to salaried journeymen—makes a significant statement about the level of production in that city. (An analysis of this topic is discussed in detail, in the introduction to Williamsburg.)

In addition to the problem of identifying chairs produced in Fredericksburg, the cases of clocks with movements signed by Thomas Walker lack a continuity of design and construction that one would expect if they had been produced in a single center. The finest case in this group was probably made in Williamsburg and has been closely examined in that section (fig. 84). Additional examples would be needed to substantiate this attribution. While other Walker clocks have the same general form, they do not show such a sophisticated understanding of architectural design or such attention to detail. In addition, the Williamsburg desk-and-bookcase (fig. 82) and the Walker clock case (fig. 84) are the lone examples of pieces from eastern Virginia with pediments made in perspective.

The remaining Walker clock cases, like the Williamsburg example, suggests that his clock movements were purchased by patrons or tradesmen from a wide geographic area, and had cases made for them in other locales. Owing to their variety in style and construction, the cases have formed the basis of this conclusion. One document survives that corroborates this pattern of patronage. William Cabell, burgess of Amherst County, recorded in his diary on December 8, 1774 that he "sent watch by P. Rose to Walker in Fredericksburg to be put in good order." His diary entry of May 27 that same year notes that he paid £2.3.7 to Joseph Kidd, a Williamsburg upholsterer, and is testimony of his patronage there as well.[6]

Since Cabell was dealing with tradesmen in both centers, his choice of Walker rather than a Williamsburg watchmaker is revealing, especially in light of the evidence that at least five watchmakers are recorded in Williamsburg in the early 1770s.[7] The survival of many clocks signed by Walker and the total absence of any from Williamsburg suggest a more highly developed clockmaking trade in Fredericksburg. This conclusion gains further credence if one compares the masterful engraving of Walker (fig. 118) with that of William Waddill, a Williamsburg goldsmith who made and engraved an escutcheon and handles for the coffin of Lord Botetourt.[8] Admittedly, it may be unfair to compare Waddill's angular roman letters and crown with the flowing script and arabesque flourishes by Walker, since the coffin plate was, by necessity, a rush order completed within four days of the governor's death. But the urgency should not have caused the many small miss-cuts and overruns that characterize the engraving. Despite the pressure for rapid production, the fitting for the Royal Governor's coffin should certainly have demanded craftsmanship of the highest quality, and, from the description of the coffin, this appears to have been the intent. Made of black walnut, it was constructed by Williamsburg carpenter Joshua Kendall and had a total of three cases—the innermost lined with lead.[9] Considering these conditions, a comparison does have merit.

The extent to which Waddill and Walker represent the state of the art within their competitive realms is difficult to know, although further observation illuminates the question considerably. Waddill was one of the very few artisans in Williamsburg to advertise specifically that he did engraving. This would normally indicate that engraving was a specialty, and the fact that his silver furniture was chosen for Lord Botetourt's coffin over the ". . .Sett of Best Japand Coffin furniture with white Shield Brestplate . . ." supplied by Benjamin Bucktrout, indicates his work was held in higher regard.[10] Considering his receipt of the commission and his newspaper advertisement, Waddill's engraving would appear to represent good, if not the best, quality work available in Williamsburg.

The work of Thomas Walker compares favorably with other American engravers. In fact, his production of bracket clocks ranks him in the highest order of American clockmaking. That he produced the highest quality metalwork in colonial Virginia is unquestionable at present, for no other examples begin to approach the excellence of his products.

Further evidence for the superior quality of Fredericksburg metalwork is also found in gunsmithing. Again, the material from Williamsburg is meager, and the surviving objects encompass only unfinished parts excavated at the Geddy site on Palace Green in Williamsburg—the same site at which Waddill once worked. (The Geddy Family had operated a shop there from the 1730s to the 1780s. Three members of the family practiced gunsmithing and foundry work, while a fourth was a silversmith.) Of these fragments, few have engraving, and of those that do, the best work is found on a portion of a trigger guard that is naive and poorly executed when compared to intact examples that survive on firearms from Fredericksburg.[11] The excavation did prove that the Geddys produced some elaborate castings, but the most artistic of these were derived from models of finished products that were most often British in origin, leaving unanswered the question of their ability to design elegant examples. The engraved trigger guard previously mentioned, a brandy warmer by James Geddy, a large quantity of spoons, and the engraved escutcheon by William Waddill all have a quality well below that achieved in Fredericksburg.[12]

117a.

117b.

117. *Tall Case Clock, Fredericksburg, circa 1775; movement*
      by Thomas Walker of Fredericksburg.
Walnut primary; chestnut, yellow pine secondary.
Height 95⅛", width 21⅝", depth 11⅛".
The Colonial Williamsburg Foundation (acc. no. 1951-578).

The preceding analysis, though based on only a few surviving examples, suggests a convincing pattern. Colonial Fredericksburg appears to have excelled in technological development and produced metalwork far superior to that of Williamsburg.

The first two clocks to be studied (fig. 117 and 118) have Thomas Walker movements. The tall case clock has an eight-day movement with a well-engraved face, cast spandrels of average quality, and a moon dial. The case is made of black walnut with yellow pine and chestnut secondary woods. It has original carved flame finials and ogee bracket feet, although the plinth has lost the raised panel that was originally glued to the front.

The overall style of the case and the workmanship are quite reminiscent of Philadelphia and Delaware Valley clocks, which exhibit a heavy baroque character. Their heaviness is not confined to style, however, since each element is made of thick pieces of wood and results in cases of great weight. This approach contrasts with the example attributed to Williamsburg (fig. 84) and with several others having Walker movements that are pictured in the files of the Museum of Early Southern Decorative Arts. These eastern Virginia clocks are formed from very thin pieces of wood and, in this respect, are much closer to English examples than those of the Delaware Valley. The Williamsburg example is thinly constructed and, in addition, the elements of its architectural design are proportionately scaled. The effect is one of refined elegance and balance—in contrast to the Delaware Valley type, which relies on boldness achieved principally from oversized and out-of-scale elements best exemplified by overpowering broken-scroll pediments. This approach, however, is also characteristic of provincial production and the question of the origin of this case's design (fig. 117) is thereby difficult to determine. In this instance, the task is complicated by the fact that some influence from Delaware Valley furniture is present in Virginia Piedmont examples. This being the case, it would not be surprising to encounter it in Fredericksburg, which is situated on the eastern portion of this area and had strong economic and social ties with the Piedmont and the Shenandoah Valley.

The bracket clock (fig. 118) has a movement of good quality housed between brass face and back plates that are decorated with bold, fine engraving. The shading is cut with a three dimensional effect, which is achieved by the simulaton of a light source coming from the left. This sophisticated engraving is seldom seen on American-made objects and is testimony to the high level of the engraver's artistic training.

*118. Bracket Clock, Fredericksburg, circa 1775; movement
   by Thomas Walker of Fredericksburg.
Mahogany primary; yellow pine secondary.
Height 19¾", width 10¹³/₁₆", depth 8".
The Colonial Williamsburg Foundation (acc. no. 1951-397).*

This engraving has, in fact, raised some questions as to the origin of the Walker clocks. Did he import movements and apply his name to them, or did he order them from England with his name and city already engraved on the dial? A study of the engravings on the three clocks illustrated here results in the conclusion that they were executed by the same hand. The engraving on this bracket clock appears to be the earliest; it is composed essentially of arabesques with only two small rococo shells and C-scrolls. The movement of the tall clock in the Williamsburg section (fig. 84) appears to be the latest, with an abundance of rococo features and a floridness typical of that style. While the change in style is strong, the technique of the engraving and

173

the small design elements show the same approach. The latest example shows some degeneration in the quality of the engraving.

The dominant feature of the bracket clock back is a classical mask having an unusual extended hair style with a large needle thrust through it (fig. 118b). Perhaps this feature is only meant as decoration, but the possibility exists that the needle is an allusion to the textile industry since the term "walker" was synonymous with "fuller" and referred to a trade within the textile industry.

Since no other colonial period bracket clocks are known from eastern Virginia, it is impossible to determine where this case was produced. It appears to be eastern Virginia and, of necessity, is presumed to be from Fredericksburg because of Walker's signature on the movement. As pointed out in the foregoing discussion, the diversity of Walker tall case clocks emphasize the hazards of such a presumption. This case is very plain and thus is somewhat incongruous with the fine movement.

While fine metalwork is often marked, this seldom occurs in furniture. The problem of Scott chairs with histories in the Fredericksburg region has spurred considerable discussion and study. However, there are other examples from that area that reveal a different approach to design and construction. This includes a walnut side chair from a set of six (fig. 119) that was bought in Alexandria in the 1930s and may be of Fredericksburg origin. No further information concerning the set's history has survived. Several other chairs with Fredericksburg histories have similar, although not identical, splats. Like chairs in the Scott group, they have parallel stiles and crests with somewhat bulbous ears. But the similarity ends here, since the shoe is a separate element and the very deep seat rails are unlike Scott's and others from Williamsburg. The simplified rosettes carved on the splat may be compared with those that terminate the scrolls of the tall clock (fig. 117a). Yet these similarities are very basic and cannot be accepted without further supporting evidence—evidence that is not forthcoming at present.

Upholstered furniture from eastern Virginia is very rare. Thus examples such as the easy chair (fig. 120) are of extreme importance. This piece, which descended in the Lewis family of Fredericksburg, is unusual in having a frame made entirely of black walnut. A Fredericksburg origin seems plausible because of the Lewis history, and its legs and feet are quite different from those of Williamsburg and the "Norfolk" group. The unusual form of the thin claw feet and high "shod" rear feet on this chair could be the key to further identification of related examples and could prove or disprove the Fredericksburg

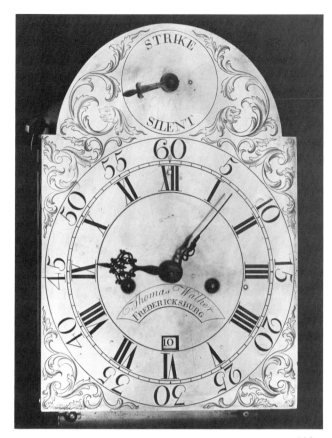

118a.

118b.

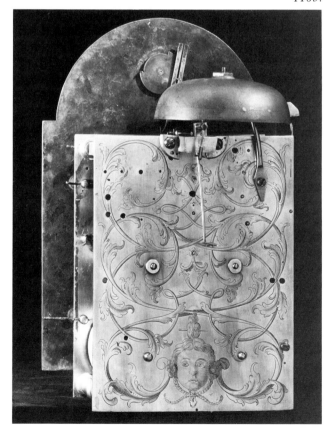

119. Side Chair (one of six), Fredericksburg, circa 1770.
Walnut primary.
Height 38⅝", width 20", depth 16".
The Colonial Williamsburg Foundation (acc. no. 1930-23).

120. Easy Chair, Fredericksburg, circa 1770.
Walnut primary; walnut secondary.
Height 44", width 36", depth 30½".
The Henry Francis duPont Wintherthur Museum
(acc. no. M51.72.1).

attribution. The lack of such examples is disturbing, although the exploration of carved furniture from Virginia is only now beginning. As an awareness of it increases, more Virginia pieces will undoubtedly be recognized in public and private collections throughout the country. It is hoped that further examples from Fredericksburg will be among them.

FOOTNOTES

1. Richard L. Morton, *Colonial Virginia* (Chapel Hill: The University of North Carolina Press, 1960), vol. 2, pp. 445-446.
2. Harold L. Peterson, *Arms and Armor in Colonial America, 1526-1783* (Harrisburg, Pennsylvania: The Stackpole Company, 1956), p. 187.
3. Alexander Craig Account Book, Manuscripts Division, Earl Gregg Swem Library, College of William and Mary, Williamsburg, Virginia. Information courtesy of Harold B. Gill, Jr.
4. Allen's 1740 date courtesy of Harold B. Gill, Jr.; George Washington Ledger A, Folio 62, courtesy of Ms. Christine Meadows, curator, Mount Vernon Ladies' Association of the Union, Mount Vernon, Virginia.
5. *The Virginia Gazette*, ed. John Dixon, October 20, 1752, p. 2.
6. Manuscript Diary of William Cabell, 1751-1795, Virginia State Library, Richmond, Virginia. Reference courtesy of Harold B. Gill, Jr.
7. From a list of Williamsburg craftsmen of the eighteenth century, compiled by Harold B. Gill, Jr., historian, Colonial Williamsburg Foundation, Williamsburg, Virginia.
8. John D. Davis, "Williamsburg: The Silver," *The Magazine Antiques* 95 (January 1969):137.
9. Mills Brown, "Cabinetmaking in the Eighteenth Century" (unpublished research report, Colonial Williamsburg Foundation, 1959), p. 142; *The Virginia Gazette*, ed. Alexander Purdie and John Dixon, October 18, 1770, supplement, p. 1.
10. Brown, "Cabinetmaking," p. 142.
11. Ivor Noel Hume, *James Geddy and Sons, Colonial Craftsmen* (Williamsburg, Virginia: Colonial Williamsburg Foundation, 1970), p. 23, fig. 17; Nathan L. Swayze, *The Rappahannock Forge* (American Society of Arms Collectors publication no. 2, 1976), pp. 21-23, figs. 18a, 18b, 18c.
12. Davis, "The Silver," p. 137.

Origin Unknown

The three examples shown here—a tea table, a candlestand, and a slab-top table (figs. 121, 122, 123)—have Virginia provenances. Although their precise origins are unknown, they are included with the hope that further examples may be found and thereby that their identity might be established. Hundreds of objects fall into this uncertain classification, although few have the refinements of carving or outstanding form seen in these examples. In addition, two of them are related to other examples with Virginia histories, and, therefore, present a greater possibility of future identification.

The tea table and the candlestand (figs. 121, 122), both made of mahogany, have the same history in the Boyd family of New Bern, North Carolina. They descended from Virginia families that migrated in the eighteenth century from southeast Virginia to the Edenton, North Carolina area. Initially these two tables appear to have little in common; only after close inspection of their bird cage pillars does their affinity to each other become apparent. The unusual pillars are identical on both tables and are visible in the illustration of the candlestand. Their form, which is constricted at the middle with a fine central ring, appears to be a degenerate development of a bold double-balustrade type on a stand with an Alexandria, Virginia history. This stand and its companion tea table are pictured in the files of the Museum of Early Southern Decorative Arts (acc. nos. S-6979 and S-6980). On the tea table, the carving of the ball-and-claw feet and the knees are quite similar to those of figure 121. The knee carving has a double-overlapped acanthus issuing from beneath an eight-petaled rosette. The entire concept is so similar to that of figure 121 that they may be by the same hand. A similarity to the Scott overlapping acanthus and ball-and-claw feet is suggested by these two carved tea tables, although the quality of design and execution is far below that of the poorest Scott examples. Perhaps they are related, having possibly been made by a cabinetmaker (or cabinetmakers) influenced by the Scott group or who represented the second or third generations of training from his shop. All four tables share interrelated details and their survival in pairs with histories so geographically separated is intriguing, although extremely difficult to interpret. They are undoubtedly Virginia products. Perhaps in time the exact location of production will be determined. It is worth pointing out that the general heaviness of design of figure 121, particularly in the upper legs, is conceptually similar to the tea table illustrated in the Norfolk section (fig. 108).

Slab-top tables from Virginia are very rare, and the example shown here (fig. 123) stands out among

them. Little is known of its background, but it was purchased in Alexandria, Virginia in 1930. Although it was long thought to be of provincial English origin, its primary wood is black walnut with corner braces and a central batten of yellow pine, thus proving its American production. The knee brackets are replacements, but the leg and the pad feet have a distinctive design that is appreciably different from others examined in this work. The white-grey marble is original and shows better workmanship than the Hay shop example (fig. 43).

121. Tea Table, origin unknown, circa 1770.
Mahogany primary.
Height 28″, diameter of top 33¾″.
Frederick R. Boyd.

121a.

122. Candlestand, origin unknown, circa 1770.
Mahogany primary.
Height 28⅝″, diameter of top 23¼″.
Frederick R. Boyd.

123. Side Table, origin unknown, circa 1735.
Walnut primary; yellow pine secondary.
Height 34″, width 54⅛″, depth 26⅜″.
The Colonial Williamsburg Foundation (acc. no. 1930-9).

Eastern Shore

The Eastern Shore of Virginia, which is separated from the Virginia mainland by the Chesapeake Bay, shows an independent development of furniture styles. Since the peninsula is shared with Maryland and Delaware, it might initially appear that a stronger influence would be felt from Pennsylvania and the Delaware Valley than Tidewater Virginia. But certain forms appear to be indigenous, suggesting an independence from outside influences, and a high level of creativity on the part of the native artisans.

That an academic urban style developed on the Eastern Shore during the colonial period seems highly improbable. Sophisticated furniture from Philadelphia and New England has been passed down through generations of Eastern Shore families, suggesting an active coastal trade. Williamsburg pieces have also been in the area since the eighteenth century (fig. 45), and presumably Norfolk, the closest major city on the mainland, will also be represented once its products are better understood. On Virginia's Eastern Shore, the largest centers were courthouse towns—Eastville in Northumberland County and Drummondtown (now Accomac) in Accomac County. These appear to have been incapable of supporting a highly specialized cabinet trade, although style-conscious furniture may be discovered, once more is known of the craft there.

The largest group of furniture currently attributable to the Eastern Shore shows an affinity to the area's architectural woodwork, particularly the many houses that incorporate complex networks of panel designs. The connection is well illustrated by a paneled blanket chest (fig. 124), one of the finest surviving examples from that area. Originally found in Westmoreland County, it was long attributed to that area, though it has also been associated with Goochland County, where doors at Tuckahoe Plantation incorporate the same motifs.[1] The only link between the doors and this chest, however, seems to be a common design source—William Salmon's *Palladio Londinensis*. Published in London in 1734, it underwent nine editions before 1774 and was the most widely used design book among the joiners of eighteenth-century Virginia. The chest's central design comes from plate XXIII, and those flanking it from plate XXVI, suggesting that those who engaged in building were often employed in the cabinet trade as well.

Blanket chests of this form are common on the Eastern Shore—though other examples seldom exhibit the pleasing combination seen here—and this piece is representative in a number of ways. It has large, single panels on either end and a back composed of horizontal boards. The corner stiles con-

124. Blanket Chest, Eastern Shore of Virginia, circa 1770.
Yellow pine with original green and white paint.
Height 24¾", width 56", depth 20".
The Colonial Williamsburg Foundation (acc. no. 1930-108).

tinue all the way to the floor and have bracket feet nailed over them. The feet flare noticeably inward at the base and have an exaggerated beak-like point. The top has thumbnail molding, overlapping ends, and battens nailed to them from beneath. The original hinges were simple wrought staples, which suggest an early date.

Much time was expended on the decorative aspects of this chest, and the techniques of its construction approximate those found on architectural paneling. Each side was conceived as a separate entity, and was joined with carefully fitted through-tenons. The front and back edges have been rabbetted to receive the sides, and the final product is simply nailed together like finished paneling is nailed to the walls of a house. The bottom is also nailed in.

The painted decoration on this chest follows the scheme on most pine pieces in this group; it serves as an effective technique for highlighting the shaped panels. Although the decoration now gives an impression of blue, it was originally green—the color that seems to have been favored. Blue is occasionally

found, however, and other colors were presumably used as well.

The clothespress (fig. 125) is made of walnut, a wood currently unknown in blanket chests but represented in other forms. Although this piece lacks the complex panels seen in the preceding example, closely related presses have doors that incorporate one of the designs found on the chest.

This clothespress first appears to be a two-part cupboard, a feature that heightens its architectural qualities—but it is actually a single unit. The corner stiles of the lower section run all the way to the floor, as they do in the blanket chest, and the brackets are nailed to them. The corner stiles of the upper portion also extend downward—all the way to the top of the feet—and form additional support behind the stiles of the lower section. With the exception of the drawers, the piece has no dovetails. The case lacks a bottom and a dust partition between the drawers.

Individuality is characteristic of the pieces in this group. Many of them do not give the two-piece impression seen in this walnut example. Some are

fitted with drawers, others are not. All have panels flanking their doors, but not all have pilasters. One piece has two doors in an area slightly larger than that covered by this one. Needless to say, there is also tremendous variety in the scheme of paneling from piece to piece.

Joiners' furniture representative of the Eastern Shore also includes a large number of architectural-style corner cupboards (fig. 126). These were made in walnut or yellow pine and are characterized by pleasing proportions with a height that is approximately twice the width. They invariably have canted corners with pilasters, often subdivided by molding to give definition to their slender proportions. The pilasters are always fluted, but it is unusual to find a paneled plinth at the base, as on this example. The pronounced waist molding, which accentuates the architectural quality of this piece, is also representative of cupboards in the group.

The lower portion of these cupboards usually has two doors, occasionally with arched panels. The upper section most often has a single one, invariably glazed, and usually with arches along the top row. The interior shelves, which are often scalloped, fall directly behind the horizontal mullions of the doors.

The large quantities of closely related joined furniture found on the Eastern Shore indicates a well developed regional style differing significantly from that of the Virginia mainland. Standardized form, construction, and proportion reveal an acute awareness of design formulas that were repeated again and again, although there is sufficient individuality to determine that these objects were made by a large number of artisans from a wide geographic area.

126. Corner Cupboard, Eastern Shore of Virginia, circa 1775.
Yellow pine throughout.
Height 90", width 43", depth 21½".
The Colonial Williamsburg Foundation (acc. no. 1965-160).

125. Clothespress, Eastern Shore of Virginia, circa 1775.
Walnut primary; yellow pine secondary.
Height 83¼", width 51¼", depth 19¾".
The Colonial Williamsburg Foundation (acc. no. 1968-750).

FOOTNOTES

1. Although doors at Tuckahoe Plantation incorporate the same panel designs seen here, blanket chests of this form are unknown in that area. These same motifs occur repeatedly in joined furniture with documented histories on the Eastern Shore. A pine cupboard found on Chincoteague Island has the outer design of the blanket chest represented in its door. (See Dean Fales, *The Furniture of Historic Deerfield* [New York: E. P. Dutton, 1976], p. 251, fig. 492). The central cross design occurs even more often in furniture there, and, according to twentieth-century vernacular usage, is sometimes called a "pie panel."

Appendix

York County Wills & Inventories Vol. 22, 1771-1783, p. 40.

The Appraisment of the Personal Estate of Major Edmund Dickenson decd. taken this 28th. July 1778.

81 Planes of different sorts £14..2..6 1 large framed Saw £5	19.. 2..6
1 small framed Saw 30/ 1 Whip Saw 60/ 1 Tenant 1 Panel 1 hand Saw 74/	8.. 4..–
3 dove tailed 1 Bow and 1 Sash Saw 30/ 47 Carving Chissels & Gouges 94/	6.. 4..–
1 Stock and 20 Bitts 60/ 6 Morticeing Chissels 20/	4.. –..–
2 Iron hold fasts 30/ 1 large Cramp 40/ 1 small Do. 20/	4..10..–
1 bench Vice 30/ 2 Oyl Stones bedstead Keys 28/	2..18..–
1 Hatchet 2/6 2 Squares Bevels & Gages 6/ 1 Tool Chest 30/	1..18..6
1 pr. Pinchers pr. Nippers Saw Sett and Punches	0..12..–
part of Case of Drawing Instruments 10/ 2 Irons 5/	0..15..–
1 black leather Trunk 30/ Grey Cloth Coat and Waistcoat 40/	3..10..–
brown Cloth Coat and Waistcoat £6 1 pr. buff Silk Stocking breeches £5	11.. –..–
3 white waistcoats and breeches £9 2 Stript tyke [tick, i.e., ticking] Waistcoats £3	12.. –..–
3 pr. Breeches and pr. Drawers £3..18/ 2 Cloth Waistcoats £3	6..18..–
pr. black Cloth Legings 12/ 1 Shirt and 3 Stocks 50/	3.. 2..–
2 pr. brown thread and 1 pr. worsted Stockings	3.. –..–
1 Case drawing Instruments 40/ 1 Tea Kettle 40/ 9 Pewter Plates 30/	5..10..–
1 Camp bedstead £5 1 Window blind £3 3 Yard Yellow Canvas 36/	9..16..–
A Marked and Tent £30 "The Preceptor" 2 Vols. £1.10/	31..10..–
Fennings Dictionary 15/ Boyers French Dictionary and Grammer 44/	2..19..–
Spectators 8 Vols. and Tatlers 4 Vols.	3.. 7..6
Age of Lewis 15th 2 Vols 18/ Wises Companion 6/	1.. 4..–
Universal Gazetteer 12/ British Merchant 18/	1..10..–
Conniosseur 4 Vols. 24/ Quintessince of Poetry 18/	2.. 2..–
Essay on health 6/ Longinus on the Sublime 4/	0..10..–
Types for marking Linnen 15/ Chippendales Designs £6	6..15..–
Gold Appulet 12/ Silver Stock buckles 15/	1.. 7..–
Masons Apron 30/ New Rifle Gun £6	7..10..–
Eminersons Machanicks	2..12..–
	£ 164.. 6..6

Aggreeable to an Order of York County Court We the Sub-scribers have appraised the Personal Estate of Major Ed-mund Dickenson decd as above to £164..6..6 current Money of Virginia.
July 28th. 1778.

Hum'y Harwood
Wm. Goodson
Benja. Bucktrout

Returned into York County Court the 17th. day of August 1778 and Ordered to be recorded.
Exd.   Teste
                  Thos. Everard Cl: Cur

References Cited

BOOKS

Beverley, Robert. *History and Present State of Virginia.* Edited by Louis B. Wright. Chapel Hill: University of North Carolina Press, 1946.

Bridenbaugh, Carl. *The Colonial Craftsman.* New York: New York University Press, 1950.

————. *Myths and Realities of the American South.* New York: Atheneum, 1963.

————. *Seat of Empire: The Political Role of Eighteenth-Century Williamsburg.* Williamsburg in America Series, Vol. 1. Williamsburg: Colonial Williamsburg Foundation, 1950.

Burroughs, Paul H. *Southern Antiques.* Richmond: Garret and Massie, 1931.

Burton, E. Milby. *Charleston Furniture 1700-1825.* Charleston, South Carolina: Charleston Museum, 1955.

Carson, Jane. *We Were There: Descriptions of Williamsburg, 1699-1859.* Williamsburg: Colonial Williamsburg Foundation, 1956.

Chippendale, Thomas. *The Gentleman and Cabinet-Maker's Director.* 3rd edition. London, 1762. Reprinted New York: Dover Publications, 1966.

Colvin, H. M., ed. *The History of the Kings Works.* Vol. 5 (1660-1782). London: Her Majesty's Stationery Office, 1976.

Comstock, Helen. *American Furniture.* New York: Viking Press, 1962.

Craven, Wayne. *Sculpture in America.* New York: Thomas Y. Crowell Co., 1968.

Ecke, Gustav. *Chinese Domestic Furniture.* Rutland, Vermont and Tokyo, Japan: Charles E. Tuttle, 1962.

Fales, Dean. *The Furniture of Historic Deerfield.* New York: E. P. Dutton, 1976.

Fitz-Gerald, Desmond, ed. *Georgian Furniture.* London: Her Majesty's Stationery Office, 1969.

Gill, Harold B., Jr. *The Gunsmith in Colonial Virginia.* Williamsburg: Colonial Williamsburg Foundation, and Charlottesville: University Press of Virginia, 1974.

Goodwin, Rutherford. *A Brief and True Report Concerning Williamsburg in Virginia.* Richmond: A. Dietz and Son, 1941.

Greenlaw, Barry. *New England Furniture at Williamsburg.* Williamsburg: Colonial Williamsburg Foundation, 1974.

Hunt-Jones, Conover. *Dolley and "the great little Madison."* Washington, D.C.: American Institute of Architects Foundation, 1977.

Illustrated Catalogue of the Rare and Extremely Choice Collection of Early American and English Furniture formed by Louis G. Myers. New York: American Art Association, 1921.

International Exhibition 1876 Official Catalogue Complete in One Volume. Philadelphia: John Nagle and Company, 1876.

Johnston, Frances Benjamin, and Waterman, Thomas Tileston. *The Early Architecture of North Carolina.* Chapel Hill: University of North Carolina Press, 1947.

Jordon, Virginia Fitzgerald. *The Captain Remembers: The Papers of Captain Richard Irby.* Blackstone, Virginia: Nottoway County Historical Association, 1975.

Kirk, John T. *American Chairs: Queen Anne and Chippendale.* New York: Alfred A. Knopf, 1972.

McIlwaine, H. R. *Journal of the Council of the State of Virginia.* Richmond: Virginia State Library, 1931.

———— and Kennedy, J. P., eds. *Journals of the House of Burgesses of Virginnia 1619-1776.* Vol. 4 (1702-1712). Richmond: Virginia State Library, 1905-15.

Morton, Richard L. *Colonial Virginia.* Vol. 2. Chapel Hill: University of North Carolina Press, 1960.

Mount Vernon Ladies' Association of the Union. *Washington Furniture at Mount Vernon.* Mount Vernon: n.p., 1966.

Museum of Early Southern Decorative Arts. Winston-Salem: Old Salem, Inc., 1970.

Noël Hume, Ivor. *James Geddy and Sons, Colonial Craftsmen.* Williamsburg: Colonial Williamsburg Foundation, 1970.

————. *Williamsburg Cabinetmakers, The Archaeological Evidence.* Colonial Williamsburg Archaeological Series No. 6. Williamsburg: Colonial Williamsburg Foundation, 1971.

Parramore, Thomas C. *Launching the Craft: The First Half-Century of Freemasonry in North Carolina.* Raleigh: Litho Industries, Inc., 1975.

Peterson, Harold L. *Arms and Armor in Colonial America, 1526-1783.* Harrisburg, Pennsylvania: Stackpole Company, 1956.

Report of the Curator 1975. Monticello: Thomas Jefferson Memorial Foundation, 1975.

Roberts, Kenneth L. *Antiquemania.* New York: Doubleday, Doran and Company, 1928.

Singleton, Esther. *The Furniture of Our Forefathers.* New York: Doubleday, Page and Company, 1900.

Society of Upholsterers, Cabinet-Makers et al. *Genteel HousHold Furniture.* 2nd edition. London: Robert Sayer, ca. 1765.

Stitt, Susan. *Museum of Early Southern Decorative Arts.* Winston-Salem: Old Salem, Inc., 1970.

Swayze, Nathan L. *The Rappahannock Forge.* American Society of Arms Collectors, 1976.

Symonds, R. W. *English Furniture from Charles II to George II.* New York: International Studio, Inc., 1929.

Waterman, Thomas T. *The Mansions of Virginia.* Chapel Hill: University of North Carolina Press, 1945.

Whiffen, Marcus. *The Public Buildings of Williamsburg.* Williamsburg: Colonial Williamsburg Foundation, 1958.

PERIODICALS

Comstock, Helen. "Furniture of Virginia, North Carolina, Georgia, and Kentucky." *The Magazine Antiques* 61 (January 1952): 58-100.

———. "Discoveries in Southern Furniture: Virginia and North Carolina." *The Magazine Antiques* 65 (February 1954): 131-134.

Dahill, Betty. "The Sharrock Family, A Newly Discovered School of Cabinetmakers." *Journal of Early Southern Decorative Arts* 2 (November 1967): 37-51.

Davis, John D. "Williamsburg: The Silver." *The Magazine Antiques* 95 (January 1969): 134-137.

Dibble, Ann W. "Fredericksburg-Falmouth Chairs in the Chippendale Style." *Journal of Early Southern Decorative Arts* 5 (May 1978): 1-24.

Dockstader, Mary Ralls. "Simple Furniture of the Old South." *The Magazine Antiques* 20 (August 1931): 83-86.

"Furniture of the Old South, 1640-1820." *The Magazine Antiques* 61 (January 1952): 38-100.

Gusler, Wallace B. "Queen Anne Style Desks from the Virginia Piedmont." *The Magazine Antiques* 104 (October 1973): 665-673.

———, and Gill, Harold B., Jr. "Some Virginia Chairs: A Preliminary Study." *The Magazine Antiques* 101 (April 1972): 716-721.

Horton, Frank L. "Carved Furniture of the Albemarle, A Tie with Architecture." *Journal of Early Southern Decorative Arts* 1 (May 1975): 14-20.

Journal of Early Southern Decorative Arts 1 (May 1975).

London Gentlemen's Magazine 48 (September 1778): 420.

Rauschenberg, Bradford L. "Two Outstanding Virginia Chairs." *Journal of Early Southern Decorative Arts* 2 (November 1976): 1-23.

Roth, Rodris. "Pieces of History: Relic Furniture of the Nineteenth Century." *The Magazine Antiques* 101 (May 1972): 874-878.

Saunders, Richard H. "Collecting American Decorative Arts in New England." *The Magazine Antiques* 109 (May 1976): 996-1003.

Semple, J. McKenzie. "Loo Table Much Traveled Piece." *Antique Monthly* 8 (October 1975): 13A.

"Will of Mrs. Mary Wilting Byrd of Westover, 1813, with a List of Westover Portraits." *Virginia Magazine of History and Biography* 6 (1899): 356.

DOCUMENTS AND MANUSCRIPTS

Brown, Mills. "Cabinetmaking in the Eighteenth Century." Unpublished research report. Williamsburg: Colonial Williamsburg Foundation, 1959.

Charlottesville. University of Virginia. Alderman Library. *Virginia Gazette* Day Book. July 27, 1751; November 7, 1751; December 31, 1751; and May 28, 1752.

Doylestown, Pa. Bucks County Historical Society. John Mercer Manuscript Ledger (1725-1750).

Durham, N. C. Duke University Library, Manuscripts Division. Robert Carter Manuscript Day Book.

———. Robert Carter Manuscript Letter Book.

London. British Records Office. Papers of John Murray, Earl of Dunmore. Manuscript T1-488, folio 101.

———. Loyalist Claim of John Murray, Earl of Dunmore. File A.O. 13-18.

Richmond, Va. Virginia State Library. Manuscript Diary of William Cabell, 1751-1795.

Richmond, Va. Virginia Historical Society. Robert Carter Papers.

———. John Custis Papers, 1711-1764.

———. The George Mason Papers. Letter from George Mason to Col. John Ott of the Virginia Historical Society, Alexandria, Virginia, July 26, 1880.

———. Col. William Bassett Manuscript Account Book (1730-1748).

Williamsburg, Va. Colonial Williamsburg Foundation. Department of Collections. *Frank Leslie's Illustrated Newspaper.* June 16, 1866.

———. Research Library. "Catalog of the Art Loan Exhibition for the Benefit of the Ladies Parish Aid Society of St. Paul's Church, Norfolk, Virginia, at Mechanics Hall, May 27, 1879."

Williamsburg, Va. College of William and Mary. Earl Gregg Swem Library. Manuscripts Division. Galt Family Papers.

———. Alexander Craig Account Book.

NEWSPAPERS

The Maryland Gazette [Annapolis]. June 24, 1762.

The Virginia Gazette [Williamsburg], ed. William Hunter. November 7, 1751; ed. John Dixon, November 28, 1751; ed. John Dixon, October 20, 1752; ed. William Hunter, March 21, and June 20, 1755; ed. Alexander Purdie and John Dixon, July 25, 1765 and Jan. 8, 1767; ed. William Rind, September 22, 1768 and February 23, 1769; ed. Alexander Purdie and John Dixon, March 9 and September 7, 1769; ed. Purdie and Dixon, October 18 (supplement) and December 13, 1770; ed. Purdie and Dixon, January 3, 17, April 4, and November 14, 1771; ed. Purdie and Dixon, July 28, 1774; ed. John Dixon, February 4, 1775; ed. John Dixon and William Hunter, December 2, 1775; ed. Alexander Purdie, January 5, 1776 (supplement) and January 26, 1776; ed. John Dixon, February 10 and March 9, 1776; ed. Alexander Purdie and John Dixon, April 18, 1776; ed. Alexander Purdie, July 26, 1776.; ed. John Dixon, August 15, 1777 and August 28 and December 11, 1779.

Index

Accomac County, Virginia: 178.

Account book, unidentified cabinetmaker's: 56 (note 21).

Adam, Robert: 7.

Albemarle region of North Carolina: 156.

Albemarle Sound, North Carolina: 157, 159.

Alexandria, Virginia: 160, 174, 176, 177.

Allen, James, cabinetmaker: 147 note 4, 170.

Ambler family: 9; furniture descended in, see Illustration Index, figs. 5 and 6.

Ambler, James: 9; furniture owned by, see Illustration Index, figs. 5 and 6.

Amelia County, Virginia: 119, 131, 135, figs. 116, 168.

American Antiquarian Society: xv.

American Wing, Metropolitan Museum: xvii.

Amherst County, Virginia: 171.

Anderson, James, public armourer: 67.

Annapolis, Maryland: xx.

Anthemion: 97.

Armory, Public, of Virginia: 67.

Art Loan Exhibition, Norfolk: xvi, 91.

Attwell, John, cabinetmaker and ship's carpenter: 3.

Augusta County, Virginia: 40.

"Back" Street: see Francis Street, Williamsburg, 25.

Baird, John: 151.

Baltimore, Maryland: xvii, xx, 6, 84.

Barroud family: 154, fig. 108.

Bassett, Col. William, account book, 27, 42, and Illustration Index, fig. 35.

Bassett family: 27, 42, and Illustration Index, 35.

Bell, Phillip, cabinetmaker: xviii, xxi note 22.

Beverley, Robert, of Blandfield, Essex County, Virginia: xviii, xix, 27, 51 and Illustration Index, figs. 40, 42.

Bible: 111

Biggs Antique Company, Richmond, Virginia: 70.

Biggs, J. F., Richmond: 70.

Bill of Rights: xvi.

Blacks, as cabinetmakers: 25, 26, 59, 61, 62; mentioned in Anthony Hay's estate, 62.

"Black-grained leather:" 144, 147 (note 4), 170.

Blair-Pollock House, Edenton, North Carolina: 157 (note 7).

"Blandfield," Essex County, Virginia: xviii, 27, 100.

Blandford, Virginia: 6, 151.

Boggs Family, Spottsylvania County, Virginia: see Illustration Index, fig. 29. Pembroke tables made by: 137 (note 5), 139.

Boston, Massachusetts: 162, 165.

Botetourt, Norborne Berkeley, Baron de: 7, 9; tenure as Governor, 71; death of, 7; coffin of, 8, 65, 171; estate of, 145; estate sale of, 119; funeral of, 65; statue of, 8, 9, 66, 97.

Boyd family, of Virginia and North Carolina: 176, and Illustration Index, figs. 121, 122.

Bragg family: 137 (note 6), and Illustration Index, fig. 91.

British: Army destroys Norfolk, Virginia, 151; House of Commons, 16.

Brodnax, John: 15.

Brodnax, Mecklenburg County, Virginia: 131.

Brown, Mills: 62.

Bruton Parish Church: 25, 26.

Bryan, Mary M. Osborne: 137 (note 6), and Illustration Index, fig. 91.

Bucktrout, Benjamin, cabinetmaker: 3, 59, 61, 62, 63–65, 66, 67, 95, 136, 147; furniture attributed to, 75–89, and Illustration Index, figs. 49–56; other Williamsburg furniture related to, 139; as journeyman, 112 (note 19); Masonic chair by, 75–79, 95, 98, 126; partnership with Kennedy, 64; retail store of, 3; as undertaker, 65.

Bucktrout funeral service: 65.

Burgesses, House of: see House of Burgesses.

Burroughs, Paul H.: xvii.

Burton, E. Milby: xvii.

Buzaglo Stove: 7, 9, 66, 97.

Byrd, William III, Charles City County, Virginia: 84.

Byrd, William Powell, Charles City County, Virginia: 84, and Illustration Index, fig. 51.

Cabell, William, of Amherst County, Virginia: 171.

Cabinetmakers: advertisements of, 3, 6; distribution in Virginia, 6; description of shops used by, 164.

Capitol of Virginia: burning and rebuilding of, 13–16; furniture from, see Illustration Index, figs. 7, 46; in Richmond, 70; in Williamsburg, 2, 8, 13–16, 63, 70, 79, 94, 144, 145.

Capitol chair: 70–79; 93, 113 (notes 52 and 55), and Illustration Index, fig. 46.

Carter family, of Shirley Plantation: 151, and Illustration Index, figs. 18, 105, 106.

Carter, Robert, of Nomini Hall: 2, 3, 27, 64, 65; coffin purchased by, 65.

Carter, Robert "King": 18, and Illustration Index, fig. 9.

Carvers, advertisements of: 61, 66.

Carvers, in Hay shop: 6.

Carving: of ball-and-claw feet, 103, 105; chip-, 100; of lion's heads, 113 (note 55); of lion's-paw feet, 103–105; punchwork in, 94, 98.

Case pieces, construction and style of:

—back: with additional batten support, 123; panelled, xix, 119, 120, 124, 129, 15; shrinkage allowances in panelled backs, 120; tongue-and-groove, 87.

—base: see molding, base.

—case construction: Eastern Shore type, 179, 181, "Scott type," 41, 43; southeast Virginia type, 160, 162; Williamsburg case pieces type, 130, 131.

—cornice: "Scott type," blocking of, 42, 129; detachable, 83, 89, 116, 117, 132, 152, 168; glued to case, 89; held by pegs, 168; in perspective, 124, 126, 171; pitch, 124, 126, 132, 168; scroll, 126, 132, 135, 168, 173.

—desk interiors: pen compartments in, 132; Piedmont Virginia type, 115, 162; "Scott type," 43, 47, 49; Williamsburg type, 115, 159 (see also drawer construction, small desk interior drawers).

—door: indented corners, in Scott furniture, 45, 47; in other furniture, 89, 91, 168; in Norfolk, differentiated, 152; with curtains, 124, 132; flat panels, dating of, 89; narrow stiles on, neoclassic, 132; "Scott type," 42, 55, 81, 117; stop-joint, 87.

—drawer construction: with batten bottom, 160; in Bucktrout examples, 81–83, 86, 87; sliding clothes trays, 87; small desk interior drawers, 42, 166; fitted desk drawer, dating of, 89; fitted dressing drawer, 81–83; in Norfolk examples, 152, 156; in Richmond, 166; in Scott furniture, 42; in Williamsburg case pieces, 115, 117, 119, 123, 129, 130, 131, 132, 136.

—drawer blade: 115, 123, 165; with exposed dovetails, 159, 162, 166.

—dust board: "full-bottom" defined, 83, 115; on furniture, 87, 115, 117, 119, 123, 130, 131, 132, 159; Norfolk type, 152, 156, 159, 166; "Scott type," 42, 87; cases made without, 159, 162, 165, 168, 179.

—fall board: southeast Virginia type, 160; with straight battens, 169; with reading-shelf molding, 163.

—fall board support: "Scott type," 42.

—foot, ball-and-claw: in Scott furniture, 47, 54.

—composite, xix; defined, 42; English derivation of, 55, 121; advantages of, 120; in Hay shop, 87; in London, 55; in Scott shop, 42, 45, 55; in Norfolk, 152; in Williamsburg case furniture, 115, 116, 119, 120, 130, 132; variations of, 131;

—dovetailed, 131, 169.

—neoclassic influence on, 132.

—ogee, in London furniture, 55; method of producing ogee bracket, 53; in Norfolk examples, 156, 159; "Scott-type"

Woods, varieties used in construction:
—beech: secondary use in Williamsburg, 10; in upholstered furniture in London and Williamsburg, 55; in secondary usage, figs. 5, 6, 16, 19, 21, 23, 27, 37, 46, 64.
—birch: in secondary usage, figure 90.
—cedar: in secondary usage, figure 56.
—cedar: Spanish, in secondary usage, fig. 114.
—cherry: absence in advertisements discussed, 54; historical reference to, 151; in primary usage, figures 18, 19, 30, 32, 33, 34, 50, 53; in secondary usage, figure 19, 84, 90.
—chestnut: in secondary usage, fig. 117.
—mahogany: use denotes quality of furniture, 57 (note 21); in veneers, 87, 126, 147, 166; used in building Hay Shop, 61; historical reference to, 65, 151; in armchairs, 3; drying time of, 65; furniture advertisement, 25; plank, 162, 26; thickness of, 65 in primary usage, figs. 5, 6, 8, 9, 11, 16, 21, 22, 31, 36, 44, 45, 46, 47, 48, 49, 51, 53, 56, 57, 59, 60, 61, 63, 64, 65, 66, 77, 78, 79, 83, 84, 87, 90, 91, 93, 94, 99, 102, 103, 104, 105, 106, 107, 108, 109, 110, 114, 115, 118, 121, 122; in secondary usage, figs. 48, 105.
—maple, curly: rare in southern furniture, 84, 85; as book-matched veneer, 84, 85; in primary usage, fig. 52; in secondary usage, fig. 52.
—oak: as secondary wood, 147; in upholstered furniture from London and Williamsburg, 55; in secondary usage, figs. 7, 8, 9, 11, 20, 30, 31, 32, 33, 34, 35, 44, 45, 52, 58, 62, 67, 84, 90, 94, 102, 103, 107, 111, 112, 116.
—pine: historical reference to, 65; plank for sale, 26; in primary usage, figures 39, 92, 124, 126; in secondary usage, figs. 7, 8, 9–14, 20, 24, 26, 31, 35, 36, 37, 39, 40, 42, 43, 44, 45, 46, 48, 50, 54, 56, 58, 75–82, 84–102, 104, 105, 106, 108, 110–118, 123–126.
—poplar: in secondary usage, figs. 7, 33, 34, 37, 45, 52, 53, 55, 56, 63, 84, 85, 88, 90, 91, 102, 104, 107, 109, 115.
—walnut: advertisements for furniture made of 25, 26; plank for sale, 26, 164; in primary usage, figs. 7, 10, 12, 13, 14, 15, 20, 23, 24, 25, 26, 27, 28, 29, 35, 37, 40, 42, 54, 58, 75, 76, 77, 80, 81, 82, 85, 86, 88, 89, 95, 96, 97, 98, 100, 101, 111, 112, 113, 116, 117, 119, 120, 123, 125; in secondary usage, figs. 8, 12, 27, 28, 29, 36, 39, 40, 42, 49, 56, 59, 60, 77, 80, 82, 85, 90, 101, 120.
"Wood Lawn," in Orange County, Virginia: 135.
Woodlawn Plantation in Alexandria, 160.
Woods, Col. Arthur: v.
Woodson, Mrs.: 62.
Worcester, Massachusetts: xv.
Wright, David, cabinetmaker, of Lancaster, England: chest signed by: 156.
Wythe, George, side chairs belonging to: 38 and Illustration Index, fig. 30.

York County, Virginia: 21.
Yorktown, Virginia: 6, 8, 65.

Zeus: 111.

INDEX OF ILLUSTRATIONS

The page numbers listed in this index indicate places in the text where illustrated items are either mentioned or discussed. Numbers in *italics* refer to pages where those items are depicted.

Cloath

T. Chippendale inv.ᵗ et del.

Pub.ᵈ according to Act of Par